Parallel Universes
Essays and Conversations

Chang Wang

the answer company™
THOMSON REUTERS®

平行集

Parallel Universes: Essays and Conversations
Copyright © 2017
by 王昶 Chang Wang, Thomson Reuters
All Rights reserved.

For information, address US-China Cultural Media Group,
1920 South 1st Street, Suite 509, Minneapolis, MN 55454.

FIRST EDITION

Book Designed by Jeff Schalles and Michael Kaufman

Thomson Reuters provides professionals with
the intelligence, technology and human expertise
they need to find trusted answers.

We enable professionals in the financial and risk, legal,
tax and accounting, and media markets to make
the decisions that matter most, all powered by the
world's most trusted news organization.

ISBN-10:0-692-82384-0
ISBN-13:978-0-692-82384-2

Printed in the United States of America

To Chinese Americans

献给华裔美国人

Table of Contents

Foreword

Parallel Universes

For the past decades, I travel between different time zones and parallel worlds: from East Asia to North America, and to Western Europe. In the past and present, simultaneously, I inhabit in parallel universes: law, business and the arts.

In the first chapter of my current life, I was trained as an artist and art critic in Beijing. When I left my hometown and my comfort zone for a second graduate degree in art history in America, where I was immediately deprived of a cultural identity. I could easily equate with Chinese artist Chen Danqing who summarized for all diaspora intellectuals— "all of your earlier accomplishments—your previous life —count nothing in the new world. You have to reborn." Chen ultimately chose to go back to China to reconnect with his previous life. I chose to stay and reborn as an attorney and counselor at law.

I've always wondered whether my relocation and rebirth were force majeure, or unconsciously self-driven by a strong sense of finding. Certain elements of Midwest, mysterically, appear to be more familiar and comforting than those of my hometown. This constant feeling of déjà vu cannot be mistaken as daily routine. It is inward, retrospective and nostalgic.

On the other hand, when I travel from west to east, commonality fades, and familiarity morphs into surrealism. I fall into the same dilemma pondered by Yung Wing (1828-1912), the first Chinese to graduate from a U.S. university:

"Would it not be strange, if an Occidental education, continually exemplified by an Occidental civilization, had not wrought upon an Oriental such a metamorphosis in his inward nature as to make him feel and act as though he were a being coming from a different world, when he confronted one so diametrically different?"

The explanation, ultimately dwells on the very existence of parallel universes, or reincarnation, or both.

Buddhists believe there are two ways in which someone can take rebirth after death: rebirth under the sway of karma and destructive emotions, and rebirth through the power of compassion and prayer. Regarding the first, due to ignorance negative and positive karma are created and their imprints remain on the consciousness. These are reactivated through craving and grasping, propelling us into the next life. We then take rebirth involuntarily in higher or lower realms. This is the way ordinary beings circle incessantly through existence like the turning of a wheel. On the other hand, superior Bodhisattvas, who have attained the path of seeing, are not reborn through the force of their karma and destructive emotions, but due to the power of their compassion for sentient beings and based on their prayers to benefit others. They are able to choose their place and time of rebirth as well as their future parents.

As an ordinary sentient being, I came to this present life from my previous lives and take rebirth again after this life. Like trillions of human beings, gazillions of sentient beings, I am recycling in the wheel of time.

Buddhist teachings on impermanence and reincarnation has a scientific equivalent — quantum physics, particularly the theory of parallel universe and multiverse. Physicist Brian Greene believes that the universe we are in is infinite. Since there are only so many ways matter can arrange itself within that infinite universe, so eventually, matter has to repeat itself and arrange itself in similar ways. If the universe is infinitely large, it is also home to infinite parallel universes. Greene argued: "Imagine a deck of cards, if you shuffle that deck, there's just so many orderings that can happen. If you shuffle that deck enough times, the orders will have to repeat. Similarly, with an infinite universe and only a finite number of complexions of matter, the way in which matter arranges itself has to repeat."

Some of the combinations of the fundamental ingredients of matter repeat itself. Life is also an arrangement of particles. In parallel universes, or multiverse, any arrangement has to repeat. Therefore, somewhere out there, there is at least one duplicate me at this precise moment, at least one duplicate me at any precise moment in the past, and at least one duplicate me at any precise moment in the future. From a multiverse perspective, time is an illusion: there is no past, no present, and no future. We do not born, live, or die. All universes parallel, all matters transient, and all sentient beings immortal.

In a parallel universe, once upon a time, I was a Tibetan Mastiff, wandering around the Sacred City of Lahsa, enjoy the brightest sunshine of the Land of the Snow, and following the footsteps of the faithful pilgrims who walked and prostrated thousands of miles from the rural area to the Seat of His Holiness the Dalai Lama.

In a parallel universe, once upon a time, I was a mouse in a Buddhist temple in Southern China, busy after dark, and hiding in plain sight during the day, listening to the peaceful chanting of the "Diamond Sutra."

In a parallel universe, once upon a time, I was an Italian chef in Firenze. I master the Toscani cuisine. I turn deceptively simple ingredients — flour, cheese, vegetables, mushrooms and fresh fruit into exquisitely profound art of delicacy, completed by a sip of Chianti Superiore.

In a parallel universe, once upon a time I was Wang Chang 王昶 (1724 – 1806) in Qing Dynasty, known as one of the "Seven Literati in Central Wu." I excelled in the Imperial Examination and was awarded a high rank civil service post. But how I will be remembered are on the 46 volumes of scholastic works on epigraphy, textology and poetics.

In a parallel universe, once upon a time, I was a beluga whale, a slow swimmer and (nicknamed by humans) a "sea canary" due to my high-pitched twitter. I am highly sociable and often join small cooperative groups of belugas to find food. We like to chase each and rub against each other. I have a great degree of curiosity. I play with objects I find in the water: wood, plants and bubbles I have created.

In a parallel universe, once upon a time, I was a white elephant in Southeast Asia. I dwell in dry thorn-scrub forests and feed myself leaves, twigs, fruit, bark, grass and roots. At midday, I rest under trees and may doze off while standing. I travel with my family, never lost.

In a parallel universe, once upon a time I was an ever-green pine tree. My bark is thick and scaly, my branches are produced in a very tight spiral but appearing like a ring of branches arising from the same point. I stand quietly on the mountain top and look down at the river below. When the heavy snow falls, small animals take refuge under my arms.

In a parallel universe, once upon a time, I was a Russian writer, and because all real Russian people are philosophers, I am a philosopher too. I write novels, novellas, novelettes, short stories, essays, pamphlets, limericks, epigrams and poems. My lengthy, psychological and sophisticated works explore such themes as depression, poverty, human manipu-lation and morality. They were never published.

In a parallel universe, once upon a time, I was a Pansori drummer in Korea. Pansori is the Korean folk version of Blues, a musical storytelling performed by one sorikkun (singer) and one gosu (drummer). I play a barrel drum called buk. The singer plays the central role through her singing, words, and body language while I, the drummer, play an accompanying role by providing the rhythm and shouting words of encouragement to add to the passion of the performance. My favorite madang (story), of course, is "Chunhyangga."

In October 2013, I interviewed Maestro Dario Fo, Italian comedian and 1997 Nobel Literature Prize laureate. His wife for 69 years, Franca Rame, just passed away a few month ago. The maestro and I discussed politics, art, love and death. I explained Buddhist theory of reincarnation to him. He listened carefully, paused for a long time, and murmured, "I just wish I had met Franca in my past life, and will meet her again in my next life."

I know he had and he will, and I know we have met in our previous lives, and we will meet again in our future lives.

ACKNOWLEDGEMENTS

This volume contains essays, conversations, reports, and interviews published in recent years (2012 - 2017) in *China Insight*, the exclusive English-language American newspaper on US-China relations; and on *Legal Current*, an official blog of the Legal businesses of Thomson Reuters, with the exceptions of two longer art essays and several law review articles.

I would like to express my deepest appreciation to my teacher and mentor Rick King, Executive Vice President and Chief Information Officer, Thomson Reuters, and to his wife Gina King. Without Rick's trust and support, none of my research projects and career accomplishments would have been possible. I am forever in debt to Rick and Gina.

I have been blessed to work with some of the best journalists and editors of *China Insight* and *Legal Current*: Elaine Dunn, Greg Hugh, Alex Cook, Scott Augustin, and Susan Martin. Their professional guidance, insightful comments, and diligent editing make these pieces worth reading.

The intellect, wisdom, and knowledge of my advisors, co-authors, colleagues, friends, and students are continuing sources of inspiration and encouragement for my writings and teachings, I want to record my sincere gratitude to:

- Professor Jonathan Fineberg, University of Illinois and the University of the Arts, and Marianne Fineberg;
- Dr. Peter Warwick, Thomson Reuters, and Helen Warwick;
- Mr. Vance Opperman, Michele Engdahl, Sharon Sayles Belton, Ed Friedland, Tom Leighton, Betsy Lulfs, Sue Lauermann, Maura Coenen; Gretchen

DeSutter, Nicole Hansen, Randy Goetz, Donna Gies, Christopher Luehr, Ken Ross, John Thomas, Lori Parizek, Pamela Jergens, Anne Thompson, and Debra Meyer, Thomson Reuters;

- Martin Hyndman, Thomson Reuters, and Tatiana Hyndman;
- Dean Joan Howland, Dr. Ryan Greenwood, Professor David Weissbrodt, Dean Robert Stein, Professor Fred Morrison, University of Minnesota Law School;
- Joe Pearman, Pamela Baker, Professor Matt Bribitzer-Stull, and Kris Nygaard, University of Minnesota Honors Program;
- President Eric Kaler, Vice President Meredith McQuaid, Joan Brzezinski, University of Minnesota;
- Nathan Madson, New York University;
- Vivian Wu, The New School and BBC;
- Ai Weiwei, the artist;
- the late Maestro Dario Fo, Chiara Porro;
- Professor Iole Fargnoli, Università degli Studi di Milano and Universität Bern;
- Professor Karl-Ludwig Kunz, Universität Bern;
- Professor Gianfranco Pistoia and Carla Pistoia;
- Professor Mauro Pasquali and Nicoletta Pasquali;
- Professor Alexander Morawa, Universität Luzern and American University Washington School of Law;
- Professor Wolfgang Mazal, Universität Wien;
- Professor Les McCrimmon, Charles Darwin University;
- Susan J. Cohen, Mintz, Levin, Cohn, Ferris, Glovsky and Popeo, P.C.;

- Professor Frank Wu, Committee of 100 and University of California Hastings College of the Law;
- Professor David Larson and Patty Larson;
- Professor David Bryden and Rebecca Bryden;
- Carlos Seoane and Susana Pérez-Castillejo, Extempore;
- John Fonder, Christensen Fonder Dardi, P.A., and Traci Fonder;
- Nathan Otremba and Kimberly Cline;
- Becky Fillinger, Federal Publications Seminars;
- Dan Gilchrist and Suzanne McCurdy;
- Al Maleson and Ann Maleson;
- Fred Gordon and Karen Gordon;
- Dr. Tsewang Ngodup and family;
- Tashi Lhewa and family;
- Sarena Lin and family;
- Cindy Cribbs and Stephen Conover;
- Michael King and Melanie Leidinger;
- Xiaolu Zhang-Coenen, Shell;
- Zhang Zhang, ZHANG.O.MUSIQ;
- Justice Paul Anderson and Janice Anderson;
- Chief Justice Lorie Gildea, Justice Barry Anderson, Justice Alan Page, and Mrs. Ginger Meyer, Minnesota Supreme Court;
- Chief Judge John R. Tunheim, Sr. Judge Michael J. Davis, Judge Wilhelmina M. Wright, Judge Tony N. Leung, United States District Court for the District of Minnesota;
- Professor Nancy Nentl, Professor Duncan McCampbell, Professor Marcia Hagen, Mr. Mark Newfield, Metropolitan State University;

- Commissioner Kevin Lindsey, Deputy Commissioner Rowzat Shipchandler, Nicholas Kor, Minnesota Department of Human Rights;
- Professor Jim Hilbert, Dean Eric Janus, Professor Ken Port, Professor Tony Winer, Mitchell Hamline School of Law;
- Alan Miller and Sharon Miller, *Access to Democracy*;
- Lee Rawles, *ABA Journal;*
- Professor Jothie Rajah, Professor Robert L. Nelson, American Bar Foundation;
- Robert Webber, Webber Law Firm, LLC;
- Abigail Pribbenow, Yinghua Academy;
- Andrew Carlson, Briggs & Morgan, and Lisa Hollingsworth;
- Laura J. Danielson, Ruilin Li, Fredrikson & Byron, P.A.;
- Dr. Yang Liu, Minneapolis Institute of Art;
- Dr. Steven Shu, *Minnesota Times*;
- Sylvia Kilchenmann, Sabine Senn-Müller, Jonas Bamert, Universität Bern;
- Julia Ruth Maria Wetzel, Universität Luzern;
- Professor Hiroshi Narita, Seijo University;
- *Neuen Zürcher Zeitung;*
- *Minnesota Lawyer;*
- Minnesota State Bar Association;
- Minnesota Zoological Board;
- Council on Asian Pacific Minnesotans;
- Minnesota Asian Pacific American Bar Association;
- New York State Bar Association;
- American Law Institute;
- American Bar Association;

– and all my students at the University of Minnesota
  Law School, University of Minnesota Honors
  Program, Mitchell Hamline School of Law,
  Metropolitan State University, Università degli Studi
  di Milano, Universität Bern, Universität Luzern,
  Universität Wien, and China University of Political
  Science and Law.

Special thanks to Jeff Schalles and Michael Kaufman for
their kind assistance in book design and typesetting.

For the safety of my colleagues and students in China, I
prefer not to list their names here, but I greatly appreciate
their wisdom, integrity, and courage.

This book is dedicated to all Chinese Americans, including my family.

Chang Wang
October, 2017

The Last Lecture in China:
To the Next Generation of International Lawyers*

First and foremost, I'd like to thank all of you for joining me to explore the fascinating world of American law and Westlaw.

As I'm sure you remember, we started our journey by comparing common law and civil law.

As a common law country, the United States and its legal system are deeply rooted in precedent, or *Stare Decisis*, relying heavily on courts' interpretations of both codified law and previous judicial opinions. This doctrine of precedent helps ensure the predictability, consistency and integrity of the American legal system.

In contrast, notwithstanding its civil law framework, current Chinese law is a "socialist legal system with Chinese characteristics," a legal system designed to support the "socialism" of the Chinese Communist Party (CPC). In China, the law is used primarily as a tool to reinforce party rules and strengthen its policies; the party itself operates outside the law.

In an attempt to prevent one branch of government from holding more power than others, the U.S. legal system incorporates a system of checks and balances, and the separation of powers. Because governmental responsibilities have been divided among different branches of government, and because the different branches of government are accountable to the American people, each branch can

---

*These were the final remarks of Chang Wang to his "Legal Research in American Law: The Westlaw Approach" class at China University of Political Science and Law. The lecture was delivered on July 4, 2014. *China Insight* published the original lecture in article form on October 1, 2014.

1

act independently, according to its own interpretation of what is best for the country. This is true even if the interpretations of the various branches of government are in conflict with one another. This is the very rationale that underscores the principle of separation of powers, especially "judicial review."

Government in China, by contrast, is founded on single-party rule. The Chinese Constitution enshrines the CPC as the Leviathan of the country, in charge of all aspects of government. The Party reviews its own actions and is above the law.

Nevertheless, the CPC has promised to strengthen the "rule of law" in China. Let's look closely at the definition of "rule of law" in *Black's Law Dictionary*, the premier legal dictionary published by Thomson Reuters. Black's defines "rule of law" as:

1) A substantive legal principle;

2) The supremacy of regular as opposed to arbitrary power;

3) The doctrine that every person is subject to the ordinary law within the jurisdiction; and

4) The doctrine that general constitutional principles are the result of judicial decisions determining the rights of private individuals in the courts."

From these definitions, you can see that as long as the CPC retains power over the Chinese legal system and judiciary, and as long as the judiciary is not independent and is denied the power to review legislative and administrative actions, there will be no "rule of law" in China. Rather, there will be "rule *by* law:" that is, the CPC will use the law as a tool of governance.

It was said that "where the law ends, tyranny begins." How, we asked, did Americans prevent tyranny? How did they "form a more perfect union, establish justice, insure domestic tranquility, provide for the common defense, promote the general welfare, and secure the blessings of liberty?" What kind of political and legal system did the founding fathers envision and devise?

We have read the United States Constitution, the Constitution of the State of Minnesota, the Freedom of Information Act (5 USCA § 552); "Public Access to Information" in the Code of Federal Regulations (1 CFR § 456.4); Federal Rules of Civil Procedure; Federal Rules of Criminal Procedure; Federal Rules of Evidence; and the Rules of the U.S. Supreme Court.

To better understand the principle of "judicial review," we have read Marbury v. Madison (5 U.S. 137), the 1803 case law that made the Supreme Court a separate branch of government, on par with the legislative and executive branches, and formally established the doctrine of

John Marshall (1755-1835), the fourth Chief Justice of the United States.

"judicial review." And, to better understand the life cycle of a litigation, we read "The Pentagon Papers Case."

In light of the recent WikiLeaks and Edward Snowden incidents, the "Pentagon Papers Case" might be of particular interest to you, including the Memorandum issued by the United States District Court for the Southern District in New York, the decision of the Second Circuit Court, and the landmark U.S. Supreme Court decision in New York Times Co. v. United States (403 U.S. 713), a triumph of the First Amendment. The ruling made it possible for the New York Times and Washington Post to continue to publish the then-classified Pentagon Papers without risking of government censorship or punishment. As Justice Hugo Black articulated in his concurring opinion:

In the First Amendment the Founding Fathers gave the free press the protection it must have to fulfill its essential role in our democracy. The press was to serve the governed, not the governors. The Government's power to censor the press was abolished so that the press would remain forever free to censure the Government. The press was protected so that it could bare the secrets of government and inform the people. Only a free and unrestrained press can effectively expose deception in government. And paramount among the responsibilities of a free press is the duty to prevent any part of the government from deceiving the people and sending them off to distant lands to die of foreign fevers and foreign shot and shell.

Let us not forget that, in China, access to information is still a *privilege*, not a right. While reading this opinion or conducting legal research on Westlaw to understand a particular statute, it is hard to fathom that Chinese scholars and journalists can be charged with "divulging state secrets" for simply publishing a CPC leader's internal speech or media censorship orders, and lawyers can be disbarred for representing those defendants.

Our task is to gain a whole picture of American law and perfect a way to find the law we need. Two hundred years ago, almost all the information a lawyer needed was contained in the American edition of Blackstone's "Commentaries on the Law of England: "the great multivolume, comprehensive law text of the 18th century. "With Blackstone, a desk, and an inkwell, you were a lawyer."

Today's lawyer is no renaissance man. We have practical working knowledge of legal rules, legal institutions and the fundamental tools of legal research as they apply to the specialized areas in which we practice.

"Legal research," as defined in *Black's Law Dictionary*, is:

1) The finding and assembling of authorities that bear on a question of law"; or

2) The field of study concerned with the effective marshaling of authorities that bear on a question of law.

The American Bar Association identifies legal research as a "fundamental lawyering skill." It is the arduous process of finding the necessary information to attempt to answer a question of law. Thus, we swim in **Westlaw,** a sea of legal information:

Primary authority—enforceable legal rules and principles that may be mandatory or persuasive—is the body of law. Primary authority includes cases, Constitutions, statutes, regulations and rules.

Secondary authority—comments upon, analyzes, discusses, interprets, and/or criticizes primary authority —includes treatises, practice materials, Restatements, periodicals, *American Law Reports* and much more.

We also learned the value of using KeyCite™ to ensure that a law is still "good law," so as to avoid citing "bad law" (i.e., law that is out-of-date) in court.

We learned how to do legal research with the help of *West's Analysis of American Law*, or the Key Number System™. The West Outline of the Law organized the entire body of American law into seven categories: Persons; Property; Contracts; Torts; Crimes; Remedies; and Government. The law is categorized into more than 400 topics and 100,000 subtopics. The Key Number System™ is the most powerful tool available to legal researchers, making it easy for them to find any and all legal resources relevant to a given issue.

The "West" in West's *Analysis of American Law* refers to Mr. John B. West, the founder of West Publishing. On Oct. 21, 1876, John B. West began publishing "The Syllabi," in St. Paul, Minn., thus starting the National Reporter System, the genesis of legal publishing in the United States.

The Syllabi, Volume 1, Number 1, published by John B. West in St. Paul, Minnesota, on Saturday, October 21, 1876.

Now we come to the question: Can China really pattern its legal system after the Anglo-American system if, as the CPC argues, the Anglo-American system does not fit China's reality and situation?

The Syllabi, Volume 1, Number 1, published by John B. West in St. Paul, Minnesota, on Saturday, October 21, 1876.

Our final research project was a daunting task: Find a Chinese legal case of interest to you, transfer the fact pattern of the Chinese case to the great state of Minnesota, find relevant state and federal case law and statutes on **Westlaw**, apply relevant American legal principles to the Chinese case, and then present your finding and analysis as if you were operating under the U.S. legal system, following its principle of precedents.

Are we subjecting ourselves to "incommensurability of paradigms?" As Thomas Kuhn, American physicist, historian, and philosopher, whose book "The Structure of Scientific Revolutions" gave rise to the term "paradigm shift" argued, proponents of different paradigms cannot fully appreciate or understand others' points of view because they live in different worlds, with different ideas, vocabularies, and experiences.

Can we reconcile the "incommensurability of paradigms" in law and legal research? Particularly when West meets East, when common law meets the "socialist legal system with Chinese characteristics"?

Perhaps we can. Perhaps we can collaborate to build, to exchange ideas, to share knowledge, and to communicate in the neutral language of the law.

In this course, we have identified legal issues; read and learned case laws, statutes, regulations and rules; examined and analyzed fact patterns and procedural postures in the light of governing laws and rules; and finally, we have reached our conclusions.

If, after weeks of searching, reading and analyzing, and being constantly challenged, you are confident you have found the right authorities, put together the right resources, and thoroughly read and analyzed all relevant materials, then the law is in your hearts and minds.

You now think like a lawyer!

In harmony with the truth expressed in Jane Austen's *Pride and Prejudice*: "it is universally acknowledged, that a single man in possession of a good fortune must be in want of a wife," we believe that a developing country with excellent potential for prosperity must be in want of some good lawyers.

The practice of law is a calling. "To our clients, we are advocates and advisors; to the courts, we are officers with a duty to speak for the justice system; to the public, we represent the rule of law and have an obligation to represent it honorably."

I share with you the Attorney's Oath I took eight years ago in St. Paul, Minnesota:

"I do swear that I will support the Constitution of the United States and that of the state of Minnesota, and will conduct myself as an attorney and counselor at law in an upright and courteous manner, to the best of my learning and ability, with all good fidelity as well to the court as to the client, and that I will use no falsehood or deceit, nor delay any person's cause for lucre or malice. So help me God."

This is the last lecture of *Legal Research in American Law: The Westlaw Approach.*

The last lecture is a hidden tradition at many esteemed universities and colleges, where the teaching professor has the liberty to depart from the subject matter of the course and share some private thoughts with the students. The fundamental presumption of any "last lecture" is: "If this were your last chance to lecture your students, what would you say?"

I was most fortunate to sit in the late Law Professor Donald Marshall's lecture at Mondale Hall, the University of Minnesota Law School, on April 27, 2005, when he shared the six clearly thought-through personal values and principles that guided his life: discrimination is wrong; service is important; you have an obligation to teach; manipulation and exploitation are wrong; you should live a healthy life; and, you should devote yourself to creating a few genuine love relationships. His last lecture has become one of the most cherished moments in the University of Minnesota Law School community's collective memory.

So please indulge me for a few minutes while I share with you a story that changed me from an artist to an attorney. I hope, however, that by doing so, I will not appear to be overly eager to be associated with the Last Lectures of past great teachers.

My story is an actual historical event which I have watched on the History Channel and which I have read about in history books.

My story is a story about the courage of a lawyer — Joseph Welch — while standing in front of the most powerful Senator Joseph McCarthy.

On June 9, 1954, on the 30th day of the Army-McCarthy hearings being held by a United States Senate subcommittee, Senator McCarthy accused Fred Fisher, a junior attorney at Welch's law firm, of associating while in law school with the National Lawyers Guild, a group for which J. Edgar Hoover had sought designation as a Communist front organization.

Welch, acting as the head counsel for the Army, dismissed the charge as a youthful indiscretion and condemned McCarthy for naming the young man before a nationwide television audience without prior warning or previous agreement to do so. Welch said to McCarthy, in an unmistakable voice:

"Until this moment, Senator, I think I have never really gauged your cruelty or your recklessness. Fred Fisher is a young man who went to the Harvard Law School and came into my firm and is starting what looks to be a brilliant career with us. Little did I dream you could be so reckless and so cruel as to do an injury to that lad. It is true he is still with Hale and Dorr. It is true that he will continue to be with Hale and Dorr. It is, I regret to say, equally true that I fear he shall always bear a scar needlessly inflicted by you. If it were in my power to forgive you for your reckless cruelty I would do so. I like to think I am a gentle man but your forgiveness will have to come from someone other than me."

When McCarthy again sought to attack Fisher, Welch interrupted him:

"Senator, may we not drop this? We know he belonged to the Lawyers Guild. Let us not assassinate this lad further, Senator. You've done enough. Have you no sense of decency, sir? At long last, have you left no sense of decency?"

McCarthy tried to ask Welch another question about Fisher, and Welch cut him off:

"Mr. McCarthy, I will not discuss this further with you. You have sat within six feet of me and could have asked me about Fred Fisher. You have seen fit to bring it out. And if there is a God in Heaven it will do neither you nor your cause any good. I will not discuss it further. I will not ask Mr. Cohn any more questions. You, Mr. Chairman, may, if you will, call the next witness."

The spectators' gallery burst into applause.

This is one of the most beautiful moments in American history, and it was the beginning of the downfall of Senator Joseph McCarthy.

When I first saw this story, while thrilled by the audacious courage of Joseph Welch, I was mostly intrigued by the question:

How could he? Didn't he fear consequences?

We all are well aware what the consequences that Joseph Welch would have faced had the hearing been held in China. In China, with their passports confiscated, the brave and outspoken cannot leave the country; the even more courageous and outspoken cannot even get out of their homes, as they suffer house arrest; and the most courageous cannot get out of the jail—as they are serving time for "inciting to subvert the state power."

Years later, I found out my question was well-asked and answered by Lee Ross and Richard E. Nisbett in the book "The Person and the Situation":

> Indeed, when we are confronted with behavior that seems to suggest exceptional personal attributes of any kind we tell ourselves to pause and

consider the situation. What were the details of the immediate context of behavior? How was the situation construed by the actor? And what was the broader social context or social system within which the actors were functioning? More pointedly, what objective situational features or subjective construals, or tension system considerations would make these seemingly exceptional actions less exceptional, and more congruent with what experience has taught us about the way ordinary people (ourselves included) generally behave?

The dramatic exchange between Welch and McCarthy led me to explore and appreciate the "broader social context or social system" in which Joseph Welch was operating: American legal system.

And I hope this story will also make you think about the reasons why you study law and why you want to become a lawyer.

11

The Last Lecture on China:
To The Next Generation of China Watchers*

At the beginning of this class, I asked you to close your eyes and tell me the first image that came to your mind when you heard "China." Today, during this last session, I am going to ask you to do the same thing again. This time the image might be the same, or it might be different. Is it clearer? Is it closer? I hope it is not just an empty chair.

As a lawyer, I gave you this disclaimer: this class is not about truth, it is about facts. I am sure that you now have sufficient background information, and you are equipped with the fundamental tools of critical and comparative analysis that you need for further investigation and research, should you wish to become a China watcher.

You have read the Preamble to the Constitution of People's Republic of China, and compared its version of modern Chinese history with the version offered in *Charter '08*. You saw that the Party presented the narrative of *100 Years of Humiliation (1840-1949)* as indisputable

*In fall semester of 2013, the University of Minnesota offered its first Honors Seminar on China to undergraduate students with strong records of academic achievement. This seminar, titled "Modern China: Law, History, and Culture," is taught by Chang Wang and attended by 12 Honors Students at the University. This Honors Seminar on China introduced American students to distinctive paradigms and discursive patterns of law and politics in China, with the intention of fostering comparative analysis and critical thinking. The course focused on modern Chinese history since 1840, paying particular attention to traditional Chinese views of the role of law in society, as well as to the legal and political aspects of early Sino-Western interaction. The course also discussed substantive laws, high profile legal cases, and major political events in the People's Republic of China today. The course concluded by examining current issues in Chinese law from both sides, and by looking into China's argument for "Beijing Consensus" without Western-style rule of law. This article is a modified version of Chang Wang's final remarks to the class on Dec. 9, 2013. *China Insight* published the original lecture in article form on January 1, 2014.

facts, which reminded us Croce's observation that "all history is contemporary history."

You read Confucius, Mencius and the Legalists. You learned to distinguish the "great man" that Mencius admired from the "true gentleman" that Confucius praised. You learned, with horror, of the First Emperor's burning of the books and burying alive of intellectuals; you then read, with a forced smile, "The Madman's Diary" by Lu Xun.

We discussed the "Ti-Yong dichotomy" ("Chinese learning for fundamental principles and Western learning for practical application") advocated by Zhang Zhidong, providing the hidden rationale that underscores ideological narratives in modern China. You were advised to read with discretion the Chinese criminal statute, which linked almost every human action with a punishment. You probably were surprised and puzzled by the "hidden rules of Chinese society," including, but not limited to, the government's right to harm its citizen and citizens' lack of individual civil rights.

You learned about two occurrences that gave great hope to the Chinese people: first, the May 4th Movement of 1919, which served as the starting point of modern Chinese culture and introduced "Mr. Democracy" and "Mr. Science" to China. Second, there was the 1980s Cultural Renaissance, which ameliorated the trauma that the Chinese people had suffered during the Cultural Revolution. However, endless civil wars, the Anti-Rightist Campaign, the Great Famine of 1959-1961, the Red Terror by the Red Guards and the Cultural Revolution, and, finally, the tragedy of 1989 (Tiananmen), crashed those hopes again and again, leading us to question the very nature of human existence and the validity of the law of *karma*.

You researched and did marvelous presentations on The Opium War; the Burning of Yuan-ming-yuan; the Boxer

Rebellion; extraterritoriality in China; Deng Xiaoping; Zhao Ziyang; Professor Fang Lizhi; the curious case of Ai Weiwei; the more curious case of Chen Guangcheng; and the most curious cases of Wang Lijun/Gu Kailai/Bo Xilai. You have proved beyond a reasonable doubt that you are not only able to locate and critically evaluate resources and materials on China's legal and political systems, history and current affairs, but you also understand the diverse philosophies and cultures within and across the society.

You found striking similarities between the Big Brother's attempts to "correct" history in George Orwell's "1984," and the Chinese authority's systematic efforts to wipe certain unpleasant memories out of the collective consciousness of the people. Using history as a mirror to reflect present and future, we traced the common characteristics shared by all kinds of autocratic regimes: suppressive, vicious, pragmatic, hypocritical, vengeful, and highly corrupt. Quoting Jorge Mario Pedro Vargas Llosa, recipient of the 2010 Nobel Prize in Literature: "A totalitarian government pollutes and destroys the whole society. Everything —including family life and love, no matter whether it is political or not—is polluted."

Despite tremendous hardship, the Chinese people have always risen above the failings of their rulers and found ways to survive and try to make a better future for their children. Nevertheless, when you did some simple math and realized that China will be governed by the generation of the Red Guards for the next decade or two, a big chill went down your spine. Are they the "same bunch of goons and thugs they have been for the last 50 years?" (Jack Cafferty)

Also in this class, you have familiarized yourself with major players on the stage of modern and contemporary China: Empress Dowager Cixi, Dr. Sun Yatsen,

Generalissimo Chiang Kaishek, Mao, Madam Mao, Deng, and Liu Xiaobo. You have also benefited from learned academics such as John King Fairbank, Jonathan Spence, Jerome Cohen, Orville Schell, Perry Link, Pei Minxin and He Weifang, as well as from the insightful and amusing commentaries of Yu Hua, Murong Xuecun, Richard McGregor and Ted Koppel.

We read news too: Ambassador Gary Locke is leaving Beijing. The Chinese people should forever be grateful to him for bringing the PM 2.5 air pollution index to China, as well as for his uncompromising commitment to improve human rights. Good news, too, from the Third Plenum Session of the 18th Communist Party of China Central Committee: the notorious reeducation- through-labor program has finally been abolished, and the "one-child" policy has been loosened. However, these are just half-hearted attempts to correct past wrongs, without admitting the wrongs. It would be misleading to interpret them as indications of a larger agenda for political reform. Finally, none of us was really surprised by the denial of visa to Paul Mooney, or by Bloomberg's decision to spike an investigative report on the questionable link between power and wealth in China.

2013, just like the year of 1587 that historian Ray Huang researched, appears to be "a year of no particular significance:" The Party, despite political and economic problems, remains firmly in power. The Great Firewall is high, the sky is gray, and the public forum quiet: "stability" is well maintained. Yet 2013 may be a year of particular significance for China, as all the signs point to either "the coming collapse of China" or "when China rules the world."

Nevertheless, while our subject is unpredictable and different in many ways, history teaches us one thing: every autocratic regime dies, because "its political order suffers from the same self-destructive dynamics: leadership degeneration, corruption, rising social tensions, and loss of government credibility." (Pei Minxin) No political force will be in charge forever, but the people will. When Chinese teachers tell children that Chinese civilization is the only "unbroken" civilization in the world, it is not entirely a lie. . . because resilience is a key feature of the Chinese character. No matter how long it has been eradicated (Yuan/Mongolian Dynasty), no matter how much damage has been done (Mao), Chinese culture always comes back and thrives. As Tang poet Bai Juyi wrote about the prairie grasses: "Wild fire could not burn them up to extirpate; Springtide zephyrs blow and they come to life again."

Shrewd pundits observe the same set of evidence but come up with completely opposite prognoses: total collapse, or the new super power. Will a sliding door guide China one way or another? Will a butterfly effect lead to random chaos? Whether it's headed toward triumph or collapse, China is undeniably undergoing tremendous change, and expecting even larger ones. At the 2013 Commencement of China University of Political Science and Law in Beijing, Professor Cong Riyun reminded the graduating class: "Black clouds are accumulating, thunderstorm is coming, make sure you choose the right position, and make sure you are on the right side of the history."

It is a deceptively simple yet daunting task.

Bei Dao, the greatest living Chinese poet, wrote in 1975: *"This universal longing/Has now become the whole cost of being a man/I have lied many times/in my life/But I have always honestly kept to/The promise I made as a child/So that the world which cannot tolerate/A child's heart/Has still not forgiven me."* Ai Weiwei, the greatest living Chinese artist, put it in a different way: "When you try to understand your motherland, you already have begun your journey to become a (thought) criminal."

In an Orwellian, Huxleyite, or Kafkaesque time, a normal citizen would appear to be a maverick. Chinese intellectuals, as a species, were exterminated in 1957 during the Anti-Rightist Campaign. In an age of no heroes, I too am a domesticated fox, the end-product of selective breeding to achieve certain preferred behavioral traits, e.g., respecting and trusting the authority. Derailed outliers can be put on the watch-list and the no-fly list, gagged, smothered, smeared, or simply disappeared.

This class attempts to provide neutral, yet critical, analysis of China. Both sides of the arguments are presented to you for you to hear and evaluate. Sometimes you may feel that you and the Chinese are living in two parallel universes: some basic matters of fact, even those knowable by empirical evaluation, are disputed: e.g., the Korean War, the Great Famine, and the tragedy of 1989.

Frequent travel and extended stays help me appreciate both China and the U.S. even more. The more I learn about China and America, the more I realize how little I know about these two great countries. I consider myself most fortunate to be able to appreciate the beauty of the Chinese language and culture. At the same time, I am able to function in the American system of justice and fundamental fairness. I feel obligated to serve as a bridge between these two countries: I am a lineal descendant of Chinese arts and intellectual tradition, and, at the same time, I am a zealous advocate for the democratic values, equal protection, and due process of the American system. In fact, there are only two things that can bring me close to tears: Chinese literature and American law.

Furthermore, living as an insider in two cultures gives me excellent vantage points from which to compare them.

As a result, I take nothing for granted. I am less susceptible to prejudice, because I know how it feels to be discriminated against; I am less willing to accept presumptions, especially when making business decisions, because I know that any presumption is rebuttable if you change your point of view ever so slightly. And, finally, I am more willing to communicate, collaborate, and compromise, because I know how easily language can be manipulated, and how easily information and ideas can get lost in translation, leading to misunderstandings.

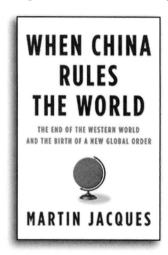

As we end our discussion and analysis of China, I would like share with you three quotes about China:

The first one is a paragraph from the preface to "My Life in China and America," the autobiography of Yung Wing, the first Chinese student to graduate from an American university: "Would it not be strange, if an Occidental education, continually exemplified by an Occidental civilization, had not wrought upon an Oriental such a metamorphosis in his inward nature as to make him feel and act as though he were a being coming from a different world, when he confronted one so diametrically different? This was precisely my case, and yet neither patriotism nor the love of my fellow countrymen had been weakened. On the contrary, they had increased in strength from sympathy."

The second one is from the late Professor Fang Lizhi: "There is no such thing as democracy with Chinese characteristics, just like there is no such thing as physics with Chinese characteristics, or science with Chinese characteristics."

The last one is from Professor Yu Yingshih, a leading Chinese philosopher and historian, who left mainland China in 1950 and spent most of his life in the US: "Wherever I go is China. Why do I need to go to that particular geographical location to find China, there is no China on that land."

It is an honor to be your instructor of this Honors Seminar on China. It is a privilege to share my thoughts on the law, history, and culture of my country and my people with you. I hope our paths will cross again in the not-too-distant future, whether in the world of things Chinese or in the world of things American, or in a place where the two great countries and cultures meet.

I Thought You Deserve Better:
Post-election Remarks to Honors Program Students, University of Minnesota*

Welcome to our first class in Trumpland.

This is a seminar on modern China, but after this election, our discussion on China is becoming more relevant to understanding the current political situation of America.

As a teacher, I feel obligated to share some of my thoughts with you: for the first time in my 16 years in the United States, I feel I am "home" — back in China.

I thought you deserve better.

It took a half century to make "political correctness" a principle of the American society. This principle embraces

A campaign sign in Polk County, Tennessee, June, 2016

civil rights, women's rights, LGBTQ rights, environmental protection, non-discrimination, tolerance, and empathy. I remember my professor in law school explained this concept in a very simple way: "This concept refers to a societal consensus that it is absolutely wrong to discriminate or exploit other people, based on their race, gender, class, religious beliefs, sexual orientation, or political affiliation." But it did take several generation's efforts and lives (Dr. Martin Luther King, RFK, Freedom Riders, and suffragettes, to name a few) to build today's "politically correct" world

*hang Wang's opening remarks to the class "Modern China:
and Culture", an Honors Seminar at the University of Minnesota,
10, 2016, two days after the 2016 presidential election. *China*
ed the remarks in the January 2017 issue.

for you. You are fortunate to be born in a world which is less violent, less discriminatory, safer, and cleaner. You automatically inherited the legacy of equal protection and due process from the past generations. It is likely that your parents put certain amounts in your bank account. But just like any inheritance, if you just sit on it and spend it, it will be depleted. Equal protection, due process, non-discrimination, freedom of speech, freedom of association. If you take all these for granted, just like clean water and clean air, you won't notice them until they become unavailable.

Elizabeth Eckford tries to flee an increasingly angry white mob outside the Little Rock Central High School, September 4, 1957

I know this because I grew up in a place where the government has a legitimate right to rule you, to exploit you, even to harm you. Individual rights do not exist, and open discrimination is accepted as a norm. Many first-generation immigrants like me came to this country for the rule of law, equal protection, due process, diversity and inclusion, for America's fundamental fairness and freedom from fear.

But I am fearful these days, and I fear for the future.

I am fearful because I hear the same rhetoric that emerged in 1949's China and in 2016's America: "I promise you land, I promise you jobs, and I promise you greatness." Millions of Chinese living in rural areas followed their leader Mao in a revolution overthrowing a democratic government, only to find themselves in a grave they dug for

21

themselves. The Chinese people lost their freedoms, their properties, and ultimately, their lives.

I am fearful because I hear the same rhetoric in 1966's China and 2016's America: "It's all their fault, the establishment, the elites, the media. They are all corrupt, all crooked. Beat them up, and lock them up!" This pattern of anti-intellectualism and anti-culture destroyed Chinese culture, arts, education, all academic institutions, and the

Mao's Red Guards torturing and humiliating intellectuals, 1960s, China

entire infrastructure of a civilization. Chinese people followed their ruthless leader Mao and engaged in a civil war against tradition, culture, and humanity.

I am fearful because I hear hate speech blaming ethnic minorities, religious groups, and undocumented workers for economic and security problems, and labeling those "others" as inferior species, thus excluded from equal protection and due process. This kind of mentality empowered numerous ethnic cleansings, religious persecutions, lynchings, and genocides in human history. It has always been "we" vs. "them", conquerors vs. barbarians, human vs. inhuman. Under this logic, xenophobia and hatred are justified, murders and mass killings are celebrated.

I am fearful because I see striking similarities of personalities in the "great" leaders: hypocritical; calculating; vengeful ("long list of enemies" and "very long memory"); ~~ ~ erly disrespectful to women, minorities, the nd anybody less fortunate, lacking empathy; science and technology; pathologically mixing

22

facts with lies; financially corrupt and morally bankrupt; and endlessly seeking power, fame, and lust. I know what these sort of "great" leaders are capable of, particularly what they can do to people's liberties and lives.

"Chairman Mao is with us forever" poster in Cultural Revolution, 1970s China

Nevertheless, America did not change on Tuesday November 8th, but America will change in the coming months and years. It is now totally up to you, your generation, to look at the ever-shrinking balance in your bank account, then decide what to do with it.

Toute nation a le gouvernement qu'elle mérite: In a democracy people get the leaders they deserve.

You deserve better; we deserve better.

University of Minnesota Students protesting in Minneapolis, November 10, 2016

Truth and Lies in Chinese Culture:
An Overview*

In her provocative book, *Lies that Bind: Chinese Truth, Other Truths,* anthropologist Susan Blum examines rules, expectations, and beliefs regarding lying and honesty in Chinese society. She argues that public lying is evaluated within Chinese society by culturally specific moral values. The Chinese, for example, might emphasize consequences of speech, while Americans would emphasize the absolute truthfulness.[1] That is because "Chinese tend to consider language a kind of action like other action, and Americans view language/speech as separate from the others."[2] The Chinese surpass Americans, Blum concludes, in manipulation of language.[3]

Blum points out that "deception and lying are distinctively cultural yet universal — inseparable from what it is to be a human being equipped with language in all its

---

*This article is a part of "Preparing to Negotiate in a Globally Diverse Environment: An Examination of Chinese and Jewish Perspectives on Truth and Lies," co. with David Larson, 33 Hamline J. Pub. L. & Pol'y 269 (2012).

[1]Susan Blum, Lies That Bind: Chinese Truth, Other Truths 4 (Rowman & Littlefield 2007).

[2]*Id.*

[3]*See id.* at 25. Blum quotes Chinese novelist Feng Jicai to illustrate Chinese wiseacre's view on truth and lying: The terms truth and falsehood contain so many subtle nuances that, if we invited the sages to debate them, even the learned ones would be unable to explain thoroughly. If there is truth, there must be falsehood; if there is falsehood, there must be truth. If truth increases, falsehood diminishes; if falsehood increases, truth diminishes. And from the beginning of history, in that area that lies between the poles of true and false, how many games have been run? How many dramas, great and small, have been played out? Play after play plays within plays, the stage is never silent. To substitute false for true is a source of great pride; to confuse true with false is a talent.

subtlety."[4] As illustrations of culturally distinctive deceptions, Blum recounts in Chapter Two a few anecdotes told by her Chinese friends to illustrate the Chinese tendency to view deception as "street smart." The stories concerned swindlers who were targeting dupes. Attempted swindles are always depicted by Chinese storytellers as examples of cleverness, and are presented not as battles of morality, but as battles of strategy. "Life in contemporary China is often depicted as filled with traps, scams, cons, misrepresentations, and other forms of danger for the unwary (especially for the greedy and gullible). Clever people (*pianzi*, cheater (s): or "swindler(s)" or "deceiver(s)")" carefully lay traps and entice dupes to their web; the dupes exercise insufficient caution — or, at most, predictable caution."[5] In one of the most popular 20th century Chinese novels, *The Deer and the Cauldron*[6], protagonist Wei Xiaobao is a lazy, illiterate,

---

But if you were fooled and took false for true, your own poor vision and thinking were to blame. Now don't go getting angry and upset. Weren't there many people who so took false for true that, even on the day they died, they still couldn't recognize the truth? And wasn't the false then true after all? As to the terms true and false, the honest, naïve people looked for the two obvious extremes. The shrewd, clever ones played the middle ground, some making a good living at it.

[4]*See generally id.* Blum correctly understands the universality of language manipulation and the potential of the language in its subtlety. *Id.* English language shall not be underestimated in this regard, *e.g.*, Sir Humphrey Appleby's famous "You told a lie" comment to Prime Minister Jim Hacker: I explain to the Prime Minister that unfortunately, although the answer was indeed simple, clear and straightforward, there was some difficulty in justifiably assigning to it the fourth of the epithets he had applied to the statement [honest] inasmuch as the precise correlation between the information he had communicated and the facts insofar as they can be determined and demonstrated is such as to cause epistemological problems of sufficient magnitude to lay upon the logical and semantic resources of the English language a heavier burden then they can reasonably be requested to bear. Jonathan Lynn & Antony Jay, *The Tangled Web*, in YES, PRIME MINISTER 409 (BBC, 1989).

[5]BLUM, *supra* note 4, at 33.

[6]*See generally* Louis Cha, THE DEER AND THE CAULDRON (John Milford trans., Oxford, 1997).

witty and sly opportunist who enjoys a number of seemingly impossible successes through sheer luck and wit. The secret of his success: Making sure that every detail is "verifiable" when telling the big lie.

The Chinese generally believe that frankness and honesty make one vulnerable to the manipulation of others. Honesty is inseparable from naiveté and could be a fatal shortcoming that invites aggression and cheating.[7] To survive in the jungle of Chinese society, according to the conventional wisdom, one should avoid the empty principle of honesty and learn from Wei Xiaobao's success.

The Chinese people's view of truth and lying is deeply rooted in traditional Confucian ethics. Confucian ethics values are *Wu Chang* (the Five Constant Virtues): *Ren* (Benevolence), *Yi* (Righteousness), *Li* (Propriety), *Zhi* (Wisdom), and *Xin* (Fidelity), listed in order of importance with *Ren* as the most basic virtue.[8] Etymologically, *Xin* is a character created by combining the two characters "people" and "speech," indicating "to persist that one said" or "one's deeds match one's words." *Xin* has a meaning similar to that of English words such as fidelity, integrity, honesty, trust, faith, and promise; however, it is not equivalent to any of them.

The Five Constant Virtues are hierarchical in nature; when one is in a situation in which two or more virtues

---

[7] *Id.* at 32.

[8] *See* Yamamoto Yasuo, *The Structure of Oriental Values and Education*, available at http://www.crvp.org/book/Series03/III-11/chapter_xxiii.htm. *See also* Tomonobu Imamichi, Wang Miaoyan & Liu Fangtongg, *The Humanization of Technology and Chinese Culture, in* ASIA VOLUME 11, CULTURAL HERITAGE AND CONTEMPORARY CHANGE, ch. XXIII (Ser. No. III), *available at* http://www.crvp.org/book/Series03/III-11/contents.htm ("There is an order of priority in the five virtues. Benevolence is first, righteousness follows, then propriety and wisdom, and finally fidelity. The criterion for this order is the benefit of each to people and society."). *See also* DAGOBERT D. RUNES, DICTIONARY OF PHILOSOPHY 338 (1983).

cannot be achieved at the same time, it is permissible to sacrifice the lower virtue for the higher virtue. This interplay of the virtues is exemplified by Confucius's *"Spring and Autumn Annals,"* a work which contains the record of the Kingdom of Lu for 242 years.[9] The 19th Century Scottish Sinologist, Dr. James Legge, attached great importance to the manner in which Confucius prioritized the virtues in this work: The fact is that the Annals are evasive and deceptive.[10] The *Spring and Autumn Annals* conceal [the truth] out of regard to the high in rank, to kinship, and to men of worth. According to Dr. Legge, this "concealing" covers the ground embraced in three English words—ignoring, concealing, and misrepresenting."[11] Despite the concealing present in the work, both Confucius and his disciple Mencius believed that the *"Spring and Autumn Annals"* was the master's greatest achievement; they understood that "it was from it [*Spring and Autumn Annals*][12] men would know him, and also condemn him."[13] Understanding that his approach would expose him to criticism, Confucius nonetheless established the precedent that it is acceptable, even noble, to sacrifice truth (fidelity) in order to preserve social status ("high in rank"), family relations ("kinship") and good reputations ("men of worth").[14]

---

[9]*See generally* SPRING AND AUTUMN ANNALS: THE FIVE CONFUCIAN CLASSICS (Michael Nylan trans., Yale University Press 2001).

[10]ARTHUR HENDERSON SMITH, CHINESE CHARACTERISTICS 278 [hereinafter CHINESE CHARACTERISTICS] (citing JAMES LEGGE, THE RELIGIONS OF CHINA: CONFUCIANISM AND DAOISM DESCRIBED AND COMPARED WITH CHRISTIANITY (Shanghai SDX Joint Publishing Company, 2007)).

[11]*Id* at 279.

[12]SPRING AND AUTUMN ANNALS: THE FIVE CONFUCIAN CLASSICS (Michael Nylan trans., Yale University Press 2001).

[13]CHINESE CHARACTERISTICS, *supra* note 13, at 278. For a full translation of ANALECTS OF CONFUCIUS, *see* ANALECTS OF CONFUCIUS (Arthur Waley, trans., Vintage 1989).

[14]*See* CHINESE CHARACTERISTICS, *supra* note 13, at 278.

Confucianism, Taoism, and Buddhism were the three most predominant religions in imperial China. Unlike Confucianism, Taoism does not speak directly on the matter of truth and lying. However, Lao-tzu, the founder of Taoism, did reflect on the complications of truth to be told: "The Tao (Truth) can be told is not the eternal Tao (truth), the name can be named is not the eternal name."[15] Similarly, "True words are not eloquent, eloquent words are not true."[16]

Chinese Buddhism has developed a comprehensive philosophical system based on the original Mahayana Buddhism. Almost all schools are committed to the fundamental ethical rules known as the "Five Precepts:" abstention from taking life; abstention from taking what is not given; abstention from sexual misconduct; abstention from false speech; and abstention from intoxication. These are the cardinal rules in Buddhist practice, for both Sanghas (ordained monks or nuns) and lay practitioners. There is no hierarchical order of the Five Precepts; they are equally important. In the *Sutta to Cunda the Silversmith (Cunda Kammaraputta Sutta)*, Buddha elaborates on the abstention from false speech by comparing "skillful mental, verbal and bodily actions" and "unskillful mental, verbal, and bodily actions." In the case of "skillful verbal action", the *Sutta* reads:

> And how is one made pure in four ways by verbal action? There is the case where a certain person, abandoning false speech, abstains from false speech. When he has been called to a town meeting, a group meeting, a gathering of his relatives, his guild, or of the royalty, if he is asked as a witness,

---

[15]Lao-tzu, Tao Te Ching: 1 (Stephen Mitchell trans., 2006).
[16]*Id*. at 81.

28

'Come & tell, good man, what you know': If he
doesn't know, he says, 'I don't know.' If he does
know, he says, 'I know.' If he hasn't seen, he says, 'I
haven't seen.' If he has seen, he says, 'I have seen.'
Thus he doesn't consciously tell a lie for his own
sake, for the sake of another, or for the sake of any
reward. Abandoning false speech, he abstains from
false speech. He speaks the truth, holds to the truth,
is firm, reliable, no deceiver of the world.[17]

In this regard, Buddhist teaching is straightforward: to
the best of one's knowledge, the truth, the whole truth,
nothing but the truth.

While Buddhist religious teachings (as distinguished
from Confucian teachings) concerning truth and lying are
well-known to Chinese people, Buddhist teachings clearly
are not reflected in every Chinese individual's attitudes
toward deception. Although an individual may intellectually
understand religious doctrine, the ways in which an individual actually practices religion, as well as secular influences,
also shape his or her attitude towards truth and lying.
According to American missionary Arthur Henderson Smith,
some Chinese have limited interest in spiritual matters and
arguably are irreligious.[18] Chinese worshippers pray mainly
for practical reasons such as financial gain, career,

---

[17]CUNDA KAMMARAPUTTA SUTTA: TO CUNDA THE SILVERSMITH, (Thanissaro Bhikkhu
trans.), *available at* http://www.accesstoinsight.org/tipitaka/an/an10/
an10.176.than.html.

[18]XINZHONG YAO & PAUL BADHAM, RELIGIOUS EXPERIENCE IN CONTEMPORARY CHINA 3
(2007) ("[F]ew Chinese think of themselves as being religious, and even
less would associate themselves with a particular religion . . . ."). *Id*. at 8.
In a recent survey, only 8.7% of Chinese considered themselves religious,
while 52.3% were non-religious, and 26.1% were firm atheists. *Id*. at 153.
China engaged in a serious undertaking to eliminate religion from society
altogether after the Communist revolution. *Id*. at 3. Arguably, though,
religion has been making a comeback in recent years. *See id.*

marriage, or rain for agricultural reasons.[19] Lower classes are mostly polytheists and pantheists who pray to the most convenient deities available in their neighborhood shrines; the upper classes appear to be pure atheists.[20] Fundamental Buddhist religious teachings are basically irrelevant to many people's daily life.[21]

When dealing with secular matters, Chinese of both the lower and upper classes adhere to pragmatic doctrines expressed in *The Art of War*.[22] In Chapter I, "Laying Plans," Sun-tzu asserts: "All warfare is based on deception."[23] "Hence, when able to attack, we must seem unable; when using our forces, we must seem inactive; when we are near, we must make the enemy believe we are far away; when far away, we must make him believe we are near. Hold out

---

[19]*See id.* at 65–66 (explaining a reason for prayer is for the god or goddess to make the praying person's wishes come true, often with an expectation that if the wishes do come true the individual will either burn incense or donate money or belongings to the temple). For example, Lord Dai is one deity whom some Chinese pray to with the belief that because Lord Dai was a physician while alive, praying to him will cure illness. *Id.* at 65. *See also id.* at 4 (explaining Chinese people who are religious generally enter into religion based on their individual circumstances and needs, with, for example, Confucianism "addressing the needs of government, family and education").

[20]*See* CHINESE CHARACTERISTICS, *supra* note 13, at ch. XXVI, "Polytheism, Pantheism, Atheism."

[21]*See* XINZHONG YAO & PAUL BADHAM, RELIGIOUS EXPERIENCE IN CONTEMPORARY CHINA 9 (William K. Kay, et al. eds., 2007) (explaining only 4.4% of Chinese identify themselves as Buddhists and only 5.3% believe in reincarnation, a central tenant of Buddhism). The core Buddhist doctrines "have been more or less confined to Buddhist scholars and high-ranking monks," while ordinary citizens "know little of them" because they "are bound up in the struggles of everyday life and direct their own [lives] only by referring to general Buddhist ideas." *Id.* at 97. Yao and Badham found that although the number of Chinese who feel a "religious experience" was fairly significant, the figures for "religious commitment" were "very low." *Id.* at 9.

[22]*See generally*, SUN TZU, THE ART OF WAR (Lionel Giles, M.A. trans., 1910) *available at* http://ctext.org/art-of-war.

[23]*Id.* at 27.

baits to entice the enemy. Feign disorder, and crush him
. . ."[24] Chapter Thirteen of *The Art of War* is devoted to
discuss *"The Use of Spies"*:[25] manipulation and deception
are necessary, and to be appreciated.

In his quintessential portrait of the Chinese national
character, *Chinese Characteristics*[26], Arthur Henderson
Smith (1845-1932) examined twenty-six Chinese personal
character traits.[27] In spite of the drastic changes in the past
110 years, the patterns of behavior and social mores of the
people are probably much the same as when this book was
written.[28] Smith identifies two traits clearly relevant to any

---

[24]*Id.*

[25]*Id.* at 88-95.

[26]*See* CHINESE CHARACTERISTICS, *supra* note 13.

[27]*Id.* The traits are: 1) Face, 2) Economy, 3) Industry, 4) Politeness, 5)
Disregard of Time, 6) Disregard of Accuracy, 7) Talent for
Misunderstanding, 8) Talent for Indirection, 9) Flexible Inflexibility, 10)
Intellectual Turbidity, 11) Absence of Nerves, 12) Contempt for
Foreigners, 13) Absence of Public Spirit, 14) Conservatism, 15)
Indifference to Comfort and Convenience, 16) Physical Vitality, 17)
Patience and Perseverance, 18) Content and Cheerfulness, 19) Filial
Piety, 20) Benevolence, 21) Absence of Sympathy, 22) Social Typhoons,
23) Mutual Responsibility and Respect for Law, 24) Mutual Suspicion,
25) Absence of Sincerity, 26) Polytheism, Pantheism, Atheism. *Id.*

[28]Kuo-Shu Yang has explained how China's agricultural economy helped
form its culture's personality. *See* KUO-SHU YANG, *Chinese Personality and its
Change, in* THE PSYCHOLOGY OF THE CHINESE PEOPLE 106, 150–51 (Michael Harris
Bond ed., 1986). With China remaining a largely agricultural economy, it's
likely that the general personality of Chinese culture has not changed
significantly, although with continued globalization and a shift toward
industrialization, this could potentially change in the near future. *See*
CHRISTINE GENZBERGER, THE PORTABLE ENCYCLOPEDIA FOR DOING BUSINESS WITH CHINA
12 (1994) (explaining that "China is still primarily an agricultural economy"
and that as recent as 1990 "the agricultural sector employed between 60
and 70 percent of China's work force."). Steve J. Kulich and Rui Zhang
suggest that even with the emergence of modern values, traditional values
continue to coexist with them. Kulich and Zhang further suggest that
scholars should study what form of value blending this eventually leads to
in the future. Steven J. Kulich & Rui Zhang, *The Multiple Frames of
'Chinese' Values: From Tradition to Modernity and Beyond, in* THE OXFORD
HANDBOOK OF CHINESE PSYCHOLOGY 241, 262 (Michael Harris Bond ed., 2010).

discussion of truth and lying: mutual suspicion and the absence of sincerity.[29]

In Chapter XXIV, Smith observes: "The firm foundation on which rest all the many city walls in China is the *distrust* which the government entertains of the people."[30] He thinks "the lofty walls which enclose all premises in Chinese, as in other Oriental cities and towns, are another exemplification of the same traits of suspicion."[31] Smith analyzed the reason why distrust is so prevalent in Chinese society: "There are said to be two reasons why people do not trust one another: first, because they do not know one another, and second, because they do. The Chinese think that they have each of these reasons for mistrust, and they act accordingly."[32] Therefore,

> [I]f any matter is to be accomplished which requires consultation and adjustment, it will not do in China, as it might in any Western land, to send a mere message to be delivered at the home of the person concerned, to the effect that such and such terms could be arranged. The principal must go himself, and he must see the principal on the other side. If the latter should not be at home, then the visit must be repeated until he is found, for otherwise no one would be sure that the matter had not been distorted in its transmission through other media.[33]

The above passage exemplifies that in order to overcome Chinese distrust, it can be important to use overtly reliable means to communicate important information. Moreover, mutual suspicion leads to the result that words are presumptively

---

[29]*See* CHINESE CHARACTERISTICS, *supra* note 13.
[30]*Id.* at 250.
[31]*Id.*
[32]*Id.* at 253.
[33]*Id.* at 257.

untrustworthy, until proven otherwise. Examples of this principle can be seen in a variety of situations:

> A countryman who meets others will be examined by them, as to his abode and its distance from a great number of other places, as if to make sure that he is not deceiving them. In the same manner, scholars are not content with inquiring of a professed literary graduate when he "entered," but he will not improbably be cross-examined upon the theme of his essay, and how he treated it. In this way it is not difficult, and is very common, to expose a fraud.[34]

In the academic context, for instance, this presumption of dishonesty is not unfounded. In China, faking academic credentials has been a practice utilized not only by academics, but also by business executives.[35] This faking diploma practice has been so rampant that employers in China regularly ask their potential employees to have their diploma notarized for authenticity.[36]

---

[34]*Id*. at 260.

[35]Zhang Jiawei, *Execs Stay Silent in Fake Diploma Scam*, CHINA DAILY USA, June 20, 2011, *available at* http://usa.chinadaily.com.cn/china/2011-06/20/content_12738092.htm.

[36]*See generally* Notarization Law of the People's Republic of China (promulgated by the Standing Comm. Nat'l People's Cong., Aug. 28, 2005, effective Mar. 1, 2006), art. 2, (notarization in China means verifying the authenticity of the document: "notarization means an act performed by a notarial institution, upon the application of a party concerned, such as certifying the authenticity and legality of a legal act, a document or a fact of legal significance according to the statutory procedures." *Id*. Author Professor Wang reminds the reader that notarization in China is different from the concept of notarization in common law jurisdictions where a notary's main functions are to administer oaths and affirmations, take affidavits and statutory declarations, witness, authenticate the execution of certain classes of documents, and take acknowledgments of deeds and other conveyances. To "notarize" means "to attest to the authenticity of (a signature, mark, etc.)." *See* "Notarize" and "Notary Public," BLACK'S LAW DICTIONARY (9th ed.2009).

In addition to deception in the academic context, Smith observes that Chinese mutual suspicion can be seen in their commercial customs. For instance, the use of third party neutrals in bargaining is common. While the buyer and seller view each other as untrustworthy, a neutral makes the bargain more reliable, because a neutral's "percentage will only be obtained by the completion of the bargain."[37] For this reason, "[n]o transaction is considered as made at all, until 'bargaining money' has been paid."[38] Similarly, because the buyer and seller do not trust each other, transactions are often viewed as incomplete before they are reduced to writing: "[i]f the matter is a more comprehensive one, something must be put into writing, for 'talk is empty, while the mark of a pen is final.'"[39]

Smith goes on to lament: "The whole history of foreign intercourse with China is a history of suspicion and prevarication on the part of the Chinese."[40]

Mutual suspicion is a result of the absence of sincerity. If we agree with Smith that "the Chinese of the present day do not differ to any great extent from the Chinese of antiquity," then "there can hardly be a doubt that the standard of the Chinese and the present standard of Western nations as to what ought to be called sincerity differ widely."[41] Nonetheless, Smith believes that the Chinese do not lie for the sake of lying, but mainly for the sake of advantages not otherwise to be had. Chinese people are "incapable of speaking of the truth, and they are equally incapable of believing it." And because "the ordinary speech of the Chinese is so full of insincerity, which yet does not rise to the dignity of falsehood, that it is very difficult to learn the truth in almost any case."[42]

---

[37]See CHINESE CHARACTERISTICS, *supra* note 13, at 263.
[38]*Id.*
[39]*Id.*
[40]*Id.* at 272.
[41]*Id.* at 276.
[42]*Id.* at 280.

The most dangerous consequence of this lack of sincerity and culture of lying is the approach of some Chinese parents towards their children, "who are taught to be insincere without consciousness of the fact either on their own part or on the part of those who teach them."[43] One study comparing how Chinese and Canadian children feel about lying and truthfulness revealed that "Chinese children rated truth telling less positively and lie telling more positively in pro-social settings than Canadian children, indicating that the emphasis on self-effacement and modesty in Chinese culture overrides Chinese children's evaluations of lying in some situations."[44] Findings of the study "suggest that, in the realm of lying and truth telling, a close relation between sociocultural practices and moral judgment exists. Specific social and cultural norms have an impact on children's developing moral judgments, which, in turn, are modified by age and experience in a particular culture."[45]

One such cultural norm in China is a "deep distrust of the system, and anyone outside one's immediate family or circle of close friends," plus an emphasis on the importance of acting in one's self-interest or the interest of one's family.[46] One observer relates this cultural emphasis on self-interest to the prevalence of deception and dishonesty, and recommends reform through increased transparency and increased use of fair dispute resolution systems.[47]

---

[43]*Id*. at 283.

[44]Kang Lee, Catherine Ann Cameron et.al, *Chinese and Canadian Children's Evaluations of Lying and Truth Telling: Similarities and Differences in the Context of Pro- and Antisocial Behaviors*, 5 CHILD DEVELOPMENT 68, 924-34 (1997), *available at* http://www.jstor.org/pss/1132042.

[45]*Id*. at 924.

[46]JAMES MCGREGOR, ONE BILLION CUSTOMERS 294 (2005).

[47]*Id*.

One consequence of this tendency towards dishonesty may be the securities scandals involving Chinese companies and the fact that some Chinese companies with shares listed in the United States financial indices falsify financial reports. "[T]hese Chinese companies that have these great numbers, they never miss a quarter of earnings. They are always right on. Their expenses are low. Their growth is tremendous, regardless of the economy."[48] This did not seem plausible, and this suspicion later was confirmed. "[T]he SEC had initiated an ongoing investigation into Chinese stock frauds in the United States . . . The frauds appear to have been orchestrated on a massive scale by Chinese companies traded on North American stock exchanges."[49] Observers found that "[t]he China Stock Frauds in the United States bear striking similarities with the Chinese corporations scandals in Singapore and the series of bankruptcy failures of P-Chips in Hong Kong."[50] Zealous investors from the U.S., Singapore, and Hong Kong have been blinded by the risks, making themselves vulnerable to deception. They have apparently ignored Smith's keen observation 110 years ago: "The almost total lack of such forms of investment as we are so familiar with in Western lands is due not more to the lack of development of the resources of the Empire, than to the general mistrust of one another among the people."[51] These investors have

---

[48]Ryan Vlastelica & Daniel Bases, *Special Report: Chinese Stock Scams Are the Latest U.S. Import*, REUTERS (May 11, 2011, 7:52 PM), http://www.reuters.com/article/2011/05/11/us-china-shortsellers-idUSTRE74A71F20110511.

[49]*China Stock Frauds*, KREUZROADS (Nov. 9, 2011), http://kreuzroads.blogspot.com/2011/11/china-stock-frauds_9707.html#more.

[50]*Id.*

[51]*See* CHINESE CHARACTERISTICS, *supra* note 13, at 255.

forgotten that the businessmen from China have studied *The Art of War*, and thus believe the fundamental principle in the book that *"All warfare is based on deception"* is totally applicable in their business practice.[52]

---

[52]*See* GEORGE T. HALEY ET AL., THE CHINESE TAO OF BUSINESS: THE LOGIC OF SUCCESSFUL BUSINESS STRATEGY 132 (2004) (explaining that while Western cultures view deception as evil, deception can be *virtuous* in Chinese business, noting that a person acts "honorably" when deceiving "to promote employers' or friends' interests," and further stating that Chinese "accept the reality of deception as a necessary element in their daily lives"); *see also* JENNY LI, PASSPORT CHINA: YOUR POCKET GUIDE TO CHINESE BUSINESS, CUSTOMS, & ETIQUETTE 55 (2nd ed. 2003) (showing that "Deception and the exploitation of weaknesses are time-honored strategies in China's business, military, and political arenas."); ALEXANDER AGEEV, *The Ethics of Political Economy, in* EDUCATING FOR DEMOCRACY: PAIDEIA IN AN AGE OF UNCERTAINTY 269-71 (Alan M. Olson et al. eds., 2004) (explaining one Chinese author's use of vivid language to illustrate how the use of military tactics such as cunning and deception will lead to triumph in business).

An Accidental Encounter with the Maestro*

If I've ever doubted that Italy is a place where all miracles are possible, or wondered if a dream can ultimately come true through uncompromised love and unequivocal devotion, or questioned the complete thoughtfulness of the "almighty," October 6, 2012 provided me with an answer.

On that Saturday afternoon, I was on a train (ES9521) from Milano Centrale to Roma Termini. While teaching a short course on Chinese law at the University of Bern as a

Dario Fo (right) and Chang Wang, October 6, 2012.

visiting professor, I had planned to spend the weekend in Rome with family friends. Unfortunately, the trains I had originally wanted to take (Bern – Milan – Rome) were all booked, so the SBB (Swiss train company) crew kindly helped me find another route from Bern to Rome, with connections in Brig and Milan, and more time on the road. While I was grateful for their help, I was not totally happy to have to catch a train at 6AM. Nevertheless, after making the last connection, I was finally on the train to Rome. I was sleepy and exhausted.

Sitting in seat 3A in Wagon 7, I was halfway to unconsciousness. As the train was about to depart, a tall, older

---

*This article originally appeared on www.dariofo.com in November, 2012. *China Insight* published this article in the January 2013 issue.

gentleman and a stunning young lady took the seats right in front of me. The gentleman's face looked so familiar. I searched my memory: *Politician? Professor? Movie star? Artist?* Suddenly, I felt as though I'd been struck by lightning: *Dario Fo! Nobel Literature Prize laureate!*

In 1997, the Nobel Prize in Literature was awarded to Dario Fo, "who emulates the jesters of the Middle Ages in scourging authority and upholding the dignity of the downtrodden." He is an Italian satirist, playwright, theatre director, actor, and composer. The Nobel Committee's press release claimed that Fo "merits the epithet of jester in the true meaning of that word. With a blend of laughter and gravity he opens our eyes to abuses and injustices in society, and also to the wider historical perspective in which they can be placed. Fo is an extremely serious satirist with a multifaceted oeuvre."

Franca Rame, Fo's wife and artistic partner, has assisted in the writing of many of the plays they have produced in their 60 years of theatre together. They share the same ideology and vision. Both are extremely talented, prolific, outspoken, and clear-sighted. Their uncompromising position has exposed them to criticism from both the left and the right, and has led them to take great risks. Nonetheless, their artistic vitality and conscience have earned them enormous respect from widely differing quarters.

As a country mesmerized with the Nobel Prizes, China was totally at loss of words when Dario Fo won the Prize in Literature. For Chinese authorities and media, Chairman Mao's *Yan'an Talks on Literature and Art* is the "Bible" that guides artistic creation, and socialist realism is the only "correct" art form. Chinese career propaganda officers judge art and literature by the standard set up by Chairman Mao in 1942 in the *Yan'an Talks*: i.e., writers should extol the bright side of life of the Socialist society and to expose the darkness of the Capitalist society. But who is Dario Fo, who criticizes conservative institutions and political corruption, but also criticized Stalinism and protested the 1989 Tiananmen tragedy? Chinese socialist authority and media were puzzled by Dario Fo, this "socialist" artist.

In 1998 and 1999, I authored and published four Chinese essays on Dario Fo: "Dario Fo and History;" "A Case Study of the Chinese Version of Dario Fo's *An Accidental Death of An Anarchist*;" "Political Correctness and Dario Fo;" and "Who is Afraid of Dario Fo?" These four essays were later included in my book *The End of the Avant-Garde: Comparative Cultural Studies*, published by Peking University Press. In my essays, I predicted that Dario Fo would be misunderstood by Chinese audiences, because his Sisyphus-like compassionate idealism, belief in human dignity and individual rights, total independence from any institution, and extremely serious satires based on the great tradition of *commedia dell'arte* are so hard to define and to comprehend by a China that was undergoing a bizarre transformation from Maoist Socialism to "Socialist" Capitalism.

But I also believe Dario Fo is extremely relevant to China and the Chinese. Everything Dario Fo and Franca Rame fight is stronger in China today than ever before: organized crime, political corruption, ideological hypocrisy, and suppression of free speech and expression. Dario Fo was and is my hero.

Hesitantly, I asked the gentleman in front of me: "Are you Mr. Dario Fo?" He smiled: "Si (Yes.)"

I extended my hand and shook his: "What a great honor! Maestro, I am a big fan of yours." I then jumped up and grabbed my backpack from the luggage compartment and pulled a copy of my book *The End of the Avant-Garde*, which by pure coincidence, brought by me from home for my Italian uncles. (One third of the book was on Italian culture.) My Italian level is limited to greetings and food ordering, so I turned to the young lady who sat next to Dario Fo: "Do you speak English, can you help me to translate?" She smiled too and answered: "Yes, I do, and I can; I am his assistant," in perfect English. Her name is Chiara Porro.

I first showed Dario Fo and Chiara the first 40 pages of the book which includes the four essays on him. He was delighted to see his picture in the book, and occasional Italian words of the names of his plays, venues, and organizations inserted in the Chinese paragraphs. After I signed and presented the book to him, he asked Chiara to scan the articles on him and put them on his online archive.

The Maestro then took from his briefcase a book entitled *Picasso Desnudo* (Picasso Naked), his most recent book published in conjunction with his and Franca Rame's lecture-performance on Pablo Picasso.

Dario Fo began to draw a picture on the front page. He completed the drawing in a few minutes, and then used his finger to blur the lines, just as Chinese ink painters normally do. He then wrote down "Storia di Qu (Story of Ah Q). Chang. Dario Fo." He explained he is working on a new play adapted from *The Story of Ah Q*, a short story masterpiece by Lu Xun (1881-1936), one of the founding fathers of Chinese modern literature. He then gave the signed book to me. I recommended another Lu Xun short story, *The Madman's Diary,* to the Maestro and explained that it probably would provide some background information as to how Lu Xun understands Chinese history.

For the next an hour and a half, from Milano to Firenze, we had a long and interesting conversation, on art, politics, and China.

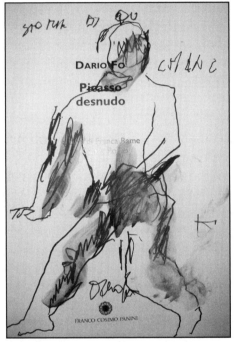

Dario Fo's drawing of Ah Q

Ognuno sta solo sul cuor della terra
trafitto da un raggio di sole:
ed è subito sera.

(Every one of us stands alone on the heart of the earth,
transfixed by a beam of sun:
and suddenly it is evening.)

When Dario Fo saw the above quotation of Salvatore Quasimodo on the front page of my book, he told me that

42

Salvatore Quasimodo, actually his good friend, was not only a great poet but also a great art critic who translated Sappho from Greek to Italian, and that I should read this important work.

Aware of the Chinese version of *The Accidental Death of an Anarchist*, Dario Fo noted that the Chinese version is a great departure from his original play: "it is a completely different story." He shrugged.

"I wanted my other play, *A Tale of a Tiger*, to be performed in China; but the Chinese authorities would not allow it." Dario Fo explained the plot of the play: During Mao's Long March across China, a revolutionary soldier is wounded. His comrades leave him behind. Gangrene sets in, and he believes that he is about to die. He drags himself into a cave and falls into a deep sleep. When he awakens, he is confronted by the sight of a female tiger and her cub. They live together, as the tiger nurses him back to health. As this develops, tiger-human communication is born — and, while he introduces the tigers to cooked meat, they in turn introduce him to the archetypal elements of their spirits.

From his description I immediately understood why the play was banned in China: The Long March, a retreat by the Red Army of the Chinese Communist Party, has been depicted as a pillar of the Chinese Communist Revolution, and has been a constant theme of communist propaganda. Propaganda officers would not appreciate Dario Fo's mix of politics, humanism, and mystic spirituality.

Very concerned with environmental protection in China, Dario Fo asked whether the government has taken any measures to reduce the pollution and encourage electric cars. I explained that GDP occupies the central position in China's economic life, and that environment is being damaged at an unprecedented scale and speed as a result of efforts to boost the GDP. Local authorities have few incentives to develop alternative energy and green cars because they already have invested interests — tax revenues and kick-backs — in current practices that guarantee steady profits for the government.

Dario Fo also asked whether workers' rights are improving in China. I explained that the current administration is extremely pro-business. Ideologically, as this regime is more on the right side than the left: independent workers' unions are impossible.

With Chiara's kind assistance, Dario Fo and I interviewed each other on the subjects that interest us most.

To make a connection to Perugia, where the Maestro would be teaching a week-long class on drama, the Maestro and Chiara got off the train at the Firenze station.

We said "Ciao" to each other. I saw them off from the train, and they quickly disappeared into the crowds on the platform.

It was almost surreal for me to sit down with Dario Fo, face to face, for a long conversation. How amazing that I would happen to be in the right place at the right time to meet my hero, and have just the right language assistance available! I can hardly believe this was pure coincidence. It is like a dream.

Only a week later, a long-time dream came true for Chinese people: The Nobel Prize in Literature in 2012 was awarded to Chinese novelist Mo Yan. He is the first Chinese citizen ever to receive this honor. He is an extremely prolific author, but ironically, "Mo Yan," the author's penname, means "Don't Speak Up."

Perhaps I can make two wishes: first, that *A Tale of a Tiger* will be able to be performed in China, and second, that all Chinese writers will be all free to speak up, in the not-too-distant future.

10 Questions for Dario Fo*

Chang Wang and Iole Fargnoli:

Dear Maestro, it is a great honor to see you again. As you may remember, it was exactly one year ago, on October 6th 2012, that Chang met you, by amazing coincidence, on a train from Milano Centrale to Firenze.

Dario Fo:

Thank you, and good to see you again, Chang. Sorry for keeping you waiting. I was on the phone with a journalist: very sad news, filmmaker Carlo Lizzani committed suicide today.

Chang Wang and Iole Fargnoli:

We are so sorry to hear that.

Chang also wanted to tell you that all of us in China and in the U.S. were deeply saddened by the sudden passing of your wife Franca. We know how little the words can do to ease the grief that this has caused you. Her passing leaves a void which will not be filled. We gained so much from her

---

*In 1997, Dario Fo, Italian maestro of theater and painting, "who emulates the jesters of the Middle Ages in scourging authority and upholding the dignity of the downtrodden," won the Nobel Prize for Literature. In addition to producing prodigious quantities of provocative creative work, Dario and his late wife Franca Rame played key roles in Italy's political life. In 2006, Franca was elected senator. Dario has run for Mayor of Milan and remained active with regard to a variety of political, social and cultural issues.

On October 5, 2013, Chang Wang (Thomson Reuters) and Professor Iole Fargnoli (University of Milan) interviewed Dario Fo in Fo's Milan residence. This interview was conducted in Italian and English. Dr. Linda De Maddalena (University of Milan) transcribed the interview in Italian, and translated it into English. Al Maleson edited the English version. The bilingual (English and Italiano) version of this conversational article first appeared on www.dariofo.com in November, 2013.

45

charisma, talent, and wisdom. We wish to express our deep sorrow and offer profound condolences to you, and to all who were close and dear to her.

At the same time, we are all thrilled to see the publication of Franca's memoir *In fuga dal Senato (Run from the Senate)*. We hope to see English and Chinese translations in the near future. We could not agree more with her observation that "we are living in a society whose basic aim is to misinform."

Dario Fo:

Franca was an unconventional senator—probably just as Lucrezia Borgia was an unconventional daughter of the Pope. The title of her book is "Run from the Senate." For its cover, I painted a picture of Franca running away from the Senate on bicycle.

Chang Wang and Iole Fargnoli:

It is a great painting, thank you for showing it to us. At this point, we have a list of questions to ask you:

1. Illegal Immigration:

At least 130 African migrants died, and many more are still missing, after a boat carrying them to Europe sank off the southern Italian island of Lampedusa on October 3rd.

It is heartbreaking to hear that many of the dead children were wearing new shoes, a sign of hope for new lives they will never have.

Do you think Italy is now facing an illegal-immigration problem, like the US?

Dario Fo:

Italians have always been a people who emigrated; after World War I, for example, more than one million Italians emigrated to the United States. Now we are becoming a people who receive migrants. And we need them! Our population is going down: the number of inhabitants, and the number of children, is falling in Italy. Illegal immigration helps us fill the gaps in our population. We are saved by illegal immigration. It's absurd, but it is so.

Chang Wang and Iole Fargnoli:

2. Pope Francis, religion, faith:

We now have a new Pope, who appears to be quite different from the last one. According to President Obama, Pope Francis knows "how to embrace people as opposed to push them away. How to find what's good in them as opposed to condemn them."

We understand you are not a big fan of organized religion. Nevertheless, we are curious to hear your comments on Pope Francis' recent remarks on homosexual, abortion, and contraception.

Dario Fo:

First of all, this is an open-minded Pope who doesn't want to impose, but wants to discuss problems. Above all, he's in favor of the dignity of poor people. He says that we must stop being afraid to get undressed, to be nude. As his first act in the cathedral of his village, San Francis threw all his clothes on the ground and said: "From this moment I'm a free man, I have nothing anymore." The Pope said yesterday that we must have the courage to get undressed, to throw our clothes away, along with the idea that richness is something that exalts you, and that one is better and touched by God only because of wealth.

Chang Wang and Iole Fargnoli:

3. Al Franken, Beppe Grillo, Ai Weiwei:

Al Franken is one of the two US Senators from the State of

Minnesota, where I live. Like Beppe Grillo, Al is a comedian turned politician.

Many people were doubtful when Franken entered politics. It has turned out, however, that he is doing pretty well as a politician.

Do you think comedians, intellectuals, and artists can be good politicians? Does playing politics require special skills that artists do not have? Should artists get involved in politics directly? Or should they just observe, comment, and criticize?

Dario Fo:

First of all a good comedian has to be a politician. A comedian must know politics and the tragedy of life. The comedian must know what honesty, poverty, desperation, and lack of justice mean. And then choose one side or the other. The one who can choose to stay at this or at the other side of a program is a politician. We live in a society of lies.

Chang Wang and Iole Fargnoli:

In 2011, Chinese artist Ai Weiwei got in trouble for criticizing Chinese authority. He spent 81 days in solitary confinement. The experience is now visualized by his installation work titled *"S.A.C.R.E.D."* on view at the Chiesa di Sant' Antonio in Venice. Did you see the installation?

Dario Fo:

No, I haven't seen the installation.

Every time you say something new, you risk being arrested. The power wants the convention — the rules and regulations. Look at those who have done something new, for example Saint Francis. Saint Francis was put in prison and banished by his brothers from the convent. All that we know about him today isn't true because it is a story created 40 years after his death. It was as the church wanted the story to be told, but isn't the real story of Saint Francis. 40 years after Saint Francis's death, the church ordered the burning of every book that had been written during his life.

At present, it wouldn't be possible to put on an opera that, although it tells the truth about the past, satirizes the authority. I put the past (the 14th century) on stage in "Mistero Buffo" and was imprisoned for it. Because, if you tell the history of the past, you offer a photo of the present. Injustice, lack of correctness, theft, fraud, corruption and violence are always the same.

The Story of Ah Q, by Chinese author Lu Xun, is the story of a poor man who doesn't have culture and is mistaken for a leader of the revolutionary party. Having taken him in prison and having condemned him to death publicly works in favor of the power. But inside the prison, Q becomes a hero, and the prisoners ask him about Utopian Communism." And Q invents it. He invents rules and ways of life, taking them from popular traditions. He describes an ideal communism, not the real communism of the bureaucrats. This imagined story of Communism charms everyone who listens to it; as did the unreal description of communism that Che Guevara offered. Had he been in the Russia, he would have been imprisoned.

Chang Wang and Iole Fargnoli:

4. Italian Politics:

Very surprisingly, Silvio Berlusconi and his People of Freedom Party supported Mr. Letta in the recent vote of confidence. Some observers say that Berlusconi is no longer able to control Italian politics, or even his own party. And he is now expected to lose his seat in the Senate.

Do you think Berlusconi will continue to play an important role in Italian politics?

Dario Fo:

Italy's problem isn't Berlusconi, but the social democratic parties, which have accepted the ideals of "berlusconismo", before Berlusconi entered politics. For 20 years, the Partito Democratico has been dancing with Berlusconi. They were a clandestine engaged couple. And now they are married and have settled everything. They sleep in the same bed!

Chang Wang and Iole Fargnoli:

5. US government shutdown:

US government is being partially shut down. Some blame Republicans; some blame Democrats; some blame both. President Obama has said that the shutdown is entirely unnecessary, and that he is 'exasperated' by the budget impasse in Congress. On the other hand, Republicans say the President refused to listen to "American people" and negotiate.

Do you have any comments and advice to the American politicians?

Dario Fo:

No, because I know little about the situation. It's a completely American conflict. However, I think the fight is a pretext: the real fight is a fight for power and for the ability to oversee and manipulate the government and the country.

Chang Wang and Iole Fargnoli:

6. Environment:

I understand that you are very concerned about the environment. Air and water pollution in China are getting very serious. Blue sky is a luxury for the residents of Beijing;

respiratory disease is the number one cause of death in China. The pollution index in Beijing is expected to soar above the "hazardous" level of 300 again this week.

In addition, one-half of all groundwater and two-thirds of all surface water in China is polluted.

Low-quality coal and gasoline, as well as the government's obsession with industrialization and urbanization, are major contributors to all this pollution. But some factions of the Chinese local and central governments benefit directly from the businesses that contribute to pollution, creating conflicts of interest.

Some environmentalists and intellectuals have begun to make connections between the environmental deterioration and China's political system. This irritates the government, of course, making the environment a very political issue in China.

Do you have any advice to China as to how to protect the environment?

Dario Fo:

It's the same as in Italy or in America. The basic problem is one of political choice. China has imitated what is done in America or in Italy. China has the possibility to derive energy from the sun and wind. However, it made the wrong choice, with coal and oil, from the beginning. Had it begun producing energy by placing solar panels on the roofs, in the fields, in the forests (it has such big spaces), it could have generated a lot of electric energy and distributed it easily, as they do in Finland, where there's a charging station for cars every 2 km. Had China developed the culture of electric and Aeolian-energy, it surely would be the healthiest country in the world. On the contrary, China followed the logic of American capitalism, buying oil at the cost of water and selling it at the cost of gold. Unfortunately, this approach doesn't generate advantages for the population; rather, it generates profits for few individuals.

Chang Wang and Iole Fargnoli:

7. Primer on Your works:

In order to understand your art, which of your works should American and Chinese college students study?

Dario Fo and Chang Wang in front of Dario Fo's painting "Franca Escapes from Senate"

Dario Fo:

Asking an artist to choose one of his works is a little bit daunting: Which helps you better to understand Shakespeare, "Romeo and Juliet" or "Measure for Measure"?

I would say, just to start, "Mistero buffo"; and soon after "Morte accidentale di un anarchico". I've written 70 operas, choosing only one is difficult. . . .

Chang Wang and Iole Fargnoli:

8. Desert Island:

For decades, BBC Radio has aired *Desert Island Discs*, a show on which guests choose and discuss the eight pieces of music, one book and one luxury item that they would take with them if they were cast away on a desert island.

Do you have a short list of books and music you would like to take with you if you were on a desert island for one year?

Dario Fo:

I really don't know . . . there's an old proverb from Lombardia that is paradoxical and says: "If my grandmother had the wheels, she would be a tram." What does it mean? It means that a paradox is inescapable, and you can't make a choice on an absurd paradox. The first thing I would do on a desert island would be to burn the books to make light and heat. The only book I would bring with me to read would be a guidebook for survival on a desert island: because the first rule on a "desert island" is surviving.

Dario Fo and Iole Fargnoli

Chang Wang and Iole Fargnoli:

9. Reincarnation:

Some people believe in reincarnation: the soul or spirit, after biological death, begins a new life in a new body that may be human, animal or spiritual depending on the moral quality of the previous life's actions. I firmly believe I was an Italian in my immediate past life. Unfortunately, however, I forgot how to speak Italian.

I know you probably do not believe in reincarnation, but could you please just imagine your previous or next life?

Dario Fo:

I'd like it very much if reincarnation existed. I've written the introduction for one of Franca's books, called "Una vita all'improvviso", where I imagine to have met her 5 times in my passed lives.

And I'd like to meet her again in my future lives.

Chang Wang and Iole Fargnoli:

10. Your next project:

Can you tell us anything about your next project?

Dario Fo:

I have lots of projects. I never start only one. I'll help some young people who are going to put on a show, then I have to finish 3 books which I'm writing at the same time and after that I will go surely to France, my second native land. Furthermore, I've big and small appointments. In the end, I will wait to rest.

10 domande per Dario Fo*

CHANG WANG e IOLE FARGNOLI:

Caro Maestro, è un grande onore rivederla. Ricorderà che esattamente un anno fa, il 6 ottobre 2012, Chang l'ha incontrata, per una sorprendente coincidenza, sul treno da Milano Centrale a Firenze.

Dario Fo:

Molte grazie, sono felice di rivederti Chang. Scusate per l'attesa. Ero al telefono con un giornalista. Una notizia molto triste, il regista Carlo Lizzani oggi si è tolto la vita.

CHANG WANG e IOLE FARGNOLI:

Siamo molto spiacenti di ricevere questa notizia.

Chang voleva inoltre dirle che tutti noi in Cina e negli Stati Uniti siamo rimasti profondamente addolorati per l'improvvisa scomparsa di Franca. So quanto poco le parole possano fare per alleviare il dolore che sta vivendo. La sua scomparsa lascia un vuoto che non potrà essere colmato. Abbiamo imparato così tanto dal suo carisma, dal suo

---

*Dario Fo è stato premio Nobel per la letteratura nel 1997, ed è maestro italiano di pittura e di teatro "che emula i giullari del Medioevo screditando l'autorità e difendendo la dignità degli oppressi". In aggiunta al comporre prodigiose quantità di provocatorie opere, Dario e sua moglie Franca Rame, da poco scomparsa, hanno rivestito ruoli chiave nella vita politica italiana. Franca Rame fu eletta senatrice nel 2006 e Dario si candidò come Sindaco di Milano ed è rimasto attivo in questioni politiche, culturali e sociali.

Il 5 ottobre 2013, Chang Wang (Thomson Reuters) e la Prof.ssa Iole Fargnoli (Università di Milano) hanno intervistato Dario Fo nella sua residenza di Milano. Questa intervista è stata condotta in lingua italiana e in lingua inglese. La Dr. Linda De Maddalena (Università di Milano) ha trascritto l'intervista in italiano e l'ha tradotta in inglese. Al Maleson ha curato l'edizione della versione inglese.

talento e dalla sua saggezza. Vorremmo esternarle il nostro profondo dispiacere e offrire le nostre più sentite e profonde condoglianze a tutti voi che le eravate vicini e cari.

Allo stesso tempo, siamo tutti entusiasti di assistere alla pubblicazione di "In Fuga dal Senato" di Franca. Speriamo di avere le traduzioni in inglese e in cinese a breve. Non possiamo che essere più che d'accordo con la sua osservazione per cui: "Viviamo in una società il cui scopo fondamentale è quello di disinformare".

Dario Fo:

Franca era una senatrice non convenzionale – probabilmente come Lucrezia Borgia era una figlia non convenzionale per un Papa—. Il titolo del suo libro è "In fuga dal Senato". Per la sua copertina, ho dipinto l'immagine di Franca che scappa dal Senato su di una bicicletta.

CHANG WANG e IOLE FARGNOLI:

É un bellissimo quadro, grazie per avercelo mostrato. A questo punto, abbiamo una lista di domande da porle:

CHANG WANG e IOLE FARGNOLI:

1. La tragedia della barca affondata nel mare di Lampedusa:

Il 3 ottobre scorso almeno 130 emigranti africani sono morti e molti altri sono dispersi dopo che la barca che li stava trasportando in Europa è affondata al largo dell'isola siciliana di Lampedusa.

È profondamente triste sapere che molti dei bambini morti indossavano scarpe nuove, un segno di speranza per la nuova vita che non avranno mai.

Pensa che l'Italia stia ora affrontando il problema dell'immigrazione illegale, come accade negli Stati Uniti?

Dario Fo:

Gli Italiani sono sempre stati un popolo di emigranti; nel primo dopoguerra, per esempio, più di un milione di abitanti italiani sono emigrati negli Stati Uniti. Ora siamo diventati un popolo che riceve gli immigrati. E abbiamo bisogno di loro! La nostra popolazione è in calo: sta scendendo il numero degli abitanti e soprattutto dei nati in Italia. L'immigrazione illegale ci aiuta a colmare il vuoto nella nostra popolazione. Noi siamo salvati dall'immigrazione illegale. É assurdo ma è così.

CHANG WANG e IOLE FARGNOLI:

2. Papa Francesco, la religione, la fede:

Ora abbiamo un nuovo Papa, che apparentemente è molto diverso dal suo predecessore. Secondo il Presidente Obama, Papa Francesco sa "come abbracciare le persone invece che spingerle via e come trovare cosa vi sia di buono in loro invece che condannarle".

Comprendiamo che lei non è un grande ammiratore delle gerarchie ecclesiastiche. Tuttavia, sono curioso di sapere i suoi commenti sulle recenti osservazioni di Papa Francesco in merito all'omosessualità, all'aborto e alla contraccezione.

Dario Fo:

Prima di tutto questo è un Papa aperto che non vuole imporre ma discutere i problemi. E soprattutto è per la dignità dei poveri. E dice che bisogna smettere con quest'abitudine a "temere di spogliarsi, di rendersi nudi", come fece San Francesco che, come primo atto nella cattedrale del suo paese, gettò tutti i suoi abiti per terra e disse "da questo momento sono un uomo libero, non ho più niente". E il Papa ieri ha detto che bisogna avere il coraggio di spogliarsi, di togliersi gli abiti, l'idea che la ricchezza sia qualcosa che ti esalta e che si è migliori e, soprattutto, dei 'toccati da Dio' solo perché si è ricchi.

CHANG WANG e IOLE FARGNOLI:

3. Al Franken, Beppe Grillo, Ai Weiwei:

Al Franken è uno dei due senatori dello Stato del Minnesota, dove io vivo. Al Franken è stato un comico prima di diventare un uomo politico, un po' come Beppe Grillo.

Molte persone erano diffidenti nei confronti di Al Franken, quando è sceso in politica. Si è rivelato, tuttavia, un buon politico.

Pensa che i comici, gli intellettuali e gli artisti possano essere buoni politici? La politica richiede una qualche speciale abilità che gli artisti non hanno? Gli artisti dovrebbero occuparsi di politica direttamente, oppure dovrebbero limitarsi a osservarla, commentarla e criticarla?

Dario Fo:

Prima di tutto un buon comico deve essere un politico. Un comico deve conoscere la politica così come la tragedia della vita e deve sapere cosa significa l'onestà, la miseria, la disperazione, la mancanza di giustizia! E quindi deve saper scegliere se stare da una parte o dall'altra. Chi sa scegliere se stare da una parte o dall'altra di un programma è un politico. Noi viviamo in una società di menzogna.

CHANG WANG e IOLE FARGNOLI:

L'artista cinese Ai Weiwei ha avuto problemi per avere criticato le autorità cinesi. Nel 2011 ha trascorso 81 giorni in isolamento. L'esperienza può ora essere letta nel suo lavoro dal titolo "S.A.C.R.E.D." in mostra presso la Chiesa di Sant' Antonio a Venezia. Ha visto l'installazione? Conosce alcuni dei suoi lavori?

Dario Fo:

No, non ho visto l'installazione.

Tutte le volte che si dice qualcosa di nuovo si rischia di andare in galera. Il potere vuole la convenzione—le regole e i regolamenti. Si vada a vedere tutti quelli che hanno fatto un qualcosa di nuovo: San Francesco, per esempio. San Francesco è finito in galera ed è stato cacciato dai suoi fratelli dal convento. Tutto quello che noi ora conosciamo di lui è falso perché è una storia inventata 40 anni dopo la sua morte. Ed è stata costruita così come piaceva alla Chiesa, ma non ha niente a che vedere con il vero San Francesco. L'ordine della Chiesa, 40 anni dopo la sua morte, era quello di bruciare tutti i testi che erano stati scritti durante la sua vita.

Dario Fo:

Oggi come oggi non sarebbe possibile mettere in scena un testo che, nonostante racconti la verità sul passato, si prende gioco dell'autorità. Io ho messo in scena il passato, il Medioevo (1300), e mi hanno incarcerato per "Mistero Buffo". Perché, se si racconta bene la storia del passato, è sempre la fotografia di quello che stai vivendo adesso. L'ingiustizia, la mancanza di correttezza, il furto, la truffa, la corruzione, la violenza, sono sempre le stesse. *La storia di Ah Q*, dell'autore cinese Lu Xun, è la storia di un pover'uomo che non ha cultura ed è scambiato per un capo del partito rivoluzionario. Aver incarcerato e condannato a morte Q pubblicamente gioca a favore del potere. Tuttavia, dentro le prigioni Q diventa un eroe e i prigionieri gli chiedono: "Cos'è il Comunismo utopistico"? E Q lo inventa. Inventa delle regole, dei modi di vivere, traendole dalla tradizione popolare. Egli descrive un Comunismo ideale, non il Comunismo dei burocrati. Questa storia inventata seduce tutti quelli che la ascoltano; come Che

Guevara offrì un'irreale descrizione di Comunismo. Se fosse stato in Russia, sarebbe stato imprigionato.

CHANG WANG e IOLE FARGNOLI:

4. Politica in Italia:

Molto sorprendentemente, Silvio Berlusconi e il suo Popolo della Libertà hanno supportato Letta nel recente voto di fiducia. Alcuni osservatori dicono che Berlusconi non è più in grado di controllare la politica italiana, e persino il suo stesso partito. E ora ci si aspetta che perda il suo seggio al Senato.

Pensa che Berlusconi continuerà a svolgere un ruolo importante nella politica italiana?

Dario Fo:

Il guaio dell'Italia non è Berlusconi, sono i partiti socialdemocratici che hanno accettato gli ideali del "berlusconismo", prima ancora che Berlusconi entrasse in politica. Da 20 anni il Partito Democratico danza con quello di Berlusconi. Erano fidanzati nascosti. E adesso si sono sposati, hanno sistemato le cose: vivono nello stesso letto!

CHANG WANG e IOLE FARGNOLI:

5. Arresto di governo ("shutdown") negli Stati Uniti:

Il Governo degli Stati Uniti sta parzialmente subendo una battuta d'arresto, per alcuni è colpa dei Repubblicani, per alcuni dei Democratici, per altri di entrambi. Il Presidente Obama ha detto che l'arresto è del tutto inutile, e che è stato "esasperato" dall'impasse di bilancio al Congresso. D'altra parte, i Repubblicani dicono che il Presidente si è rifiutato di ascoltare "il popolo americano " e di negoziare con esso.

Ha eventualmente commenti e consigli per i politici americani?

Dario Fo:

No, perché conosco poco la situazione, è un conflitto del tutto americano. Tuttavia penso che sia pretestuale: il vero conflitto è una lotta per il potere e per avere l'opportunità di gestire e manovrare il governo e la nazione.

CHANG WANG e IOLE FARGNOLI:

6. Ambiente:

So che lei è molto sensibile al tema dell'ambiente. L'inquinamento atmosferico e delle acque in Cina è sempre più grave. Vedere il cielo blu è un lusso per i residenti di Pechino; le malattie respiratorie sono la prima causa di morte in Cina. Si prevede che l'indice di PM2,5 sarà di oltre 300 milligrammi per metro cubo ancora una volta questa settimana, un livello pericolosissimo.

Inoltre in Cina la metà di tutte le acque sotterranee e 2/3 di tutte le acque di superficie è inquinata.

La scarsa qualità di carbone e benzina, così come l'osses-sione del governo per l'industrializzazione e l'urbanizza-zione, sono le principali cause di tutto questo inquinamento. Tuttavia alcune fazioni del governo cinese locale e centrale beneficiano direttamente dal business che contribuisce all'inquinamento, creando conflitti d'interesse.

Alcuni ambientalisti e intellettuali hanno cominciato a fare collegamenti tra il degrado ambientale e il sistema politico in Cina. Questo irrita il governo, ovviamente, e rende l'in-quinamento in Cina una vera questione politica.

Ha qualche consiglio per la Cina in merito a come proteg-gere l'ambiente?

Dario Fo:

È lo stesso che succede in Italia, o in America. Il problema fondamentale è una scelta politica. La Cina ha ricalcato quello che si fa in America o in Italia. La Cina ha la possibilità di trarre energia dal sole e dal vento. Tuttavia ha fatto la scelta sbagliata dall'inizio, con carbone e benzina. Se avesse cominciato a produrre energia mettendo i pannelli solari sui tetti, nei prati, nelle foreste (ha degli spazi immensi) avrebbe potuto avere e distribuire facilmente tanta energia elettrica, come fanno in Finlandia, dove ogni 2 km c'è un distributore di energia elettrica per caricare le macchine. Se la Cina avesse sviluppato una cultura dell'energia elettrica ed eolica, sarebbe di sicuro il paese più salubre del mondo. Invece la Cina ha cavalcato la logica del capitalismo, comprando la benzina al prezzo dell'acqua e vendendola a quello dell'oro. Sfortunatamente quest'approccio non genera vantaggi per la popolazione; piuttosto ciò genera profitti per pochi individui.

CHANG WANG e IOLE FARGNOLI:

7. Un testo di base fra le sue opere:

Quale tra le sue opere dovrebbero conoscere gli studenti dei college americani e cinesi per comprendere la sua arte?

Dario Fo:

Chiedere a un artista di scegliere un'opera è un po — riduttivo: per capire Shakespeare è meglio "Romeo e Giulietta" o "Misura per Misura"? Io, solo per cominciare, direi "Mistero buffo"; poi subito dopo "Morte accidentale di un anarchico". Ho scritto 70 commedie, scegliere è difficile . . .

CHANG WANG e IOLE FARGNOLI:

8. Isola deserta:

Per decenni, la BBC Radio ha mandato in onda *Desert Island Discs*, uno spettacolo in cui gli ospiti scelgono e discutono otto pezzi di musica, un libro e un bene di lusso che porterebbero con loro se fossero naufraghi su di un'isola deserta.

Ha un breve elenco di libri e musiche che porterebbe con lei se fosse su di un'isola deserta per un anno ?

Dario Fo:

Non so proprio . . . C'è un vecchio detto lombardo che è paradossale e dice: "Se mia nonna avesse le ruote sarebbe un tramvai"; cosa vuol dire? Significa che un paradosso è ineluttabile, e non si può fare una scelta su di un paradosso assurdo. La prima cosa che farei su di un'isola deserta sarebbe prendere i libri e bruciarli per fare luce e calore. Il solo libro che mi porterei da leggere sarebbe una guida alla sopravvivenza in un'isola deserta: perché la prima regola su di un' "isola deserta" è sopravvivere.

CHANG WANG e IOLE FARGNOLI:

9. Reincarnazione:

Alcune persone credono nella reincarnazione- l'anima o lo spirito, dopo la morte biologica, inizia una nuova vita in un nuovo corpo che può essere umano, animale o spirituale, sulla base della qualità morale delle azioni della vita precedente -. Sono fermamente convinto di essere stato un italiano nella mia vita precedente. Purtroppo, però, mi sono dimenticato la lingua italiana.

So che probabilmente lei non crede nella reincarnazione, ma potrebbe per favore solo immaginare la sua precedente o prossima vita?

Dario Fo:

Mi piacerebbe tanto che esistesse la reincarnazione. Ho scritto l'introduzione per un libro di Franca, che si chiama "Una vita all'improvviso", dove immagino di averla incontrata 5 volte nelle mie vite precedenti; e mi piacerebbe incontrarla ancora nelle mie future vite.

CHANG WANG e IOLE FARGNOLI:

10. Il suo prossimo progetto:

Puoi dirci qualcosa del suo prossimo progetto?

Dario Fo:

Ho tanti progetti, io non ne comincio mai uno solo. Aiuterò dei ragazzi che metteranno in scena un'opera, poi devo finire tre libri che sto scrivendo contemporaneamente e poi andrò sicuramente in Francia, la mia seconda patria. E poi ho tanti piccoli e grandi appuntamenti. E, infine, aspetterò di potermi riposare per sempre.

On Roberto Rossellini's *Il Messia*

I. Rossellini and the Road to *Il Messia*

*Noble acts and momentous events
happen in the same way and produce the
same impression as the ordinary facts.*

— Roberto Rossellini

Neorealism and Rossellini

Italian Neorealism, French New Wave, and New German Cinema represent the high achievements of post-war cinema. The importance of the role that Italian Neorealism has played cannot be overstated. It has been argued that "art film" started with Italian Neorealism and Roberto Rossellini.

Rossellini was regarded as one of the best filmmakers of all time. He, and other maestros after WWII, created the groundbreaking "Neorealism;" his films *Rome, Open City* (1945) and *Paisan* (1946) defined the genre "neorealism;" his career re-defined the meaning of "art film;" his generation elevated film to a level equivalent to other major art forms. He is an *auteur* (film author) in the full sense of the term. *Rome, Open City* was considered the perfect exemplar of the new mode of cinematic creation: neorealism whose established critical definition was given by André Bazin. Bazin argued that neorealism portrays truth, naturalness, authenticity, and is a cinema of duration. The necessary characteristics of neo-realism in film include: a definite social context, a sense of historical actuality and immediacy, political commitment to progressive, even violent, social change, authentic on-location shooting as opposed to the artificial studio, the rejection of classical Hollywood acting styles, extensive use of non-professional actors as much as possible, and a documentary style of cinematography. Andre Bazin argued: "Neorealism is a description of reality conceived as a whole by a consciousness disposed to see things as a whole. Neorealism contrasts with the realist aesthetics that preceded it, in particular with naturalism and verism, in that its realism is not so much concerned with the choice of subject as with a particular way of regarding things."[1] Bazin had no doubt that Rossellini's contribution to the genre placed him in a prominent place in film history: "That of all Italian directors Rossellini has done the most to extend the frontiers of the newrealist aesthetic. I have said there is no such thing as pure neorealism. The newrealist attitude is an ideal that one can approach to a greater or lesser degree." Bazin said "Rossellini directs facts. It is as if his characters were haunted by some demon of movement. His little brothers of Saint Francis seem to have no better way of glorying God than to run races."[2] The originality of Rossellini is his minimal approach to the reality,

---

[1]Andre Bazin, *What is Cinema?* (Berkeley and Los Angles: University of California Press, 1971), 97.
[2]Ibid,100.

his objectivity, and his calm. Objectivity is not for objectivity' sake; it has a meaningful purpose, Bazin argued: "The world of Rossellini is a world of pure acts, unimportant in themselves but preparing the way (as if unbeknownst to God himself) for the sudden dazzling revelation of their meaning."[3]

The Question of Religion and the Road to *Il Messia*

Even though Rossellini put his religious background behind him, his Catholic education and the Catholicism of Italian culture and society had a profound influence on his works. There are many religious themes and elements in his films, and four out of his twenty-eight feature films have explicit religious subject matters.

In 1948, Rossellini directed the controversial *The Miracle,* a film about a woman (played by the legendary Anna Magnani) who sleeps with a bum (played by Maestro Federico Fellini) and, thinking he is a saint, assumes her pregnancy is a miracle. This film is noteworthy because a distributor who wanted to show the film in New York challenged the state's laws banning "sacrilegious" films, which led to a landmark 1952 US Supreme Court decision that granted the cinema the same protections under the First Amendment that were already enjoyed by books and newspapers. The Supreme Court ultimately chose to abandon its own longstanding determination that film comprised a mere "business" unworthy of free-speech rights, declaring for the first time that the First Amendment barred government from banning any film as "sacrilegious."[4]

---

[3]Ibid.

[4]See William Bruce Johnson, *Miracles and Sacrilege: Robert Rossellini, the Church, and Film Censorship in Hollywood* (Toronto: University of Toronto Press, 2008).

However, it appeared that Rossellini had taken a quite different approach to religion in *Francesco, Giullare di Dio* (1950). Shooting primarily in exterior spaces, using unobtrusive camerawork, and incorporating a natural environment with a cast of nonprofessional actors Roberto Rossellini "creates a sense of timelessness and contemporary relevance to the universal themes of humility, compassion, faith, sacrifice, and community" in this masterpiece of humanity. "By portraying St. Francis and his disciples within the context of everyday human struggle through all its simple joys and disappointments, celebrations and travails, the film presents a remarkably lucid and accessible portrait of the interrelation between humanity and spiritual enlightenment."[5] *Francesco* is a tremendous work that locates the point where Italian humanism and spiritual faith cross.

Rossellini's later work, *Il Messia,* in tone and affect, style and content, belongs to his didactic approach works. He directed *Acts of the Apostles* for Italian TV in 1969, and this was followed by made-for-TV biographies of *Socrates* and *Saint Augustine*. *Il Messia* has to be understood within this context of Rossellini's later, "didactic" films.

In an interview, Rossellini explained the rationale behind *Il Messia* and this overly religious theme:

Question: So you began The Messiah at a historic moment of rupture, of confrontation?

Answer: It's Jesus, the history of Jesus, that's all. I made The Messiah with a great deal of respect for everyone. What is great in Jesus' message is his faith in man. That is what is irreplaceable, even though I am a complete atheist.

---

[5] Strictly Film School , *Roberto Rossellini*, http://www.filmref.com/directors/dirpages/rossellini.html

Question: People usually think just the opposite.

Answer: Everyone is permitted to fool himself however he wants. If someone just wants to place me, he can always say that I am a Christian without knowing it. But one can also perhaps place oneself, and ask why one is interpreting incorrectly.[6]

In another interview Rossellini says, "I'm not religious at all. I'm the product of a society that is religious among other things, and I deal with religion as a reality."[7] Rossellini further declared: "I always thought that this would have to be the point of arrival. In my maniacal search for an abecedarium of wisdom I had to put down so many letters to reach, sooner or later, the highest point, the compendium of everything."[8]

Rossellini announced he would do *Marx* after *Il Messia* and insisted on the similarity of Christ and Marx. He told Pope Paul that he was a non-believer and wanted to make *Il Messia* for non-believers.[9]

[6]Jacques Grant, Cinema 76, no. 206 (February 1976), 68.
[7]Ibid, 90.
[8]Interview in *Avvenire* (October 26, 1975).
[9]Tag Gallagher, *The Adventures of Roberto Rossellini*, Da Capo Press, 1998.

II *Il Messia*

*I have laid out — without personal
interpretation and without emotional stimulation,
but as the result of careful study — the life and, above
all, the thought of Jesus of Nazareth.*

— Roberto Rossellini

Il Messia and Other Jesus Films

Rossellini took "a pedagogical look at a great man in history, usually representative of an age in which some profound psychological shift in human consciousness took place."[10] Rossellini's basic idea in *Il Messia* was to represent the historical Jesus in so much as he is known from the gospels, in as objective and dispassionate a manner as possible, in order to inform the viewers, to teach who Jesus was and what he said, in order to edify them and show them the way to wisdom. This is a radical departure from the traditionally reverent Jesus-film tradition.

It is worth noting that an earlier masterpiece of the same subject matter, Pier Paolo Pasolini's *The Gospel According to St. Matthew* (1964), also had a very different approach in telling the "greatest story ever told." The film was carefully filmed by Pasolini, and beautifully photographed in black and white. Pasolini, a Marxist and a humanist, stressed Christ's legacy of socialism and humane activism, so the film was full of passion and opinion. On the other hand, *Il*

---

[10]Bondanella, Peter, The Films of Roberto Rossellini (Cambridge: Cambridge University Press, 1993), 25.

Messia is tranquil, peaceful, and serene. Rossellini's attitude is logical and didactic, stressing more the message of Jesus than his figure, more the words of Jesus than his person. This film is an austere cinema of prose, the traditional and essential dramatic spectacle in Jesus-film is diminished by intention. The right-wrong dichotomy is abandoned, negative characteristics are purified, and intellectual stimuli enriched, thus "involving the spectator not sentimentally but intellectually."[11]

Rossellini's Jesus is worldly, an eloquent preacher and a wise teacher. "In wanting to guide the viewer in search for meaning in the life of Jesus, Rossellini wants the eyes to move, not towards the heights of the heavens . . . but along the surface of this dusty planet."[12]

The film was shot in 42 days in June and July 1975, mostly in Tunisia, where Rossellini had previously filmed the biblical *Acts of the Apostles.*

Story/Screenplay

When was asked "What is *Il Messia* based on", Rossellini answered: "On the Messiah!"

Rossellini gives *Il Messia* a structure which promotes the priority of the protagonist, a structure which is linear and not dramatic. There is no rising and falling action, no suspense, no turning point or climax. The episodes in the film are swift transcriptions, without any emotional emphasis or dramatic construction. The film follows the experiences of Jesus day by day, as if it were a chronicle. But this linear structure of narrative did make the film fast-moving, leaving an impression that it was straightforward, uncomplicated.

---

[11]Rodolino, Gianni, Roberto Rossellini (Firenze: La Nuova Italia, 1977), 118.

[12]Virgilio Fantuzzi, '*Il Messia di Roberto Rossellini*," *La Civilta Cattolica* an. 126, n.4, qd.3010 (15 November 1975): 341.

In Rossellini's own words, it is an "accurate historical reconstruction . . . of daily life, of the most normal data, into which environment is situated the event . . . everything becomes very simple."[13]

Il Messia has a prefatory condensation of Hebrew history, reaching all the way back to the first Hebrew king, Saul. Exploring its sources by opening the film in 1050 B.C., that is far earlier than most conventional depictions. Rossellini explained the historic context of waiting for the Messiah; it was the rationale behind the prefatory condensation of history at the beginning of the film: "The idea of the film is that the tribe of Israel was living in a patriarchal society and so there were no chiefs. They were confronting different powers, kings and armies and things like that. And they wanted also to be like that. They asked Samuel, who was the spiritual leader in a sense—a judge—to have a king, a power established like the others. . . . In the period of the king started all the movements of prophets who were protesting against the kings and waiting for someone who would bring back justice, in the large sense. And finally Christ arrived who is just an expression of the human being, simpler, the most humble. And that is the reason why he was not identified with that idea of justice, like an avenging angel with sword in hand."[14]

After the first 20 minutes (a concise history of the Jews), the life begins. It is the life of Jesus without the miracles. Like the priest in *Open City*, Rossellini understands that the struggle is to live a good life. The film's tendency to downplay miracles is perhaps made most explicit when John

[13]"Conversazione con Roberto Rossellini," edited by Edoardo Bruno, Alessandro Cappabianca, Enrico Magrelli, and Michele Mancini, Film Critica v.27, nn.264-2654 (May-June, 1976): 134.

[14]Rossellini, Roberto, My Method: Writings and Interviews (Marsilio Publishers, 1995), 241.

the Baptist sends his messengers to ask if Jesus is really the one he's been waiting for, and it is Peter, not Jesus, who replies by rattling off all the miracles that have taken place. Jesus then holds him back or interrupts him and tells John's messengers that the poor have been given good news. Matching this typical de-dramatized presentation of "facts" is Rossellini's portrayal of a Christ who is, unsurprisingly, a thinking Christ, a humanist Christ (Rossellini told one interviewer that he saw Christ as "the perfect man," rather than as God). Accordingly, the director accentuates Christ's loving, human side and pays little attention to the divine, especially as it might be revealed in miracles.

Rossellini's de-dramatized approach again echoes the fundamental principle of neorealism: "Neorealism looks on reality as a whole, not incomprehensible, certainly, but inseparably one. This is why neorealism, although not necessarily anti-spectacular (though spectacle is to all intents and purposes alien to it) is at least basically anti-theatrical."[15]

The film shows a "real-life" Christ, one who was familiar with work. (For example, he does some carpentry.) Similarly, we see fishermen casting nets, Mary making bread, and other constant emphases on the unspectacular events and activities of daily life. Much of this quotidian imagery derives almost directly from *Acts of the Apostles* (1969), as does the film's emphasis on community. "For example, the scene of Christ walking on the water is omitted, as is the usually mandatory and highly emotional *via crucifix*, Christ's carrying his cross to the site of his crucifixion on Golgotha. For Rossellini, including the latter scene would have been not only too dramatic, but also inessential when compared with

---

[15]Andre Bazin, *What is Cinema?* (Berkeley and Los Angles: University of California Press) 1971,97.

Christ's words.[16] "Rossellini did not purposefully negate a divine side of Christ, but simply attempted to de-spectacularize his life. To viewers not accustomed to Rossellini's severely understated style, this minimalism can be pretty disappointing.

In an interview with the editors of *Filmcritica* , Rossellini elevated this anti-spectacular technique almost into a metaphysics, saying that he "wanted a reconstruction of everyday life, of the most normal data, and then to set the event in this context. Everything then becomes extremely simple. . . . This data is the reality on which everything is based. All the parables, even though they have an abstract meaning, aren't really abstract in the least; they all refer to the small facts of everyday life, the facts that we have lost, that we no longer know."[17]

Dialogue

In the film, Jesus speaks in a formal and slightly archaic tone. His words and actions are always performed in the concrete circumstances of the material world in which Jesus lives. Comparing the words in *Il Messia* and Pasolini's *The Gospel According to Saint Matthew*, a film critic pointed out: "Different from what happens in *The Gospel According to Saint Matthew* of Pasolini, in *Il Messia*, the word does not assault. Rossellini defuses whatever dogmatic force it might have by putting it on the lips of Jesus while he is busy with carpentry work or talking to a small group."[18]

Also in this film, Jesus preaches constantly, audaciously, with authority, and here he teaches others to teach, a

---

[16]Bondanella, Peter, The Films of Roberto Rossellini (Cambridge: Cambridge University Press, 1993), 343.
[17]Interview, Filmcritica , nos. 264-65 (May—June 1976).
[18]Luigi Bini, "*Il Messia di Roberto Rossellini*," Letture v.31, qd.326 (April 1976): 312.

unique theme in the Jesus-film tradition. The story of Jesus is taken from the Bible; the dialogue closely follows the text. There is a great deal of dialogue. The film was actually originally in English, then dubbed in Italian. Since the actors were already speaking English quickly, and since the Italian language had to be spoken even more quickly because it required more syllables to say the same thing, the dialogue appears rich and quick. Critic Claudio Sorgi has pointed out that "the true protagonist of the entire film is the Word of Jesus, as the penetrating, clear, incontestable realization of the ancient word. A word that is received by the disciples, taken up, and amplified."[19] According to Sorgi, *Il Messia* follows the theory known as *"Formgeschichtliche Methode,"* which holds that the Gospels were born as oral tradition between the time of Christ's death and their actual writing.[20] Sorgi believes that the principal source for the film is the *Gospel of Mark*, mainly because of its popularism and its accent on the mystery of messianism, but "the fundamental theory of the film derives from Matthew: Jesus seen as the realization of promises and the continuous correlation between what Jesus does and says and what was predicted of him".[21]

It should also be pointed out that Rossellini's insistence on the actual "real" words of the Bible whenever possible paradoxically almost guarantees the artificiality and stiffness, the lack of "realism" that many have complained about in this film. The words of the Bible are written words, after all, and will never sound like actual speech. The result of this strict adherence to biblical language is a further

---

[19]Claudio Sorgi, "Il Messia," Rivista del cinematografo (December 1975), 543.
[20]Ibid.
[21] Ibid, p543.

self-reflexxive distancing that accords well with the film's general strategy of de-dramatization.[22]

Directing

Rossellini's treatment of the familiar story is refreshingly astringent, and the typical strategies of de-dramatized acting and anti-spectacular *mise-en-scène* here find their perfect subject.[23]

Rossellini took a directing approach that has been described as "minimalistic", because the film clearly downplays the miracles. This approach is based on Rossellini's philosophical belief in the enlightened humanity of Jesus the teacher, so he makes an effort to remove every supernatural element from the narrative. This approach also reflects the way most people at the time of Jesus would have learned of his miracles and in a way it reflects the oral tradition already active during Jesus' lifetime.

Rossellini wanted to avoid "romantic touch, created by marvels," he explained: "If you show miracles in a film, you can do anything, even flying carpets. So what kind of credibility can you give the thing seen? I wanted to make a film that would be appreciated by people of our time. . . . If I had underlined more the prodigious aspects of the Gospel, I would have alienated the non-believer. But I think that even believers can find sufficient moments for their faith in the film."[24]

Rossellini's Jesus is well integrated in the world, full of the joy of living and of being with other people. Rossellini

---

[22]Peter Bondanella, *The Films of Roberto Rossellini* (Cambridge: Cambridge University Press, 1993), 344.

[23]Peter Brunette, Roberto Rossellini (Berkley and Los Angles: University of California Press, 1996), 341.

[24]Fantuzzi, "*Il Messia di Robert Rossellini*," 312.

clearly rejects the dramatic effect, for which the Gospel narrative provides plenty of opportunities. At the beginning of the film, for example, he represents the slaughter of the innocents in a discrete, almost un-dramatic way, a choice consciously made, says Rossellini, to counter a contemporary habit: "Of course, showing the slaughter of the innocents today can be a major dramatic scene, in the sadomasochistic style of film-making so in vogue today." For Rossellini, rejecting artificially dramatic effects, though they are clearly pleasing to the audience which wants thrills and chills even from the life of Jesus Christ, is the "rejection of seduction." In the film-essay, there is no need for seduction: the truth speaks for itself.

In the film, Rossellini constantly chooses the anti-spectacular approach to focus more clearly on the essentiality of the message. His matured directing style is austere, rigorous, almost documentary-like clean, sober, and scientific. This style provides a transparent network of images and sounds.

Cinematography

Mise en scène means "telling a story", both in a visual way, and through a thematic way of directing the cinematography.

The camera in *Il Messia* holds a "social realist" style that eschews close-ups and montage and stylized lighting in favor of longer, wider shots in which people roam about the landscape and the camera generally remains in one place while zooming in, zooming out, and pointing this way and that. One of the interesting things about this approach is that it creates a sort of tension between the filmmaker and the unique aspects of the subject of the film, namely Jesus' life, both in terms of the miracles he performed (which the film almost ignores), and the centrality of his own self to his own message.

The cinematographic style in *Il Messia* is also very minimal. There are a lot of long takes, which made the images very contextual. Long take, as opposed to to close up, prevents filmmakers from leading audiences in a specific direction. Artificial manipulation is being reduced to a minimal level.

Every shot, every composition, every camera movement of *Il Messia* is precise: "Rossellini reached a level of essentialness almost unimaginable, totally void of all emphatic or rhetorical accentuation."[25] Very different from Hollywood and perhaps inspired by the icon-painters, Rossellini makes visual references to popular iconic images, but he carefully purifies them of possible mannerism. In one of the final sequences of the film, after Jesus is taken down from the cross, Rossellini has his body rest in the ever-young Mary's lap. The reference to Michelangelo's Pieta is clear and quite striking, but Rossellini keeps it from becoming sentimental.

The camera work furnishes a great quantity of contextual data. Rossellini believed that the long take and zoom had a special neutrality, beyond that of the regular shot. Rossellini believed a level of concretization is needed in order to faithfully present the data: "The concrete is the synthesis of many determinations. If you want to get to the concrete, you must present a quantity of determinations which everyone can synthesize according to his own personality, his own nature. The plan-séquence allows me to present all this data, without falling into the 'privileged' point of view of the fixed shot."[26]

Rossellini's interest in the "essential image" also reaches its zenith, resulting in a new emphasis on visual beauty, and the cinematographer Mario Montuori's striking compositions and luminous color photography, coupled with the

[25]Fantuzzi, "Il Messia di Roberto Rossellini," 343.
[26]Interview, Filmcritica , nos. 264-65 (May—June 1976).

magnificent Tunisian locations, easily make this Rossellini's most beautifully photographed film.[27]

For example, in long-shot, from the vantage of Jesus's witnessing mother, Rossellini simply records the crucified man's head quickly, silently dropping—a mysterious moment, perhaps, but one nevertheless matter-of-fact, deepening Rossellini's sense of the moment into a hint of timelessness.

The zoom seems to flatten out perspective, insisting more strongly than ever on the two-dimensionality of the screen image. Rossellini often counters this tendency by arranging groups and objects in semicircles that the zoom then penetrates optically, at least, to give an impression of depth and three-dimensionality. The vast majority of the shots are exteriors, and in enormous spaces, this effect of spatial penetration is lacking. The result of this flattening is to insist on the painterliness of Rossellini's compositions, and to suggest self-reflexively, once again, the sources of his iconography and even his choice of events to dramatize, since the visual traditions of Western art had long isolated certain "photogenic" events for treatment. A scene like Christ driving the money changers from the temple, for example, seems clearly based on late Renaissance prototypes, specifically Titian and Tintoretto.[28]

Editing

The increased cutting and the greatly enlarged number of scenes (some eighty or ninety) make *Il Messia* move much faster and thus seem less ponderous than some of the other history films, especially in terms of the long

---

[27]Peter Brunette, Roberto Rossellini (Berkley and Los Angles: University of California Press, 1996), 342.
[28]Ibid, 346.

speeches. But the film limits its editing intentionally: no flashbacks, no parallel subplots, no introspective or fantasy sequences. The characters move quickly, the camera follows like an attentive and mobile observer, the editing puts actions in a sequence, no further elaboration.

Acting

Most of the actors in the film were amateurs, with the exceptions of actors Pier Maria Rossi, who played Jesus, and Mita Ungaro (Mary).

Rossellini's Mary is a sixteen-year-old who still looks sixteen at the end because, Rossellini explained, in popular imagination virgins do not age, for example, in Micelangelo's Pieta,[29] and he says the actor playing Jesus recites his words "in a formal and slightly archaic tone, almost as if removed from the events, almost like the words of an oratorio, declaimed by actors seated on stools on an empty stage."[30] The effect of Mary's youthfulness is to disturb the surface realism of the film text and, like the minimalist *mise-en-scène* and the biblical language, to foreground its artificiality.[31] This detail accentuates Mary's symbolic and meta-historical significance.

Conclusion

Rossellini's Jesus is without a divine dimension, a normal person among normal people. All of Jesus' actions have an everyday, antiheroic quality, these miracles are never

---

[29]Tag Gallagher, *The Adventures of Roberto Rossellini*, Da Capo Press, 1998.
[30]Ibid.
[31]Peter Brunette, Roberto Rossellini (Berkley and Los Angles: University of California Press, 1996), 347.

denied, never confirmed, and insofar as they are, in a very limited, indirect way represented, they are human actions.[32]

In Rossellini's film, *il messia* is meant as a message, not as salvation in itself. This *messia* identifies with the workers, the poor, the powerless. An innovator who wants to change things, to renew the culture, his words often indicate an attitude of breaking with the traditions of his society.[33] This Jesus is certainly a Messia of liberation, in his way revolutionary, uncompromising in his opposition to the legalism of the religious and social ideas of his time. Rossellini's Jesus is a "carrier of a word of dignity and of love: a word to contemplate as a sublime ideal of humanity. The Jesus of the Gospel is not only this: he is the Word who saves, call to conversion, communication of life and not only of wisdoms."[34]

Critics have praised *Il Messia* as a great film, not because Rossellini is a believer, but because he moved away from the dogmatic formulas in which he was educated.[35] A certain degree of distance is actually makes this film more believable. As Rossellini himself clearly stated: "I believe that the greatness of Jesus is unique, even for one who does not have the faith. All his preaching has to do with the raising up of human beings, of their dignity."[36]

---

[32]Stefano Masi and Enrico Lancia, *I Film di Roberto Rossellini* (Roma: Gremese Editore, 1987),133.
[33]Fantuzzi, "Il Messia di Roberto Rossellini," 337.
[34]Bini, "Il Messia di Roberto Rossellini,"314.
[35]Fantuzzi, "Il Messia di Roberto Rossellini," 349.
[36]Bini, "Il Messia di Roberto Rossellini,"311.

Borrowing Your Enemy's Arrows:
On Cai Guoqiang

1. Practicing Art Diaspora

The New York artist Cai Guoqiang was born and educated in China, partially trained in Japan, and worked in
Japan, Europe and the United States. He represents a new
kind of artist in the era of transnationalism and globalization.
A member of the first generation of Chinese post-socialist[1]
avant-garde artists, Cai works outside China and yet continues to be identified as a "Chinese artist." Indeed, part of his
vanguard stature depends upon the way in which he inte-
grates a Chinese cultural identity into the new transnational
and cultural pluralism of the contemporary art world. A
successful contemporary artist, Cai's work deals with many
of the cutting-edge fields of concern in the art world and the
academy: identity, cultural differences, post-colonialism,
postmodern conceptualism, and political appropriation.
Dana Friis-Hansen, a curator at the Contemporary Arts
Museum in Houston, compares Cai to other "third world"
artists "who address spiritual, political, and social issues, in a
broad international framework."[2] Cai draws heavily on
emblems of traditional Chinese culture, incorporating gunpowder, acupuncture, herbal medicine and teas, historical
figures, and characters from myth and folk culture, to exhibit
an evocative image of Chinese culture to Westerners.

---

[1]Contemporary Chinese art and culture after 1978 are generally considered
"post-socialist." Socialist-realism is still respected, but is no longer the exclusive
official ideology.
[2]Carol Lutfy, "Flame and Fortune," *Art News* (December 1997):144.

In 1999, Cai presented *Venice's Rent Collection Courtyard* at the 48th Venice Biennale. In this work, he did not use references to traditional culture but instead, partially reconstructed a popular socialist-realist sculpture from Communist China's Proletarian Cultural Revolution of 1966 to 1976. Cai won the Biennale's Golden Lion, its highest award, for the piece, but his work and the prize raised a tremendous controversy in Mainland China, with the sculptors of the socialist-realist original threatening to bring legal action against Cai and the Biennale for copyright infringement. Some art historians and critics as well as journalists and lawyers also joined the debate, criticizing Cai's work. The work, and the ensuing arguments, became a multi-dimensional controversy involving hundreds of people in a complex cultural, art historical, legal, and economic debate. Although it is still difficult to sort out the significance and logic of this event, the post-socialist, post-colonialist, and post-modernist threads of the argument all merit investigation. The *Venice Rent Collection Courtyard* focused on itself an interesting heated clash of the cultural logics of late capitalism (post-modernism), socialist- realism and post-socialism.

The fashion for "transnational" cultural representation in the international art market paradoxically relies on the aura of ethnic authenticity combined with universal accessibility in the global marketplace. It is not difficult to discern the overload of cultural symbols and ethnic elements in the work of such artists as Japanese filmmaker Akira Kurosawa [fig. 1.1], the first Japanese film director to be "discovered" abroad, yet Kurosawa is often considered the "least Japanese" filmmaker in Japan.[3] Similarly, Cai achieved

---

[3]2002 <http://www.usc.edu/isd/archives/asianfilm/japan/kurosawa.html>.

worldwide prominence as a "Chinese artist" while at the same time garnering criticism as a symptom of "post-colonial cultural imperialism,"[4] for manipulating Chinese cultural references for the tastes of the Western art world. Some cynical critics even argued that Cai induced the cultural signifiers in his work solely for this purpose. Thus, they insist that "cultural capital" is created, received, recognized, experienced, and acquired. According to Pierre Bourdieu's theory of cultural practice, one would conclude that the ethnic elements in Cai's work are particular cultural codes designed and produced for the appreciation of the viewers who own the cultural capital.[5]

Contemporary Chinese artists overseas do not necessarily preserve Chinese characteristics in a manner faithful to their source. Their objective is to make their own Chinese cultural experience into an efficient and personally identifiable language for writing national allegory into their own artistic persona. These artists each face the challenge of finding their own unique place in the world. In reaction to a sense of being marginal, nameless, and alternative, and in reaction to the dominant strains of global culture they have strategically mined their native culture for the shared experience and cultural capital from which to establish an "imagined community."[6] One purpose of this is to survive in the international art market, but another is to construct an

---

[4]Dao Zi, "The Duplication and Post-modernism of Venice's Rent Collection Courtyard," 2000 <http://arts.tom.com/Archive/2001/3/26-83242.html>.
[5]Pierre Bourdieu, *Distinction: A Social Critique of the Judgement of Taste*, trans. R. Nice. (Cambridge: Harvard University Press, 1986).
[6]In *Imagined Communities: Reflections on the Origin and Spread of Nationalism* (London: Verso Books, 1991), Benedict Anderson examines the forces that shaped the nation, and also makes some assertions as to nationalism's origins. The diasporic ethnic group is always built in the same way that Anderson's "imagined community" became a nation, in addition, the group's activities may have considerable cultural references to its national culture.

identity that will viably retain its integrity in the dynamic dis-
locations of global culture. On the other hand, many third
word transnational artists use this strategy to establish their
cultural identity. In "Third-World Literature in the Era of
Multinational Capital," Jameson argues that, in contrast to
the first-world cultural texts, within which the unconscious
structures of national allegory are often embedded, third
world national allegories are conscious and overt.[7]

We may speak of a Chinese diaspora in the United
States. The term "diaspora" originally describes the disper-
sion of Jews outside of Israel when they were exiled in the
sixth century B.C. and it usually implies displacement. But
the word has come to refer more broadly to the disper-
sion of an originally homogeneous cultural entity, whether
Africans across the Atlantic or Chinese immigrants relocated
to the United States,[8] and the issue of homelessness has to
be reassessed in relation to the new pervasive itinerary of
individuals in a world of global mobility. Since the United
States, in particular, is a country of immigrants, immigrant
cultures normally do not view themselves as isolated and
independent; rather they strive to become an active part of
the mainstream cultural landscape while in some way also
preserving their heritage. Cultural identity is a constantly
shifting paradigm that goes beyond the traditional identity
of nation and community, redefining itself in the changing
conditions of the new environment through an ongoing
negotiation between the individual and all kinds of historical
exigencies. Many diasporic artists use their cultural heritage

---

[7]Frederic Jameson, "Third World Literature in the Era of Multinational
Capitalism." *Social Text: Theory/Culture/Ideology* 15 (1986): 65-88.
[8]Rey Chow uses "Diaspora" to contemporary Chinese culture for the first time.
See *Writing Diaspora: Tactics of Intervention in Contemporary Cultural Studies*
(Bloomington: Indiana University Press, 1993).

and alternative perspective as strategies to gain recognition as new and fresh. But in an article on Chinese artists in diaspora, art critic Wang Nanming complained that this "new and fresh" is at most "Chinatown-like;" it does not contribute to the development of domestic Chinese art, nor promote the "real communication" between China and West.[9]

Cai was first noticed by the mainstream art world for his cultural difference, but gradually viewers came to understand the critique of art discourse in his work and the subversive effect on the mainstream achieved by incorporating more and more Chinese cultural references into it. Eventually, the incorporation of cultures at the margins into the center of artistic discourse became an accustomed practice rather than an avant-garde stance, resulting in what Jonathan Fineberg has called the "the academy of the Avant-Garde."[10] For Cai, this incorporation of his indigenous cultural references resulted in the construction of a hybrid Chinese identity for Cai's artistic persona that includes both traditional elements and the acquisitions of an international art practice, replete with a sophisticated appreciation of the production, exhibition, and consumption of "otherness" as a commodity.

The contemporary Chinese art diaspora may be seen as part of a broad international postmodernism in which the artists fully take advantage of postmodern techniques of representation—collage, pastiche, and parody. In appropriating postmodernism, the artists find a new way to actively engage the multi-faceted, fast-changing realities of post-socialist China. At the same time, they bring to the foreground

---

[9]Wang Nanming, "Chinatown Culture: The Contemporary Chinese Art on the International Stage," 2000 <http://www.oh100.com/teach/shucaiku/back_info/meishu/200207/1702070108340.html>.

[10]Jonathan Fineberg, *Art Since 1940: The Strategy of Being* (London: Laurence King, 2000): 484.

the theme of cultural identity and the problematic "the self" and "the other." For some artists, Chinese art must possess a local flavor, an indigenous appeal, a certain "Chinese-ness." China and Chinese art are positioned as the cultural other, an alternative to the art system and life of the West. More importantly, the artists also began to experiment with ways in which to question and unmask the "Orientalist" habits of thinking about China and the East both among Chinese artists themselves and in the Western audience. Even as it fabricates images of "Chinese-ness" in the global contexts of exhibition and reception, this post-orientalist art cross-examines and disengages from those conventional Orientalist notions of the self, the other, China, and the West.

2. Cai Guoqiang's Works

Quanzhou, in Fujian province, was traditionally a busy port of international trade. From the Ming dynasty (1368-1644) forward, the people of Quanzhou City have traveled to Japan, Korea, and all around South Asia to buy and sell tea, silk, crafts, and other merchandise. As the hometown of Cai Guoqiang, Quanzhou's regional culture provides a footnote to Cai's overseas art practice. The multiethnic, multi-religious backdrop that shaped his art making origi-nated from the cultural melting pot and open-mindedness that characterize Quanzhou culture. Cai admits: "More than China, it is my hometown that has informed my work. I am interested in mining that microcosm of my culture for sym-bols that can be universally understood."[11]

Cai Guoqiang was born in 1957, eight years after the Chinese Communist Party established the Peoples'

---

[11]Carol Lutfy, "Flame and Fortune," *Art News* (December 1997): 145.

Republic. Like millions of children who were "born in the New China, grew up under the Red Flag,"[12] Cai had been educated in orthodox Communist doctrine and socialist-realist aesthetics. He joined a local Gao Jia opera performance group in the late 1970s and became a major figure of the local art world.

The first generation of Chinese post-socialist avant-garde artists emerged at the end of the1970s. The desire for change (in the academy, the art world, and society) underpins this generation's art, distinguishing it from the next generation and from its Western peers. At the center of the "1985 New Art Movement"[13] which summed up the first-generation artists' experiments, was the driving impulse to remake or restate the culture, to burst out of the existing perimeters and to take on the world. In this sense, Chinese post-socialist art always shares some characteristics with contemporary political movements. Individual artists may resist the notion that a specific political agenda underlies their work, but no one would deny that the overall change of the political and cultural environment made their practices possible. This non-traditional, or "experimental" art in China began with the first stage of China's "open-door" policy in the late 1970s. New Chinese artists regard the "open-door" as a unique opportunity to catch up with the world, to make China live up to international standards.[14] At that time, China had just survived the "Cultural Revolution,"

---

[12]Idiom in Chinese "Sheng zai xin zhongguo, zhang zai hongqi xia" refers to the Chinese people born after 1949, grew up under the Communism.

[13]1985 was a milestone year for the Chinese avant-garde. The government embarked on a series of liberal reforms; avant-gardism flourished across the arts- literature, film, visual arts, music- a phenomenon soon to be dubbed the "1985 New Art Movement." For a comprehensive analysis, see Gao Minglu, *Zhongguo Dangdai Meishu Shi 1985- 1986 (History of Chinese Contemporary Art, 1985-1986)* (Shanghai: Shanghai People's Press, 1991).

[14]The following sentences appeared in the preface of the second "Star, Star" exhibition (1980) catalogue, ". . . as the world gets smaller, there is no corner

a ten-year civil war that almost totally destroyed China's economy and traditional culture. In the period after 1979, modern Western philosophical and aesthetic ideas began flourishing in China, giving rise to new art trends and movements. The fine arts of the late 1970s and early 1980s was characterized by a double aspiration: artists sought a dialogue with the "outside," chiefly modern Western culture, and a rediscovery of the traditional cultural identity which had been mostly suppressed since the establishment in 1949 of the Communist regime and its official doctrine of socialist-realism.

The new art was regarded as highly political, a revolution against the mainstream of "proletarian" art. In China, art and literature have long been regarded as "the vehicle of truth" and "the weapon for resistance."[15] Literature and art are not simply vehicles for expressing the emotions, an art for art's sake, rather the literati and artists have historically been respected as the voice of justice; they have long been looked to for moral principles and advocated for freedom. This idea, ironically, was accepted both by the official socialist-realists and the new experimental artists. The socialist-realist artists regarded the proletarian art as a revolt against the traditional literati and art as well as the art of a corrupt capitalism; the experimental artists regard their new avant-garde art as a rebellion against the oppression of socialist- realism. Yet these experimental artists were educated in the socialist aesthetics of China's art institutions

---

of the earth where man has not left behind his footprints; there are no new continents to discover. Today, the new world exists inside the self. With each new angle, each new choice we make, the world moves forward accordingly. . . ." Gao Minglu, *Zhongguo Dangdai Meishu Shi 1985- 1986 (History of Chinese Contemporary Art, 1985-1986)* (Shanghai: Shanghai People's Press, 1991): 125.

[15]Chinese idioms "Wen Yi Zai Dao," "Bu Ping Ze Ming."

and their aesthetic weapons against the socialist- realist establishment were ironically derived from the arsenals of that establishment. The incursion of these experimental artists into the communist Chinese establishment was loudly proclaimed by the first exhibition of "Star, Star Group" in 1979. This was followed by literally hundreds of new art movements over the next two decades. The artistic styles of these movements were variously inspired by 20th century Western art and traditional Chinese culture.

From 1979 to 1989, Chinese art went through the influences of modern Western art history in an accelerated sequence from impressionism through post-impressionism, expressionism, cubism, futurism, dada and surrealism, and abstract expressionism; each held the Chinese art stage for a fleeting moment [fig.2.1, 2.2]. In Cai Guoqiang's words: "The influence of Western ideas and trends became a weapon for Chinese artists to use against their own tradition, politically and socially speaking. What influenced me most when we began to learn about Western contemporary art in the 1980s was not a particular work, tendency or idea, but rather the huge amount of information suddenly made available: this vast hundred-year span of modern and contemporary Western art."[16]

A new wave of performance and conceptual art held sway in China from 1985 until 1989. Then in 1989 avant-garde art was unofficially banned in Mainland China for four years. When China re-opened its doors in 1993, Chinese artists found themselves at a loss, facing a different art world, infused with post-colonialist and post-modern theory.

The political openness and cultural renaissance which characterized the 1980s allowed the existence of

---

[16]Dana Friis- Hansen, Octavio Zaya, Serizawa Takashi, *Cai Guoqiang* (London: Phaidon Press, 2002): 10.

90

an avant-garde movement, a period of enthusiasm from roughly 1979- 1985. Two new phenomena appeared on the horizon of contemporary Chinese art in the 1990s: disillusionment over the political ineffectiveness of art during the suppression of 1989- 1993, and the international commerce of the international art market, which enabled contemporary Chinese artists to go abroad and sell work in America and Europe.

Cai Guoqiang studied in the Department of Stage Design, Shanghai Drama Academy, from 1981 to 1985. He went to Japan in 1986 for advanced studies in fine arts and became a Japanese citizen. As a critical port for Western philosophy, art, and popular culture, Japan was a popular destination for Chinese visual artists in the 1980s. They went to Japan to study the most recent Western techniques, as well as to re-discover traditional Asian aesthetics, which were preserved and appreciated in Japan. In retrospect, Cai admitted his Japanese sojourn was critical to him intellectually, giving him insight into Western thought and sensibilities without severing his ties with the East.[17] In Japan, Cai became known for staging happenings, selling gunpowder drawings, and later using gunpowder to create visually orchestrated site-specific explosions on a large scale. His obsession with gunpowder is indebted to his hometown of Quanzhou, where firecrackers were widely manufactured for festivities, and where he grew up under the vague but persistent threat of war with Taiwan ("The Republic of China").[18]

---

[17]Dana Friis- Hansen, Octavio Zaya, Serizawa Takashi, *Cai Guoqiang* (London: Phaidon Press, 2002): 14.

[18]In Cai's childhood, 1960s and 1970s, Fujian Province, which was dubbed as the "Fujian Front," was the front base of the People's Republic of China against Taiwan, i.e., the Republic of China, whose nationalists lost the Civil War of (1945 – 1949) to the communists.

For Cai, the flashes emitted from the gunpowder explosions made an impression of both violence and beauty. In the late 1990s, he initiated *The Century of Mushroom Clouds: Projects for the 20th Century,* which was a series of performances, documented in a set of crisp photographs. The artist detonated small-scale mushroom clouds with hand-held devices in places significant to the development of the atom bomb, such as the Nevada nuclear test site. To underscore the global vulnerability that the development of nuclear weapons create, Cai detonated symbolic explosions above various New York sites. His mushroom clouds rose in the sky like mysterious emblem. Beneath them, Cai modestly raises his hand. The viewer could begin to feel the fear of an Armageddon in seeing the photographs of his projects, noticing the same cloud appearing in all sorts of places from the Nevada desert to New York.

The Century of Mushroom Clouds: Projects for the 20th Century and many of Cai's other works of the 1990s, have multiple references. This work not only refers to the nuclear threat in the 20th century but also redundant to the traditional Chinese philosophy of change and *Tao.* The concept of the exchangeability of destruction and creation, of violence and beauty is founded on Taoism. For Lao Tzu, the founder of Taoist philosophy, each and every existence in this world—from humans to other living beings to lifeless beings—consists of *Qi,* an invisible energy or spirit. *Qi* is the origin of life, constantly in motion and ever changing. Because *Qi* is so strong and omnipresent, according to Chuang Tzu (the disciple of Lao Tzu), the true phase of being is chaos. Only the human mind can control *Qi;* the way to achieve that is called "Tao." For Cai, an explosion is the simplest form in which to observe *Qi,* to understand the chaos, and to practice Tao. *The Century of Mushroom Clouds: Projects for the 20th Century* illustrated Taoist philosophy and echoed the threat of nuclear war during the Cold War era.

After moving from Japan to New York, Cai began to address more issues that were tied to fashionable currents in the international art world, involving himself in debates on environmental issues, post-colonialism, multi-cultural-ism, and cultural conflict. *Cry Dragon/ Cry Wolf: The Ark of Genghis Khan* was inspired by the story of "The Boy Who Cried Wolf." The work aims to deride the idea of "China threat" which was a popular misconception among people at the Pentagon and even among the American people. Despite the fact that China is the biggest market in the world and the biggest business partner of the United States, China is still not viewed as a strategic friend, but a long-term adversary.[19] Cai said: "*Cry Dragon/ Cry Wolf* is a relatively large-scale work for my first US museum exhibition. At the time of the exhibition, the Asian economy was very prosperous and China was just emerging as a new world power. . . . Often the dragon was used as a symbol of China and its assertion of power in relation to the West."[20]

The work was made of 108 sheepskin bags and three Toyota engines, configured in a form that rises from the front (the engines) to the back like a dragon tail pointing up in the air. The engine motors powered the entire floating dragon from behind, giving a sense of threat and excess. The work has two significant references. The first was a reference to Genghis Khan's soldiers, who carried air-filled sheepskins as floatation devices for crossing the rivers; the

[19]There are two most representative books of this "China Threat School": Richard Bernstein and Ross Munro, *The Coming Conflict with China* (Philadelphia: Vintage Books, 1998); Bill Gertz, *China Threat: How the People's Republic Targets America* (Washington DC: Regnery Publishing, Inc., 2000).

[20]Dana Friis- Hansen, Octavio Zaya, Serizawa Takashi, *Cai Guoqiang* (London: Phaidon Press, 2002); 25.

second was a reference to the "invasion" of Japanese cars, a modern version of the Asian "invasion." (Before China, the rise of Japan was being similarly described as an inevitable adversary of the United States.) But the immobility of the dragon implied that the "China threat" and Asian invasion are largely imaginary. By appropriating historically charged materials and themes, the inflated sheepskins and Toyota engines, Cai made an ironic comment on the Sinophobic belief in a "Yellow Peril" threatening the Western world.

Cai has mostly made installations since he moved to New York. He found that installation is a medium in which he can more effectively explore his concern with social life and immerse his audience visually in it. In his 1997 installation *Cultural Melting Bath: Project for the 20th Century.* Cai Guoqiang made full use of the Queen's Museum's largest gallery of approximately 2,000 square feet. Within a tent-like enclosure of translucent Chinese netting, he created his own version of a traditional garden of the Chinese elite. It has live finches, well-shaped, strategically placed Chinese rocks, and a Jacuzzi bath with the roots of a banyan tree suspended above it. Cai infused the bath with a soothing herbal concoction in which visitors were invited to soak. Cai offered the visitor an impressionistic sense of the traditional life of the Chinese elite. Once in the bath, visitors found themselves with people of totally different cultures and backgrounds. Appropriating the remarkable diversity of Queens, *Cultural Melting Bath* set up a direct relationship with the conditions of American life, giving the term "melting pot" a literal rendering.

Borrowing Your Enemy's Arrows (Caochuan jiejian) [fig. 2.3, 2.4] is a sculpture that was harshly criticized by Holland Cotter in the *The New York Times* for a "distinctly

94

nationalistic and implicitly anti-Western bent."[21] But Cotter completely misunderstood this work. Cai derived the title, "borrowing your enemy's arrows" from a well-known phrase in the classic Chinese novel *Romance of The Three Kingdoms (San Guo Yan Yi):* "straw boats borrow arrows."

As the story goes, during the great Chibi War in the third century C.E., the allied navies of the Shu and Wu State were preparing to fight with the Wei State's navy. The allied Commander General Zhou (Wu) realized that he lacked enough arrows for the upcoming battle and he pressed Master Zhuge Liang (Shu) to make 100,000 arrows in ten days. Zhuge, renowned for his wisdom, made three hundred boats of straw with straw figures on them and sailed them toward Wei's navy on a misty morning. Thinking they were under attack, the Wei navy peppered the boats with thousands and thousands of arrows. These arrows embedded in the straw bags became General Zhou's weapons for the upcoming battle. Making reference to this traditional story, Cai constructed a large wooden boat- about 5 feet high and 27 feet long, festooned with 3,000 arrows, like a porcupine. Cai added a red Chinese national flag at the stern, blown by a small electric fan and suspended the boat in mid-air.

Cai Guoqiang again made double references in this work. First, it is a work about traditional Eastern wisdom. As in the traditional Japanese proverb "Willows are weak, yet they bind other wood," Eastern wisdom values winning by exploiting the opponent's power. The Taoist martial art Tai Chi, or Pushing Hands, is based on the principle of "borrowing your enemy's strength, empower yourself, then strike back." The spirit of Pushing Hands is like water: subtle,

---

[21]Holland Cotter, "Art That's a Dragon With Two Heads", *The New York Times Art Review*, 13 Sdec. 1998.

shapeless, but unbeatable. This idea came from Lao Tzu. In his book *Dao De Jing,* Lao Tzu wrote: "Nothing in the world is as soft and yielding as water, yet nothing can better overcome the hard and strong. For they can neither control nor do away with it. The soft overcomes the hard; the yielding overcomes the strong."[22] Second, the work not only points to the shrewdness of the exchange of power, but also symbolizes the pain caused by a multitude of unavoidable foreign influences that infiltrate a nation. The boat is China, and the arrows represent foreign influences over it today. In Cai's own words: " I was thinking mostly of the trauma of cultural conflict and the price you pay for opening up."[23]

Borrowing Your Enemy's Arrows is also a very personal work, symbolizing Cai's own struggle and strategy. First and foremost, it is about Cai's simultaneous battles with the competitive fashions of the global art world on the one hand and the aesthetic dogmas of socialist-realism on the other. The personal references in Cai's works are not as obvious as the historical, philosophical, and contemporary references, but they are equally critical. Understanding the subtext, being caught between the two idioms, *Borrowing Your Enemy's Arrows* is an essential backdrop to Cai's controversial *Venice's Rent Collection Courtyard.*

3. Rent Collection Courtyard

In 1999, Cai presented his "fluid installation" *Venice's Rent Collection Courtyard* at the Venice Biennale. The work is a partial reproduction of *Rent Collection Courtyard*, one

---

[22]Lao Tze, *Tao Te Ching: A Book About the Way and the Power of the Way.* Trans. Ursula K. Le Guin. (London: Shambhala Publications, 1998).

[23]Dana Friis- Hansen, Octavio Zaya, Serizawa Takashi, *Cai Guoqiang* (London: Phaidon Press, 2002); 28.

of the most celebrated proletarian realist sculptures of the Chinese Cultural Revolution of 1965. The controversy over Cai's appropriation of the work, further inflamed by his winning the Biennale's International Award, centered on an intense debate in China about the meaning of art, originality and the avant-garde.

The original large sculpture group *Rent Collection Courtyard* was held up as the "model" sculpture of the Cultural Revolution, and was widely acclaimed as the climax of official Chinese socialist-realist art. [fig. 3.1, 3.2, 3.3, 3.4, 3.5, 3.6] The first version of this sculpture, completed in Sichuan in 1965 by faculty members and senior sculpture students of the Sichuan Academy of Fine Arts, consisted of a series of life-sized clay figures arranged in the mansion of a pre-revolutionary landlord. The *Rent Collection Courtyard* is a massive project comprising 114 figures and 108 real props, sub-divided into seven tableaux, that extend almost 100 meters from end to end. The seven groupings depict: *Bringing the Rent*, *Examining the Rent*, *Measuring the Grain*, the *Struggle*, *Calculating the Rent*, *Demanding the Rent*, and *Revolt*, and within these there are over twenty-six separate scenes. It remains a singular sculptural monument in China's art history.

In the *Rent Collection Courtyard,* the figure of the landlord dispassionately surveys an array of starving peasants struggling to pay the portion of grain demanded as rent. Pathetic figures indicate the horrors of life under the former feudal society. The artists employed found objects such as farm tools, tables and chairs to create the tableaux of starving, beaten or enslaved peasants forced to turn over their last grain of rice. The purpose of the sculptural installation was to remind viewers of the terrible life peasants faced before the Revolution, and was meant to contrast with the benefits of life under Communism. The work was acclaimed as a classic and a great "textbook" for communist education. The sculpture won the approval of Chairman Mao's wife, Jiang Qing who served as the general director of the propaganda campaign of the Cultural Revolution, but was arrested in 1979 after Mao's death and was sentenced to death (later commuted to life in prison) for treason and conspiracy. According to the prosecutor, Jiang Qing also committed the crime of "destroying Chinese culture and art."

Though mainly regarded as a work of propaganda after the Cultural Revolution, the *Rent Collection Courtyard* was still respected for its ambition and regarded as a landmark of the socialist-realism of the 1960s. Like many didactic art works of the period, *Rent Collection Courtyard* was reproduced for display in various cities throughout China.

It was replicated in Beijing for both the Chinese National Gallery and then again for the Palace Museum (1965-1966). Similar sculptural groups were constructed in other cities, and at that time, there was no concept of "intellectual property" or copyright in Mainland China. An artwork could be reproduced, copied, or imitated freely because personal ownership of cultural property ran counter to the concept of a socialist society. Indeed, the popular duplication of a contemporary artwork was regarded as an honor. Besides the countless copies and imitations, additional sets of the sculpture were made and sent to China's socialist allies, Albania, North Korea, and North Vietnam, as cultural gifts. *Rent Collection Courtyard* reached a prominence during the Cultural Revolution that could only be compared to the statues of Chairman Mao.

The original sculpture was displayed in the actual courtyard in Dayi County, Sichuan, that was portrayed in the story. The courtyard belonged to an allegedly reviled landlord, Liu Wencai, though later historical documents revealed that the landlord was not as heartless as he was portrayed in the work.[24] The rent collection scene was mostly a condensation and imaginary embellishment, recreated under the socialist-realist doctrine of "picking the most representative to depict the daily life." The land-lord's whole mansion was converted into a "people's museum" after the Cultural Revolution.

4. Venice's Rent Collection Courtyard

The 48th Venice Biennale opened on June 12th, 1999. On the same day, the Biennale curator Harald Szeemann declared that Cai Guoqiang had won the *Leone d'Oro*, one of the three International Awards presented to indi-vidual artists participating in the Biennale, for his installa-tion-in-progress. The work consisted of a large room in the old renaissance shipyards filled with clay figures made by a group of sculptors whom Cai had brought from China with the help of several Italian sculpture students whom Cai hired. [fig. 4.1, 4.2] In the introduction to the exhibition catalogue, Szeemann wrote: "It's playful, the East, . . . It's propaganda mocked, It's Chinese performance . . . It's the suffering and rebellion of the clay peasants . . ."[25]

Harald Szeemann had already had a history with the *Rent Collection Courtyard*. In 1972, he was appointed cura-tor of *Documenta 5* in Kassel, Germany to which he invited artists like Joseph Beuys, Bruce Nauman, and Vito Acconci to contribute work. Among the many works Szeemann requested was the original *Rent Collection Courtyard* of the

---

[24]According to a television news of Sichuan TV of July, 2000, after Sichuan Academy of Fine Arts published a new *Rent Collection Courtyard* catalogue in 2000, Liu Wencai's live relatives threatened to bring lawsuit against Sichuan Academy of Fine Arts for "defamation of character" for the "inappropriate depiction of Liu Wencai" in the *Rent Collection Couryard.*
[25]Harald Szeemann, *d'Apertutto* (Venice: Venice Biennale, 1999):2.

sixties. The Chinese authorities declined Szeemann's invitation. Szeemann viewed *Rent Collection Courtyard* as an avant-garde work.[26] To an art historian in 1970s, the *Rent Collection Courtyard* was characterized by the inclusion of many real objects, connecting it to the much-discussed history of the ready-made, and by a "super-realist" technique which related to the new "hyper realism" of seventies artists in the West like Johan de Andrea and Duane Hanson.

The *Venice Rent Collection Courtyard*, according to Cai Guoqiang, was a time-based installation, a "fluid installation" or "movable installation" which indicates his emphasis on the act of making the work rather than on a finished figure ensemble. Cai invited Long Xuli, one of the sculptors of the original *Rent Collection Courtyard,* and seven other artisan sculptors from Mainland China to Venice and together they reproduced part of the original work. For the opening, the eight Chinese sculptors and several students from Venice's *Accademia* were still modeling the sixty tons of raw clay into copies of the great Proletarian tableaux before a curious audience. The group had already been working on the project for one and a half months. Immediately after the opening— some said as soon as Cai was awarded the *Leone d'Oro*— he stopped the work and sent the Chinese sculptors home. The sculptures were left unfired, so over the course of the exhibition, the figures dried out, cracked, and crumbled off the wire matrices, eventually disintegrating completely. Cai presented this disintegration as an integral part of the concept of the work. The laudatory jury of the Biennale stated that "The artist questions the history, function and the epic of art through

---

[26]Sichuan Academy of Fine Arts, "The Rent Collection Courtyard Copyright Breached Overseas: Sichuan Academy of Fine Arts Sues Venice Biennale (Press Release)."

temporal and physical contextual isolation . . . the work is strong and surprising and perfectly balanced in its space" Critic Britta Erikson explained: "Cai Guoqiang has co-opted that style in order to create a metaphor for the failed promise of socialism in China. Superficially, it appeared to work, but in the end, it crumbled."[27]

The event stirred outrage in the Sichuan Academy of Fine Arts, where some of the original sculptors worked, and in the Chinese press. The debate reached a dramatic climax when the Sichuan Academy of Fine Arts threatened to bring legal action against Cai, Harald Szeemann, and the 48th Venice Biennale for copyright infringement.

At first, the controversy focused on the originality and the legitimacy of Cai's authorship, the copyright issue, and on the award from a post-colonialist and post-Orientalist perspective.[28] Professor Wang Guanyi was one of the sculptors of the original *Rent Collection Courtyard*. He claimed that "Cai Guoqiang has violated our creative rights; he did this without our approval. He might say that this is common in the world of modern art, but as far as I am concerned he did nothing creative. Cai Guoqiang has exploited the weighty and profound impact of the original *Rent Collection Courtyard*."[29]

Several intellectual property lawyers questioned *Venice's Rent Collection Courtyard*'s "originality". "Originality" in copyright law means that the work must be independently

---

[27]Britta Erickson, "Cai Guoqiang takes the Rent Collection Courtyard from Cultural Revelution model sculpture to winner of the 48th Venice Biennale international award," *Chinese Art at the End of the Millennium: Chinese-Art. Com 1998-1999*, ed. John Clark (Hong Kong: New Art Media Limited, 2000).

[28]For a comprehensive view of the debate, see the special on-line edition of Fine Arts Association of Tom. Com, *Venice's Rent Collection Courtyard* discussion, 2000 <http://arts.tom.com/Archive/2001/3/23-666.html>.

[29]Wang Guanyi, "Three Questions Regarding Cai Guoqiang's Award," 2000 <http://arts.tom.com/Archive/2001/3/26-25104.html>.

created—that is, not copied from another work. In addition, to be an original work, the artwork must be fixed in a tangible medium of expression. According to these principles, *Venice's Rent Collection Courtyard* is not considered "original" because it is a rough copy of the original *Rent Collection Courtyard*, and it is not "fixed in a tangible medium of expression." (Neither installation nor performance art are officially accepted as art genres in China.) Ma Jianjun, a Shanghai intellectual property attorney, raised questions about Cai's work, while admitting that the copyright issue is extremely vague in this case since it involves a collectively produced work of public art made in an era when the very idea of intellectual property was not legally defined in Mainland China.[30]

Leaving aside whether the earlier copies of the *Rent Collection Courtyard* in the Cultural Revolution or the lack of copyright statutes in China when the work was made may have put it into the common domain, Cai's work does reproduce parts of the earlier work; and, in the Western context into which he introduced his work, it would constitute an infringement of copyright unless he could demonstrate "fair use," which includes reproduction for the purpose of "criticism, comment, etc."[31] For Szeemann, Cai's *Venice's Rent Collection Courtyard* is a criticism of the Chinese Cultural Revolution, which constitutes a "fair use."

In an interview with a Japanese art critic in 2002, Cai Guoqiang told the interviewer that "on the legal front, the court ruled that works created during the Cultural Revolution could not be granted copyright."[32] In fact, there

---

[30]Ma Jianjun, Keynote address on *Venice's Rent Collection Courtyard* Event, Venice's Rent Collection Courtyard Event Colloquium in Beijing, June 20, 2000. 2000 <http://arts.tom.com/Archive/2001/3/23-45277.html>.
[31]The Copyright Revision Act of 1976, Section 107.

had been no actual court ruling on this. Cai was stating his conviction that copyright did not apply. On the other hand, the lawyers for the Sichuan Academy of Fine Arts have never decided in what legal venue, if any, they can proceed. The original *Rent Collection Courtyard* was made in China; Cai was a Japanese citizen who domiciles in the United States; the alleged copyright violation happened in Italy. Furthermore, *Rent Collection Courtyard*'s copyright had not been registered at Sichuan Copyright Bureau until Cai's copy appeared.

Dao Zi, an art critic and professor at the Sichuan Academy of Fine Arts, viewed Cai's work from a post-colonialist perspective. He revealed Cai's collaboration with Harald Szeemann, who had been fascinated by the original *Rent Collection Courtyard* and encouraged Cai to take on the project. Dai Zi called this event an example of post-colonial cultural imperialism in which China is demonized as backward and despotic. Dai Zi pointed out that winning awards at an important international art exhibition appeared to be a short-cut to "success" for a Chinese artist, especially a Chinese artist overseas. In the works of these artists, a representation of "the Orient" must be intelligible for Western viewers. The resulting internalization of this Western cultural perspective — the aesthetic preference of international curators and exhibition juries — induced Chinese artists to reconstruct their work according to projected Western expectations. For Dao Zi and his colleagues, Cai is a symptom of post-modern, post-colonial Orientalism.[33]

---

[32]Kay Itoi, "Inside Cai Guoqiang", interview with Cai Guoqiang. 2001 <http://www.artnet.com/magazine/features/itoi/itoi5-17-02.asp#1>.

[33]Dao Zi, "The Appropriation and Post-modernism of *Venice's Rent Collection Courtyard*", 2000 (http://arts.tom.com/Archive/2001/3/26-83242.html).

Cai Guoqiang defended himself on both artistic and ideological grounds. In an interview with Octavio Zaya, Cai said he had long been thinking of an installation based on the fluidity of time and that he was attracted by the narrative qualities of the original *Rent Collection Courtyard*, which he saw as a youth. He wanted to utilize "what I call 'fluid installation' or 'movable installation'— installation based on time."[34] The final physical presence of the sculpture was not important to Cai; instead, he wanted to show the process by which the work took shape (and disintegrated). Cai said, "apart from the narrative depicted in the story, the sculptural process was also depicted as a story."[35] Harald Szeemann also told an interviewer that Cai Guoqiang did not violate the copyright law because what he presented at Venice was the work-in-process, not a copy of the original *Rent Collection Courtyard.*[36]

In addition, Cai believed his work evoked the relationship between art and politics: *"Venice's Rent Collection Courtyard* expresses a number of different things. One of them is the tragedy of time, of people, of artists who were once full of passion and conviction in their beliefs. Reflecting upon the artist's work in particular, we see the discrepancy between ideology and reality, the tragedy of it all."[37] The partly completed work was finally left unfired and disintegrating; Cai said that it evoked "a life and death cycle."[38] This cycle is also illustrated by the experiment and

---

[34]Dana Friis- Hansen, Octavio Zaya, Serizawa Takashi, *Cai Guoqiang* (London: Phaidon Press, 2002):6.

[35]Dana Friis- Hansen, Octavio Zaya, Serizawa Takashi, *Cai Guoqiang* (London: Phaidon Press, 2002):8.

[36]Yu Xiaohui, "Interview with Harald Szeemann", 2000 (http://arts.tom.com/Archive/2001/3/26-38581.html).

[37]Dana Friis- Hansen, Octavio Zaya, Serizawa Takashi, *Cai Guoqiang* (London: Phaidon Press, 2002):7.

[38]Ibid.

104

failure of socialism in the 20th century.[39] As many participants in the debate realized at the time, the dispute not only
reflects different understandings of what constitutes art and
how art relates to society, politics and law, but the dialogue also revealed an anachronism (from a post-modern
perspective) problematic of the internal incompatibility of
styles: socialist-realism versus post-modern art practice.

5. Borrowing Your Enemy's Arrows

In *The End of History and the Last Man*, Francis
Fukuyama proposed that the liberal democratic system
operating a capitalist system is the end point of the political
history; he based his analysis on the collapse of Soviet
Union and the East European communist regimes.[40] However, he made the questionable assumption that the liberal
democracy may constitute "the end point of mankind's
ideological evolution" given the end of Communism. He did
not expect that economic progress has come with a revival
of nationalism, as has happened in the post-socialist China.

In *Postmodernism, or, The Cultural Logic of Late
Capitalism,* Frederic Jameson argued "the senses of the
end of this or that (the end of ideology, art, or social class;
the "crisis" of Leninism, social democracy, or the welfare
state, etc.)" constituted postmodernism, which is the cultural logic of late capitalism.[41] Jameson is concerned with
the cultural expressions and aesthetics associated with the
different systems of production.

---

[39]Dana Friis- Hansen, Octavio Zaya, Serizawa Takashi, *Cai Guoqiang* (London: Phaidon Press, 2002):9.

[40]Francis Fukuyama, *The End of History and the Last Man,* (The Free Press, 1992).

[41]Frederic Jameson, *Postmodernism, or, The Cultural Logic of Late Capitalism* (London: Verso, 1991).

The anachronistic clash of different ideologies appeared in China when post-socialism encountered the newly introduced late capitalism, both in the arena of politics and economy and in the realm of culture and art. *Venice's Rent Collection Courtyard,* a post-modernist installation made by a Chinese artist working overseas, was perceived by some as an example of post-colonial cultural imperialism and stirred nationalist outrage in the artist's homeland; the event itself is a postmodern phenomenon. To Cai, Szeemann, and Western viewers who are accustomed to conceptual art and the role that appropriation plays in contemporary art, the controversy around *Venice's Rent Collection Courtyard* may appear naïve and inappropriate. However, for the sculptors who made the original *Rent Collection Courtyard,* appropriation and the exploitation of the socialist cultural heritage without due respect to its aesthetic value—indeed done with irony—was unacceptable. In a sense, Wang Guanyi and Dao Zi's outrage are reasonable because they perfectly understand Cai's work is a total denial of the socialist-realist legacy that they still cherish. What Cai's work brings to the post-socialist Chinese art world are the commercialism of global art, deconstructionist postmodern parody, and the logics of late capitalism, which these Chinese artists are not yet ready to embrace.

Cai Guoqiang has benefited from the development of a global art world infrastructure. He sets his perspective in the midst of transnationalism and globalization from which he looks at the significance of art in culture, politics, and society. He attempts to establish an artistic language and a style of representation that merge the protocols of contemporary Western art with his cultural identity, including aspects of traditional, pre-socialist, Chinese culture.

For Cai Guoqiang's one-man exhibition "Flying Dragon in the Heaven," at the Louisiana Museum of Modern Art in 1997, he took the title from *I Ching,* the Taoist classic. Cai Guoqiang revealed the fundamental contradiction of contemporary Chinese culture and art. The first room of the exhibition featured four stone dragons arranged symmetrically on the floor. On the surrounding walls hung some of Andy Warhol's images of Mao. In the center of the room, the hull of a derelict dinghy was suspended from the ceiling, festooned with red lanterns, casting light upon the Warhols. The juxtaposition suggested the confrontations between traditional Chinese culture and socialism, and the prospect of deconstructing the socialist legacy and returning to traditional culture. For Cai, socialist-realism is just a raw material for his postmodern parody, the same as Warhol's Mao.

Cai Guoqiang's cultural strategy echoed Zhang Zhidong's teaching of the late Qing Daynasty. Zhang was the key figure of the 1898 "Reform Campaign." His famous statement "Chinese learning for the fundamental principles and Western learning for practical application"[42] is widely used to illustrate the reformer's strategy of fitting into international standards from a practical perspective while holding fast to the cultural heritage of traditional Chinese values underneath. Zhang Zhidong's teaching echoes the traditional wisdom of "borrowing your enemy's arrows." Cai Guoqiang has been borrowing arrows from both sides: from Chinese culture and from the Western culture, but neither are really his enemies.

---

[42]Zhang Zhidong, "Exhortation to Learing (*Quan Xue Pian,*" Samuel I. Woodbridge ed., *China's Only Hope: an Appeal by her Greatest Viceroy Chang Chih-tung* (New York, Fleming H. Revell 1900).

Illustrations

1.1 Akira Kurosawa's film Ran (1985) was full of Japanese cultural references, but the story was based on Shakespeare's King Lear.

2.1 Huang Yongping, The History of Chinese Art and The History of Modern Art . . . after Two Minutes in the Washing Machine. 1987. Huang was the key figure of the avant-garde group "Xia Men Dada" of 1980s in Xianmen City, Fujian Province. The group's name "Xiamen Dada" and its anti-art activities signal an unmistakable desire to link itself to its Western predecessor. © Huang Yongping

2.2 Wu Shanzhuan, Red Humor: Big Characters, Swearing. 1987. Performance. Wu Shanzhuan's "Red Humor" series is a strong cultural critique to the socialist ideology. He was an admirer of Robert Rauschenberg. © Wu Shanzhuan

2.3, 2.4 Cai Guoqiang, *Borrowing Your Enemy's Arrows, installation. The Museum of Modern Art, 1998.* © Cai Guoqiang

3.1, 3.2, 3.3, 3.4, 3.5, 3.6 Wang Guanyi, etc.,
Rent Collection Courtyard, Dayi, Sichuan, China, 1965.

4.1, 4.2 Cai Guoqiang, *Venice's Rent Collection Courtyard, Venice, 1999.*
© Cai Guoqiang

110

Cries and Whispers

As a typical 70s-generation Chinese, I grew up witnessing China's economic reform, cultural renaissance, and the
bumpy road towards the rule of law without being exposed
to different narratives of modern Chinese history, especially
the Civil War, the Cultural Revolution, and the struggle in
Tibet. Before high school, I had only heard of the Dalai
Lama and Tibet a few times in the news; most of the time
the authorities were accusing the Dalai Lama of "separating
the homeland" or "sabotaging ethnic unity".

We had quite a few Tibetan students in my high school.
Very soon we learned that all of them were affiliated with
high Tibetan officials who served on the Beijing-controlled
Tibet local government. We joked that they were "hostages",
but indeed they were called, and treated as, brothers. One
of them, "D.", became my buddy.

D. was taciturn, partly because his Chinese vocabulary
was limited, partly because his high-profile parents advised
him not to talk too much with his fellow Chinese students.
Shortly after graduation, we hung out in a Tibetan restaurant in Beijing. After several rounds of beer, D. began to
sing. It was a very sad song, in Tibetan, so the few Chinese
in the restaurant (including me) had no idea what the lyrics
were about. We applauded at the last note. I asked D. what
the song was about, but he just showed a forced smile.
Then he began to mutter, very slowly, about his recent
mountaineering with two prominent Tibetan mountaineers
who were members of the national athletic team. Three of
them successfully climbed a 6000-metre peak in Tibet. "We
made it, and . . ." D. whispered to me, "We mounted the
Snow Mountain and Lion Flag on the peak." I was shocked

111

because I knew the Flag was the national flag of Tibet and the emblem of the Tibetan Government-in-Exile, and therefore, it was banned in China. I was speechless and I felt a flush of shame on my face. But D. continued, "Then the three of us cried our hearts out . . ."

In the following year, D. loaned me many books on Tibet and Tibetan Buddhism. To my surprise, the books included the Chinese translations of *The Opening of the Wisdom Eye* by His Holiness the 14th Dalai Lama and *In Exile from the Land of Snows: The Definitive Account of the Dalai Lama and Tibet Since the Chinese Conquest* by John F. Avedon. All these readings and a monthly visit to the Lama Temple in downtown Beijing ultimately led up to my visits to Tibet and my belief in the Four Noble Truths.

China was in a religious and spiritual vacuum in the 1990s: the communist ideology had collapsed; indigenous religions were largely devastated during the Cultural Revolution; and Chinese Buddhist and Taoist institutions were heavily regulated and distorted. Nonetheless, Christianity and Catholicism revisited rural China and thrived, while many Chinese intellectuals, artists, and professionals in metropolitan cities took up Tibetan Buddhism, the official state religion of the Mongol Yuan dynasty (1271–1368, A.D.) and the Manchu Qing dynasty (1644–1912, A.D.) that ruled China.

Wang Lixiong, a leading Chinese novelist and historian, believes that the phenomena of so many Chinese being fascinated by Tibetan culture and Tibetan Buddhism cannot be solely explained by the mysterious reincarnation stories and metaphysical inspiration of Mandala. Other factors must include the close ties of Tibetan and Chinese spirituality in history, and the tremendous integrity and the big hearts of the high gurus, HHDL in particular. In the wake of recent rioting in Tibet in 2008, Wang and a dozen Chinese intellectuals signed a petition to call for open, direct dialogue with HHDL. "We support the Dalai Lama's appeal for peace," said the petition letter, "and hope that the ethnic conflict can be dealt with according to the principles of goodwill, peace, and non-violence." The petition echoes the HHDL's Middle-Way Approach to resolve the issue of Tibet. Unfortunately, the petition, like many previous calls, was rendered futile in the chaos of nationalist hysteria. Over the past half-century, a gigantic "anti-separatist" machine was built to crack down on any attempts of rational negotiation and due process. A personal attack on HHDL and his non-violence principles is among the machine's favorite weaponry.

In his book *Dialogues with the Dalai Lama*, Wang Lixiong described his first meeting with HHDL. He was overwhelmed by the energy, solidity, generosity, and warmth of this "simple monk". Wang felt extremely sorry for the Chinese for want of a secular and spiritual leader of that caliber, with his incredible integrity, wisdom, conscience, knowledge, experience, international recognition and reputation.

When I return to China for business or to visit family, I generally spare a few hours for shopping. During my last trip in January, I stopped by a Tibetan handcraft store in Beijing's Central Business District. The owner is a pleasant young Tibetan, "L.", who speaks broken Chinese. After he greeted me "*Tashi Delek*", or "good luck" in Tibetan, he delightedly showed me his impressive collection of Buddhist instruments and Tibetan souvenirs. Among the mantra prayer wheels

and sutra scripts, I found a very small photo of HHDL placed scrupulously and respectfully on the corner of a Thangka, an embroidered Buddhist banner. This is highly unusual because it is generally considered an offense to display the photo of the HHDL in China, both in public and in private places. I nodded to L., unbuttoned the top button of my shirt and showed him my amulet with a small portrait of HHDL, which I have worn for more than a decade. I immediately noticed there was a light in L.'s eye and a lump in his throat. What happened next seemed both dramatic and ironic. L. tried to give me everything in his store I was interested in for free, and I stiffly refused his kind offer. I felt a flush on my face. When I finally escaped from the store, I said *"Tashi Delek"* to him. L. approached me and whispered, firmly and proudly, "I have seen His Holiness, in person, last year in India. I sat in one of his teaching sessions. I walked three weeks, and finally arrived."

Many years after I heard D.'s sad song for the first time, I came to know and understand that it is a folk song, an elegy, one of the songs Tibetan refugees sing upon leaving Tibet, and going into exile.

Today D. is married to the descendant of a Chinese leader. He has moved overseas and probably lives under a new identity. We have lost contact.

The Case of Tenzin Delek Rinpoche

On December 11th, 2002, I signed my name on *The Petition to the National People's Congress of China, Supreme People's Court, and Sichuan Supreme Court for a Fair Appeal Process for Tenzin Delek Rinpoche and Lobsang Dondrub*. December 12th was the deadline for an appeal for the two Tibetans who were sentenced to death by the Karze Intermediate People's Court of Sichuan on December 2nd. Lobsang Dondrub was sentenced to death for "committing crimes of explosions, inciting separatism." Tenzin Delek Rinpoche, the reincarnation of a Tibetan Buddhist high monk and the spiritual leader of the local Tibetan community, was sen-  tenced to death with a two-year suspension for "causing explosions and inciting separatism." They were denied access to lawyers in the summary trial.

The petition highlights three points. First, in accordance with Chinese Criminal Law, the defendants should be offered access to attorneys. Considering the financial hardship of Ven. Tenzin Delek Rinpoche's family, the signers planned to hire independent lawyers for him and Lobsang Dondrub. Second, the local Communist Party Committee

115

that supervises the court launched a campaign against "the convicted terrorists Tenzin Delek and his attendant Lobsang Dondrub" four months *before* the verdict; therefore people had reasonable doubt with concern to the fairness of the trial. Third, to prevent a possible negative impact on the on-going negotiations between His Holiness the Dalai Lama and Beijing, delegates of the Tibetan Government-in-Exile should have been allowed to come to Sichuan to observe the entire judicial process.

As a protest against the threat made by the local government officials that "whoever supports Tenzin Delek will be treated as guilty as Tenzin Delek himself," all signers have signed their real name on the petition. The petition has been co-signed by forty-nine Chinese and Tibetan scholars, journalists and artists. In China, those taking part in such petition-signing activities, especially group petitions involving "sensitive" issues, could be charged with "jeopardizing the national security" by the law enforcement authorities, though such a charge does not have any ground in the Chinese Constitution and Criminal Law. I signed the petition not as a political dissident, but as a law-abiding citizen who believes in procedural justice. I did not make up my mind to be involved in human rights activities overnight. Indeed, this idea has developed over thirteen years.

June 4th, 1989 was the turning point for my generation. On that day, the People's Liberation Army opened fire upon unarmed students and civilians who had been protesting governmental corruption and demanding freedom of speech for months. Hundreds, possibly thousands were killed on Tiananmen Square and Long Peace Boulevard, as casualty numbers were never released. Jiang Jielian, my schoolmate in People's University High who was just one month older than me, was also killed. No one has ever been charged with the June 4th Massacre. No public memorial activities for the victims were ever allowed. Two lower rank national security agents (Mr. Gong and Mr. Xu, who only told me their last names) "interviewed" me six times after my school proctor reported to the local National Security Office that I had edited a June 4th memorial edition of my school's magazine. Our magazine was later shut down.

Nine years later, when I was writing an article for the thirtieth anniversary of the French students movement of 1968 for *Reading (Dushu)*, the most prominent academic journal in China, I alluded to the 1989 student protest in every sentence. The article was published in the May 1998 issue as a featured article and was very well received by the Chinese academia. This time, no one interviewed me.

In China, art and literature have been long regarded as "the vehicle of truth" and "the weapon for resistance." Literature and art are not simply vehicles for expressing the emotions, or "art for art's sake," but largely the ways literati and artists address social injustices. The function of literature and art is to convey moral principles and to cry for freedom. These Confucian ideas and the concept of the "organic intellectual" have been engraved in my heart since my childhood when I learned Tang Poetry with my grandfather.

I grew up in an intellectual family ("book-reading people" in Chinese). My grandfather was the editor-in-chief of *Henan Daily*, a popular newspaper in central China. He was a strong supporter of President Liu Shaoqi's social democratic policy. President Liu, the nominal national leader that ranked No. 5 in the Chinese Communist Party, was murdered by the Party Chairman Mao's "Red Guards" at Henan in 1969 during the "Cultural Revolution" which was instigated by Mao as a main effort to establish his dictatorship. President Liu was labeled a "traitor" from his death until 1980. I remember before President Liu's reputation was formally rehabilitated, my grandfather showed me the pictures of him interviewing President Liu in the 60's. He also told me that the President was a very good statesman. When President Liu's ashes were moved from Henan to Beijing on May 14th of 1980 after the central government dismissed all wrongful charges against him, the former first lady Wang Guangmei told the press that her husband, the President of the People's Republic, desperately clung to a copy of the *Constitution of China* as he was beaten to death by the "Red Guards." My grandfather cried his heart out when he heard that on TV. That was the first and the only time I ever saw my grandfather cry.

China has witnessed too many revolutions, civil wars, and coups in the past century. Violence and mayhem have been carried out in the name of the people and "substantial justice." Without the general acceptance of Constitutionalism, without respect to the due process, the law could only be an instrument manipulated by powerful interest groups. The leaders of China promised to continue the economic marketization and to further implement the institutional and judicial reforms. In the new century, the world is becoming increasingly interdependent. It is impossible for China to join the international free market community while keeping its legal system in isolation. Law has always been critically important for promoting human rights as well as economic development. It is my generation's responsibility to work together to make China's political and legal system live up to international standards, to realize the peaceful evolution of democratization, to make China a "Red Corner" no more.

On July 12, 2015, Tenzin Delek Rinpoche died in prison.

Ai Weiwei vs. China:
Moot Court Considers Activist's Fate*

For 81 days in 2011, the Chinese government detained Ai Weiwei, the prominent artist and dissident who helped design the iconic Bird's Nest stadium for the Beijing Olympics. After Ai's detention and a subsequent investigation, the government accused Ai Weiwei's company, Beijing Fake Design Cultural Development Company, of tax evasion and levied a fine amounting to over $2.4 million. Ai and his lawyers, maintaining that the investigation was a government attempt to harass and detain a high-profile political activist, brought a lawsuit against the tax authority, alleging a litany of legal shortcomings and procedural errors. Ai lost in the district court and the appellate court; the penalty stood.

On April 23 and 24, 2013, however, this case made its way to the Courtroom of Minnesota Supreme Court, where Justice Paul Anderson and other justices presided over an appeal before the "Constitutional Court of the People's Republic of China." No strange procedural wrinkle brought the case from Beijing to Saint Paul; the proceedings were a moot court exercise, serving as the final exam for Professor Chang Wang's Chinese law courses at the University of Minnesota Law School and William Mitchell College of Law.

"All Rise! All persons having business before the Honorable, the Constitutional Court of the People's Republic of China, are admonished to draw near and give

*This article, co-authored with Andrew Hart, covers a moot court competition that formed the culminating exercise for one of Chang Wang's Chinese law courses at the University of Minnesota. It originally appeared in *Minnesota Lawyer* on May 3rd, 2013. A modified version was published in June, 2016 issue of *China Insight*.

their attention, for the Court is now sitting. The honorable Chief Justice Paul Anderson is now presiding over the oral arguments." As the gavel hit the judge's desk, court was called into session.

In the two days of moot court competition, eight teams of 47 law students from both schools representing the artist Ai Weiwei, appellant, and Beijing Tax Bureau, respondent, conducted four mock appeals. Each team authored a legal brief and presented oral arguments to the imaginary "Chinese Constitutional Court." On the first day, two teams from the University of Minnesota represented Ai Weiwei against two William Mitchell teams presenting the tax bureau's argument. On the second day, two other William Mitchell represented Ai, and two other U of M teams represented the government.

In addition to Justice Anderson, a legendary Minnesota Supreme Court justice who has lectured at Supreme People's Court of China and top Chinese law schools in recent years, other distinguished justices on the "Imaginary Constitutional Court" included:

- Alexander Morawa, expert in comparative constitutional law and Associate Dean for Internationalization and Chair in Comparative and Anglo-American Law at the University of Lucerne School of Law in Switzerland

- Rick King, Chief Operating Officer for Technology at Thomson Reuters and a leader in national technology community

- Joan Howland, Roger F. Noreen Professor of Law and Associate Dean for Information and Technology at the University of Minnesota Law School

- Tom Leighton, Vice President of Content Acquisition and Government Relations at West, a Thomson Reuters company

- Jay Erstling, professor of international and comparative intellectual property law at William Mitchell College of Law
- Jim Hilbert, Executive Director of the Center for Negotiation and Justice and adjunct professor at William Mitchell
- Alan Miller, host of the television program *Access to Democracy*
- Nathan Madson, an expert in international human rights law and an attorney at Findlaw, a Thomson Reuters business
- Professor Chang Wang, Chief Research and Academic Officer at Thomson Reuters and adjunct professor at both the University of Minnesota Law School and William Mitchell College of Law.

The tax ruling that Ai Weiwei was appealing did not actually begin as a tax case. Rather, it began as a criminal investigation, based on suspicion of Ai Weiwei's political activities. Ai had been detained at Beijing International Airport on April 3, 2011, as he was about to board a plane to Hong Kong. For the next 81 days, he was held in state custody and interrogated as to whether he had been involved in "inciting to subvert the state power." Partly as a result of international pressure, Ai was finally released in June. By then, the criminal element of the case had faded, and the case had morphed into a charge tax evasion, an administrative-law case. After his losses in the administrative hearing, district court, and appellate court, Ai Weiwei's case fully run its course in Chinese judicial system, with no avenue of appeal remaining. But the moot court assignment imagined a "Chinese Constitutional Court" that could review the case under the Chinese Constitution.

The complexities of the case forced the students to master Chinese constitutional, criminal, administrative, and evidentiary law, and to consider China's obligations under international human rights treaties—topics they had studied during a semester-long course Chinese law course taught by Professor Chang Wang. The legal teams had to wrestle over such issues as whether Ai's detention violated criminal-law procedure, whether evidence gathered by the tax bureau was valid and sufficient to convict Ai's company, and whether the tax-penalty hearing violated administrative and evidentiary procedure. Another issue confronting the teams was whether it had been proper to detain Ai —whose role with Fake was limited to that of minority shareholder and "consultant"—during what was ostensibly an investigation of the company itself. The implication of International Covenant on Civil and Political Rights (ICCPR), to which China is a signatory, in this case was also debated.

The justices challenged all eight teams with incisive questions. During a discussion of profit margins, a discussion stemming from the tax bureau's factual findings, Justice Anderson honed in on the standard of review, asking the teams to articulate the level of deference with which the court was required to treat the factual findings of the tax bureau and the district court. Justice Morawa persistently reminded the teams that they were before a constitutional court, and required students to find constitutional justification for their statutory arguments.

The student counselors made their arguments by fielding difficult questions from the bench. The Justices constantly challenged the counselors to articulate a particular point of law or to respond to a hypothesis that contained slightly twisted fact patterns. Indeed the justices and the counselors acted together to explore the nuances of complex legal issues. The courtroom was filled with almost palpable tension: zealous advocacy, probing questions and constant wrestling with fine legal points. The student counselors appreciated and benefited from this unique opportunity to make cases in front of a high profile team of senior judges, top business executives, and learned law professors.

China Law Moot Court: Justice Paul Anderson, Rick King, Tom Leighton, Dean Joan Howland, Chang Wang, and other justices judged the China Law Moot Court competition between the U of M Law School and William Mitchell College of Law at the Minnesota Supreme Court in April 2013.

The students largely withstood the onslaught of questions from the justices. Despite the talent of the justices for picking apart arguments, the students were overwhelmingly able to cite to the relevant provisions of Chinese and international law. At the conclusion of the arguments, the justices offered feedback to the students, who were honored to receive praise and constructive criticism from a distinguished panel.

At the end of the second day of arguments, the moot court participants were treated to a special moment when Rick King and Tom Leighton of Thomson Reuters commemorated Justice Anderson's judicial career by presenting him with nine bound volumes that contained more than 600 of the opinions Justice Anderson had authored during his tenure on the bench. Justice Anderson is about to retire from Minnesota Supreme Court at the end of May, when he reaches 70, the mandatory retirement age by state law.

Thomson Reuters, known as West by most Minnesotans, is a leading intelligent information provider, specializing in legal and other professional information. West was established in 1872 in St. Paul and became the nation's most respected publisher of judicial opinions and annotated statutes.

"You are so lucky to witness history today, as Justice Anderson receives these volumes compiled by West," Justice Jim Hilbert told the students, "And you also participated in history by arguing before him in the Minnesota Supreme Court shortly before his retirement."

This Chinese law moot court competition is the first ever inter-collegiate moot court competition in the United States on Chinese law. It provides a unique opportunity for American law students who have studied Chinese law to develop a better understanding of the legal system of China from a comparative perspective, and learn to predict legal actions and outcomes across cultures from a practical point of view.

After the moot court concluded, Professor Chang Wang praised the students for their arguments and poise before the court. "This was a complex and difficult set of facts, but the students researched and performed very well," Professor Chang stated. "Ai Weiwei and Beijing Tax Bureau might be amused to hear your arguments on behalf of them at this imaginary 'Chinese Constitutional Court'."

The Curious Case of Ai Weiwei*

From left to right: Pu Zhiqiang, Ai Weiwei, Meng Tang, Chang Wang

On 3 April 2011, the world-renowned Chinese artist Ai Weiwei was taken into custody at Beijing Capital International Airport as he was about to fly to Hong Kong. For the next 81 days, he was held in secret detention while his friends, family and the international art community demanded information about his condition and asked for his release. Ai's detention is interesting in that its legal basis fell under administrative law, yet the tactics utilized by Chinese authorities often fell far outside typical administrative

---

*This article, co-authored with Nathan Madson, reviews Chinese government's detention and prosecution of artist and dissident Ai Weiwei. It was first published in Chapter 8 of *Inside China's Legal System*, Chandos Publishing, 2013.

procedures.[1] The timeline of his case also lends credence to the argument that the government used a retroactive application of tax law following Ai's detention to 'legitimize' its actions.[2]

Timeline

Prior to Ai's arrest at 8:30 pm on 3 April, police officers went to his Beijing studio, Fake Cultural Development Company, to question staff members and search the studio.[3] Shortly after his arrest, four new officers arrived to search the studio and did not leave until after midnight. During the searches, over 100 pieces of property were taken, all of which were documented on a list that was then given to Ai's wife, Lu Qing. The following day Lu and Ai's assistants were released from custody after being detained. Upon their release, only Ai and his friend Wen Tao were still missing, but within one day of Ai's arrest representatives from Germany, France and the United Kingdom had all voiced their opposition to his arrest and the way China has handled its dissidents.

By 5 April 2011, Ai's mother and sister, Gao Ying and Gao Ge, had still not heard anything about Ai. Lu issued a public request for legal help, and Gao Ying and Gao Ge circulated a missing person's notice.[4] Wen's family also filed a report with the Beijing Nangao police, but the request for information was summarily rejected. A day after the governments of Germany, France and the United

[1]'The Fake case'; available at: *http://fakecase.com/case* (accessed: 9 August 2013).
[2]Ibid.
[3]Ibid.
[4]Evan Osnos (2011) 'Ai WeiWei and the law', *New Yorker*, 7 April; available at: *www.newyorker.com/online/blogs/evanosnos/2011/04/ai-weiwei-and-the-law.html* (accessed: 9 August 2013).

Kingdom issued statements regarding Ai's disappearance, the European Union and the US government both requested the artist's release.[5] Adding his voice to the mix was Zhao Lianhai, a human rights activist who was jailed for his role in the 2008 melamine-tainted milk scandal in China.

It was not until the next day that the first state-controlled media organization, the *Global Times*, even acknowledged Ai's detention. On 7 April, however, the government news source, Xinhua News, published a report claiming Ai was being held under suspicion of 'economic crimes'; the report was deleted shortly after its publication. At approximately the same time that Xinhua was breaking this news, a Foreign Ministry spokesman confirmed at a press meeting that Ai was indeed being detained for economic crimes. He also warned other countries not to interfere in the investigation. When the official transcript of the meeting was released several hours later, however, all mention of Ai had been removed.[6]

Over the next few days Lu made public a letter asking police for information on her husband, while the accountant for Ai's studio, Hu Minfen, and Ai's driver, Zhang Jingsong, both went missing.[7] By 11 April, Liu Zhenggang, Ai's partner at Fake, was also missing. In their first trip to the accounting office, the Beijing Public Security Bureau spent three hours searching the office and seized bookkeeping records, the office computer, and more than RMB20,000 in cash.

The Hong Kong radio station RTHK reported that Lu Qing had been asked to bring tax documents to the Beijing

---

[5]Ibid.
[6]note 1 above.
[7]Ibid.

127

Taxation Bureau as part of the investigation.[8] The documents had previously been confiscated by authorities, however, and it was unclear if she was able to provide the paperwork the taxation bureau was after. This request was shortly followed by a story in the pro-Beijing Hong Kong newspaper *Wei Wen Po* claiming Ai was being investigated for bigamy and disseminating pornography, in addition to the charge of tax evasion. Lu and other family members denied the charges.

Twelve days after his initial disappearance, Ai's family and Fake staff and volunteers published an open letter requesting that police look into the disappearance of Ai, his colleagues and friends, including the lawyer Liu Xiaoyuan, who had disappeared the day before.[9] The letter, which was originally posted on the website Sina Weibo, the Chinese equivalent of Twitter, asked authorities to follow the normal legal procedures throughout the investigation. Without releasing any information about his or anyone else's disappearance, Liu Xiaoyuan reappeared on 19 April.

By 9 May 2011, 37 days had passed since Ai was escorted from Beijing airport. This marked an important milestone, as the Criminal Procedure Law allows authorities to hold an individual for 37 days at most before they must release the detainee or file an official charge.[10] According to Jerome Cohen, the law allows police to detain someone for three days without releasing him or her or filing for an

---

[8]Radio Television Hong Kong (2011) 'Ai Weiwei to fight tax bill', RTHK, 11 November; available at: *http://rthk.hk/rthk/news/english-news/20111111/news_20111111_56_797318.htm* (accessed 9: August 2013).

[9]'Public letter from Ai Weiwei's family'; available at: *www.scribd.com/doc/53066441/Public-Letter-from-Ai-Weiwei-Studio*。

[10]Ai Weiwei's lawyers (2012) 'The Ai Weiwei papers', *New Statesman*, 18 October; available at: *www.newstatesman.com/politics/politics/2012/10/ai-weiwei-papers* (accessed: 9 August 2013).

arrest warrant with the prosecutors.[11] In certain cases, however, authorities can take up to seven or 30 days to file for a warrant. Because prosecutors can take up to seven days more to approve an arrest warrant, the maximum amount of time someone can be held under current Chinese law is 37 days.

Despite being in custody for 37 days, authorities did not release Ai, nor did they provide any information about his detention or on what charges he was being held. It was another six days before Lu was finally able to visit her husband on 15 May.

On 21 May the first reports emerged indicating that Fake studio was responsible for not paying taxes and destroying evidence of its tax evasion.[12] Though the reports spoke of an investigation of Ai's studio, neither he nor his other disappeared friends and associates were released. By 11 June Lu and the other families had not received any news on their relatives' disappearances, so they filed a joint letter with the public security departments in Beijing.[13] The letter specifically requested that officials properly investigate the kidnappings.

In mid-to-late June several artists cancelled their openings at Chinese museums and studios in solidarity with Ai.[14] At the same time, many renowned art museums throughout the world, including the Museum of Modern Art, Tate Modern, the Guggenheim Museum and others, pushed for Ai's release. They created a campaign on Change.org,

---

[11]Jerome Cohen (2012) 'An introduction to the Ai Weiwei papers', *New Statesman*, 18 October; available at: *www.newstatesman.com/politics/politics/2012/10/ai-weiwei-papers* (accessed: 9 August 2013).

[12]Ai Weiwei's lawyers, note 10 above.

[13]Lu Qing et al. (2011) 'Joint letter', trans. Jennifer Ng, 10 June; available at: *www.scribd.com/doc/58150935/June-11-Joint-Letter* (accessed: 9 August 2013).

[14]Ai Weiwei's lawyers, note 10 above.

which collected more than 143,422 signatures demanding Ai's release.[15]

On 22 June 2011, after 81 days of imprisonment, Ai was finally released. Within the next few days, his driver Zhang Jinsong, the manager Liu Zhenggang, the accountant Hu Mingfen, and Ai's friend Wen Tao were also released from custody. Upon his release, Ai was instructed to have limited or no contact with several of his colleagues, including his personal videographer Zhao Zhao.[16] Ai was also unable to get in touch with his manager, Liu, who had suffered a heart attack during interrogation.[17]

On 27 June, officers from the taxation bureau came to Ai's studio and asked him to sign a document agreeing to pay an alleged RMB12 million in penalties and unpaid taxes.[18] Ai attempted to get in contact with Liu Zhenggang and Hu, but was unable to reach them and so refused to sign.[19] The next day lawyers Pu Zhiqiang and Xia Lin announced they were officially representing Fake in the tax evasion case.

The first thing the lawyers did was submit an appeal to the taxation bureau seeking an accounting of the evidence for the case against Fake. The hearing was on 14 July 2011, but it was not open and public as it should have been under law. The government insisted on a closed hearing.[20]

Fake's first appeal was unsuccessful and, on 7 November 2011, the government ordered the studio to pay RMB15 million within 15 days.[21] Though it was Fake that was being

[15]Solomon R. Guggenheim Foundation (2011) 'Call for the release of Ai Weiwei', June; available at: *www.change.org/petitions/call-for-the-release-of-ai-weiwei* (accessed: ????).
[16]Ai Weiwei's lawyers, note 10 above.
[17]Liu Yanping (@duyanpili) (2011) 'Tweet', 26 July.
[18]Ai Weiwei's lawyers, note 10 above.
[19]Liu, note 17 above.
[20]Ai Weiwei's lawyers, note 10 above.
[21]Ibid.

ordered to pay the tax bill and accused of evading taxes, Pu said that Ai could be sent back to prison if the RMB15 million was not paid.[22] Remarkably, Fake was able to raise the money through donations. Several thousand people donated to pay the fine, at times throwing the money over the wall of Ai's compound.

On 29 March 2012, the Beijing Local Taxation Bureau turned down a request for a review. On 13 April 2012, Fake sued the Beijing Local Taxation Bureau Second Tax Inspection Bureau at the Chaoyang District People's Court as a matter of administrative litigation; the district court actually heard the tax case on 20 June 2012. On 20 July, it ruled against Fake and Ai Weiwei.

On 3 August 2012 Fake lodged an appeal at Beijing No. 2 Intermediate People's Court, and on 27 September 2012 the court upheld the tax evasion conviction and fine against Fake.[23] Ai's second appeal focused primarily on the fine, alleging that the tax bureau had improperly gathered evidence, erred in its examination of company accounts, and mishandled witnesses. He also argued that the government had not complied with China's basic criminal and administrative procedures. The appellate court, however, again rejected Ai's arguments.

Finally, on 1 October 2012, the government stripped Fake of its business license, stating that it had failed to meet its registration requirements.[24] It is true that the company was unable to comply with these requirements, but it was

---

[22]*Washington Post* (2011) 'In China, putting a price on democracy', *Washington Post*, 7 November; available at: *www.washingtonpost. com/opinions/in-china-putting-a-price-on-democracy/2011/11/07/ gIQA6xUHxM_story.html*

[23]Ai Weiwei's lawyers, note 10 above.

[24]*Huffington Post* (2012) 'Ai Weiwei's design license revoked by Chinese officials', *Huffington Post*, 2 October; available at: *www.huffington-post.com/2012/10/02/ai-weiweis-design-license_n_1931840.html*

because police officers had taken nearly all the studio's materials and its stamp when they first arrested Ai. Ai's lawyer, Liu Xiaoyuan, filed a request for a hearing to resolve the matter.[25]

Procedure

International human rights organizations, such as Human Rights Watch, have publicly questioned the tax case against Ai Weiwei, calling it 'an 11th hour pretext pulled out of a hat by the government to justify Ai's unlawful arrest and secret detention for 81 days'.[26] The belief is that the CPC is creating small bureaucratic and administrative hurdles for Ai to punish him for his activism. If this is true, the Chinese government has blurred the line between criminal and administrative law.[27]

In 1996 the Chinese Criminal Procedure Law was revised to give more rights to suspected criminals and defendants.[28] Though this law was revised again in 2012, the changes did not go into effect until 2013, meaning Ai's arrest and detention fell under the 1996 revisions. According to Andrea J. Worden, the 1996 changes, such as ensuring that suspects had earlier access to a defense attorney, would put China more in line with internationally recognized human rights standards, but the courts, police and procuracy resisted implementation.[29] It took until 2000 before the National People's Congress looked at whether

[25]Tania Branigan (2012) 'Ai Weiwei studio to be closed down by Chinese authorities', *The Guardian*, 1 October; available at: *www. guardian.co.uk/world/2012/oct/01/ai-weiwei-firm-closed-china*
[26]Ibid.
[27]Ibid.
[28]Andrea J. Worden (2009) '"A fair game"? of law and politics and politics in China, and the "sensitive" case of democracy activist Yang JianLie', *Georgetown Journal of International Law*, 40: 447.
[29]Ibid.

the changes had been successfully implemented. The committee investigating the revised Criminal Procedure Law found three 'chronic diseases' still prevalent in the criminal justice system: 'confessions coerced through torture (*xingxun bigong*) . . . unlawful extended detention (*chaoqi jiya*), and . . . obstacles facing criminal defense lawyers in providing representation to their clients (*lüshi bianhu nan*)'.[30] Lawyers went on to list the 'three difficulties' that hindered them from representing their clients: 'meeting criminal suspects . . . obtaining access to case files, and . . . collecting evidence and cross-examining witnesses at trial'.[31]

Criminal defense lawyers have also been restricted by the perjury statute, which they refer to as 'Big Stick 306'.[32] Article 306 of the Criminal Law of the People's Republic of China reads: 'During the course of criminal procedure, any defender, law agent destroys, falsifies evidence, assist parties concerned in destroying, falsifying evidence, threatening, luring witnesses to contravene facts, change their testimony or make false testimony is to be sentenced to [prison].'

Worden describes this statute as giving the procuracy 'unlimited power' to jail lawyers for presenting evidence that contradicts government evidence.[33] Many lawyers and academics have asked for the repeal of Article 306, as it is what many scholars believe stands in the way of lawyers taking on criminal defense cases. The case of Li Zhuang, a

---

[30]Ibid.
[31]Ibid.
[32]*New York Times* (2011) 'Editorial: the Big Stick 306 and China's contempt for the law', *New York Times*, 6 May; available at: *www. nytimes.com/2011/05/06/opinion/06fri3.html?_r=0*
[33]Worden, note 28 above.

Beijing lawyer who was convicted under this statute, was discussed in Chapter 5 of *Inside China's Legal System*.

In addition to regulations and procedures that should give criminal defense attorneys better access to their clients, the Criminal Procedure Law's 1996 revisions contained provisions on notice of and limits to detention. Article 64 states that police are required to notify an individual's family or work unit within 24 hours of the individual's arrest, the reason for detention and where he or she is being held. The article does list some exceptions, one such being where notification would impede the investigation.

There is some debate, however, as to whether written notice of detention must actually be provided. Some scholars believe that local police refrain from providing a written notice to deter defense attorneys from representing a client.[34] Police and prosecutors often insist on a written notice of detention before allowing an attorney to meet with a client, despite no provision in the Criminal Procedure Law requiring such. For Ai, it was clear that the Chinese government failed to provide any notice, written or otherwise, about his detention, his whereabouts or on what charges he was being held. Gradually, information was revealed, but it did not happen within the 24-hour time period required by the Criminal Procedure Law.

Another aspect of Ai's case that raised questions within the international legal community was the length of his detention. According to the Criminal Procedure Law, there are strict time limits on how long the criminal justice process can take. As Cohen commented: 'Although the Criminal Procedure Law in most cases gives the police only three days to hold someone before deciding whether to release him or apply to the prosecutors for an arrest

---

[34]Ibid.

warrant, exceptions allow them up to seven days and in very limited circumstances up to thirty days.'[35]

Many of these limits can be extended and there is often no way to question an extension, but there is a clear, maximum time limit for how long a suspect can be detained. As described above, Ai was held well past the limit during the pre-arrest and investigation stages of his case, even with extensions.

Several months after Ai's arrest, the NPC Standing Committee made public its draft revisions to the Criminal Procedure Law.[36] One of the changes focused on pre-arraignment and pre-conviction deprivations of liberty, mainly through residential surveillance and detention. Residential surveillance, or *jiasnshi juzhu* (监视居住), is not necessarily surveillance at a suspect's residence, and the draft revision permits police to keep someone under surveillance without notifying the individual's family.[37] Detention, or *juliu* (拘 留), and residential surveillance are acceptable in cases of suspected terrorism, bribery or endangerment of state security.

After the initial draft provisions were published, there was an outcry about this deprivation of liberty clause. There were concerns about the lack of notice, so the authorities changed the notice provision to read 'except where notification cannot be processed that there should be notification to the family'.[38] Though the change provided for notification,

---

[35](2011) 'Jerome Cohen on the detention of Ai Weiwei'; available at: *www.usasialaw.org/2011/04/jerome-cohen-on-the-detention-of-ai-weiwei/*

[36]Elizabeth M. Lynch (2012) 'Who will be watched: Margaret K. Lewis on China's new CPL & residential surveillance', *China Law & Policy*, 25 September; available at: *http://chinalawandpolicy.com/2012/09/25/who-will-be-watched-margaret-k-lewis-on-chinas-new-cpl-residential-surveillance/*

[37]Ibid.

[38]Ibid.

there are still critics inside and outside of China who believe authorities will not provide sufficient information, such as the location of the detained suspect.[39] The other major concern was that suspected bribery could qualify someone for this deprivation of liberty, and thus the law was changed to make residential surveillance or detention acceptable only for cases of extremely serious bribery.

While there is still a provision requiring family members to be notified within 24 hours of a suspect being taken into custody, Amendment 36, which has unofficially been dubbed the 'Ai Weiwei clause', precludes notification when the detainee is believed to have been involved in crimes of terrorism, threats to national security or any other serious offense and the notice could hinder the investigation.[40] Some scholars see this amendment as a way to legalize retroactively the detention of Ai Weiwei and hundreds of others who were arrested in the so-called Jasmine Revolution of 2011.[41]

Not only was the 81-day secret detention of Ai Weiwei in violation of the notice requirement of Article 91 of the Criminal Procedure Law, but it also violated Article 37 of the Constitution stating 'unlawful detention or deprivation or restriction of citizen's freedom of the person by other means is prohibited'.[42] Furthermore, the secret detention conflicts with Article 9 of the International Covenant on Civil and Political Rights, which China has signed but not ratified, requiring citizens to be arrested only 'in

[39]Ibid.
[40]Ibid.
[41]Guo Zhiyuan (2011) 'Presentation chance and challenge for Chinese Criminal Procedure Law reform', 19 September; available at: *www. usasialaw.org/wp-content/uploads/2011/09/20110926-Chance-and-Challenge-for-Chinese-Criminal-Procedure-Law-Reform.pdf*
[42]Constitution of the People's Republic of China, Article 37.

accordance with such procedures as are established by law'.[43] Ai's arrest and detention were not proper under China's own criminal procedure, and thus not legal under Article 9 of the ICCPR. In addition, the ICCPR requires anyone 'arrested or detained on a criminal charge' to be 'brought promptly before a judge or other officer . . . [and] entitled to a trial within a reasonable time or to release'.[44] Ai Weiwei's 81-day detention was clearly not in line with this requirement.

On 8 April 2011 the UN Working Group on Enforced or Involuntary Disappearances, after receiving multiple reports of persons being subject to enforced disappearance, including Ai Weiwei and a number of civil rights lawyers, issued a warning to the Chinese government: 'Enforced disappearance is a crime under international law. Even short-term secret detentions can qualify as enforced disappearances, there can never be an excuse to disappear people, especially when those persons are peacefully expressing their dissent with the Government of their country.'[45] The working group stressed: 'China has an obligation to abide by the strictest standards in the field of human rights. It also should fully cooperate with the UN special procedures and in particular with the Working Group.'[46]

The 'Tax' Case

On 18 November 2011 the lawyer for Fake, Pu Zhiqiang, wrote a legal opinion letter in which he attempted to lay out

---

[43]International Covenant on Civil and Political Rights, Article 9.
[44]Ibid.
[45]'China: UN expert body concerned about recent wave of enforced disappearances'; available at: *www.ohchr.org/en/NewsEvents/Pages/ DisplayNews.aspx?NewsID=10928&LangID=E*
[46]Ibid.

the legal points of Ai and Fake's case.[47] He suggested that Fake should not pay the back taxes the government alleged it owed, as it disputed the legal decision of the tax authority.[48] He further recommended that Fake request an administrative hearing to raise the procedural concerns within its tax case.

In his letter, Pu questioned the tactics used by authorities in the investigation of the tax evasion. In addition to the numerous disappearances of those close to Ai and in management positions at Fake (see the timeline above), Pu noted that 12 people had been taken into custody by police, including Ai himself, before officers from the Beijing Local Taxation Bureau and Beijing Public Security Bureau first went to the accounting office that was responsible for Fake.[49] Between 3 April (the date of Ai's arrest) and 6 April (the first official notice that Ai was being investigated for 'economic crimes'), police treated this more as a criminal investigation against Ai than an administrative procedure against Fake Company.

When officers went to Beijing Huxin Financial and Accounting Services Limited, they took 'original vouchers, accounting vouchers, accounting documents, tax vouchers, balance sheets, and profit/loss statements and other accounting documents of Fake Company dating from 2000 until February 2011'.[50] The next day, the Beijing Public Security Bureau Economic Crime Investigation Unit first questioned Fake's accountant, Hu Mingfen. As described above, she was then put in secret detention until 13 June

---

[47]Pu Zhiqiang (2011) 'Initial opinions regarding the "Fake tax case" (translation)', Siweiluozi's Blog, 11 November; available at: *www.siweiluozi.net/2011/11/pu-zhiqiang-initial-opinions-regarding.html* (accessed: 7 August 2013).
[48]Ibid.
[49]Ibid.
[50]Ibid.

2011, and released upon the condition that she no longer contact anyone associated with Fake. It was not until 8 April, however, that agents with the Beijing Local Taxation Bureau first issued Fake Company a tax inspection notice and inquiry notice.[51]

It should also be noted that tax officials failed to provide Fake with a list of the documents seized, as required by Article 25 of the Tax Inspection Work Procedures: whenever officials retrieve account books, accounting vouchers, statements and other relevant information, a notice for retrieving account books and documents should be issued to the target of the inspection and an inventory of retrieved account books and documents completed for the target's signature after being checked and confirmed. Furthermore, the accounting materials that were taken were not returned within the statutory timeframe dictated by Article 25 of the Tax Inspection Work Procedures, which mandate they be returned within three months or 30 days, depending on whether they were more or less than a year old.

Authorities continued to arrest, detain and question people involved with Fake and close to Ai, but on 22 June 2011, the day Ai was released, Xinhua News announced that Fake, which it claimed was controlled by Ai Weiwei, had committed the crime of tax evasion and intentionally destroyed some of its financial documents.[52] In addition, Xinhua reported, 'In light of Ai Weiwei's good attitude in admitting his crimes and the fact that he suffers from chronic illness, combined with his multiple expressions of

---

[51]Article 59 of the Law of the People's Republic of China Concerning the Administration of Tax Collection states that 'When making tax inspection, the officials of the tax authorities shall produce . . . tax inspectional notices', yet officials searched both Ai and Beijing Huxin Ltd prior to the first time notices were presented.
[52]Quoted in Pu, note 49 above.

willingness to pay the taxes owed, Ai Weiwei has been released on guarantee pending further investigation in accordance with the law.'[53]

Five days later, however, the Beijing Local Taxation Bureau made it clear that it was Fake Company and not Ai that was being punished for tax evasion.[54] The bureau issued a notice of administrative penalty for taxation ordering Fake to pay RMB12.21 million as a penalty for tax evasion. Given the government had stated this was not an investigation into Ai Weiwei's actions, but rather the alleged economic crimes committed by Fake Company, it is surprising, Pu notes, that Ai said much of the questioning he endured while in detention was in regard to being suspected of inciting subversion of state power.[55]

Pu also described the relationship between Ai Weiwei and Fake, naming Ai as 'merely a designer'.[56] He was not one of the original founders of the company, he did not donate the capital to start it and nor was he the legal representative or the individual in charge of the finances. Beyond Liu Zhenggang, the individual Pu names as in charge of financial and taxation matters, Fake had been using Beijing Huxin Financial and Accounting Services since 2000 to file taxes and handle other accounting issues.

Pu went into further detail about Ai's role with the company in an attempt to show that he was not a 'person of primary responsibility or other directly responsible person' under Article 31 of the Criminal Law. According to the lawyer, 'The Tax Management Law does not provide for holding anyone other than the taxpayer (which in this case is Fake Company) responsible, so there is clearly no factual

[53]Quoted in ibid.
[54]Ibid.
[55]Ibid.
[56]Ibid.

or legal basis for the Ministry of Foreign Affairs or the Xinhua News Agency to say that "Ai Weiwei is suspected of economic crimes." ' [57]

Pu concluded his first argument — 'The detention of Ai Weiwei et al. appears to have "exceeded authority" and been in violation of the law' by stating that, because this was an administrative matter, the police had no authority to intervene.[58] The only situation that would give the public security organ the legal authority to handle these taxation issues would be if Fake Company refused to comply with an administrative penalty and administrative authorities relinquished their authority to the police.[59] According to Pu, 'there was no legal basis for the public security organ to step in before taxation authorities had begun investigating the "Fake tax case" . . . [By doing so,] they exceeded their authority and violated the law in their handling of the case.'[60]

Pu's legal opinion letter also argued that the 'Beijing taxation authorities' handling of the "Fake tax case" involves multiple procedural violations and unclear factual determinations, and its administrative act lacks legality and should be revoked in accordance with the law'.[61] One of his largest grievances was the seizure of Fake Company's accounts and papers by police. Since public security is not authorized to deal with tax cases, Fake's financial records should never have been stored at the Shibalidian police station in Chaoyang district.

Because the public security organ had the financial records, the taxation bureau's evidence of tax evasion was based on photocopies of the originals. Pu and Fake

---

[57]Ibid.
[58]Ibid.
[59]Criminal Law of the People's Republic of China (1997), Article 201(4).
[60]Pu, note 49 above.
[61]Ibid.

reiterated that they were unable to determine whether the evidence was authentic or accurate from a photocopy, but the taxation bureau did not or could not retrieve the original records from the police. When Fake asked for its records to be 'returned in full', the bureau merely confirmed that the records were with police.

Pu also noted that Fake protested the taxation bureau's refusal to hold a public hearing.[62] According to Pu's letter, the lack of a public hearing is a violation of the law, but the bureau insisted it could only hold a private hearing because the case involved the 'commercial secrets' of a third party.[63] When the No. 2 Audit Office held its private hearing, only appointed counsel and Fake's legal representative were allowed to attend. Not only did the taxation bureau rely on reproductions of the financial records, but it was also unable to show any evidence that a third party had requested that its financial situation be kept secret.[64]

Though the Audit Office ordered Fake to pay over RMB15.22 million in taxes and penalties (approximately RMB8.45 million in missed taxes and RMB6.77 million in fines) on 1 November 2011, Pu 'maintain[s] that the afore-mentioned decisions were based on factual findings that are not clear and serious procedural violations and that the [tax] authorities were clearly cleaning up for the public security organ's "Ai Weiwei case"'.[65]

The letter ends with the procedures Pu took to protect Fake's legal interests and the seemingly arbitrary and extra-legal roadblocks the local administrative organs erected. Pu first recommended Fake only pay a tax guarantee, which would give it the 'right to pursue review and litigation

---

[62]Ibid.
[63]Ibid.
[64]Ibid.
[65]Ibid.

without resulting in outside misunderstanding and misinterpretation'.[66] In an effort to raise the money to pay the guarantee, Ai's mother and brother mortgaged Ai's father's home, yet the government rejected the mortgage, claiming Fake was 'unable in fact to mortgage Ai Qing's [Ai's father] former residence as a taxation guarantee'.[67] So, after over 8.69 million yuan were donated to Ai and Fake, Fake pledged its 'bank book' as a guarantee, but the taxation bureau claimed 'bank regulations prohibit an administrative organ like the local taxation bureau from acting as the lawful recipient of a pledge, so it would be impossible to put up the bank book as a pledge'.[68] The only way Fake was able to get an administrative review was by putting money into a tax guarantee funds account, as requested by the local taxation bureau.

Lu Qing and Ai's wife filed an application for administrative reconsideration on 29 December after Fake was issued a written decision on administrative punishment on 21 November.[69] In it, they argue that the Beijing Local Taxation Bureau erred in using the Notice of the State Administration of Taxation on Some Issues Concerning the Punishments for Acts in Violation of the Regulations on Stamp Tax, thus Fake wanted a review of the decision and the written decision to be cancelled.

Relying on a close reading of the law, Fake's first application for administrative reconsideration dissected the written decision for errors of law. It highlights part 2(1) of the decision, noting that because the company did 'not affix

[66]Ibid.
[67]Ibid.
[68]Ibid.
[69](2011) 'Application for administrative reconsideration, Fake Design Culture Development Ltd, Ai Weiwei, Google+ Account', 29 November; available at: *https://plus.google. com/106372800511710859472/posts*

tax stamps according to relevant provisions' of the Law on the Administration of Tax Collection and the Notice of the State Administration of Taxation on Some Issues Concerning the Punishments for Acts in Violation of the Regulations on Stamp Tax, it was to be fined three times the amount of stamp tax owed.[70] The problem, it argues, is that the ambiguous language of the Tax Law has 'produc[ed] three abnormal situations (i.e. a lower level law contravenes a higher level law, administrative regulations are inconsistent, provisions are inappropriate), because of issuance of the new law and regulation'.[71]

The first situation, a lower-level law contravening a higher-level law, arose because of contradictions between the Law of the People's Republic of China on the Administration of Tax Collection and the Provisional Regulations on Stamp Duty, and between the Detailed Rules for the Implementation of the Law of People's Republic of China to Administer the Levying and Collection of Taxes and the Detailed Rules for Implementation of Provisional Regulations on Stamp Tax. According to Fake, when there is such dissonance, Articles 87 and 88 of the Legislation Law of the People's Republic of China provide that 'laws, administrative regulations, local regulations, autonomous regulations and separate regulations and rules' may be revoked by the NPC Standing Committee:

> *The Standing Committee of the National*
> *People's Congress has the right to revoke adminis-*
> *trative regulations which conflict with the*
> *Constitution and the law, has the right to revoke*
> *local regulations which conflict with the*
> *Constitution, laws and administrative regulations,*

---

[70]Ibid.
[71]Ibid.

and has the right to revoke autonomous regulations and separate regulations which are approved by the standing committee of the people's congress in provinces, autonomous regions and municipalities but conflict with the Constitution and provisions of Article 66(2) in this Law.[72]

In addition, 'the State Council has the right to change or revoke inappropriate regulations in departments and local governments'.[73]

Fake insisted these regulations specify that the NPC Standing Committee can change the Provisional Regulations on Stamp Duty and the State Council can change Detailed Rules for Implementation of Provisional Regulations on Stamp Tax. Neither of these rules and regulations, however, can be changed by the State Administration of Taxation that promulgated Guo Shui Fa [2004] 15.

The second situation, in which rules and regulations are inconsistent, focuses on the Detailed Rules for the Implementation of Law to Administer the Levying and Collection of Taxes and the Provisional Regulations on Stamp Duty. As 'both of them are on the same level as administrative regulations', it is up to the State Council to choose whether the newer or older provision is applicable, as decreed by Article 85(2) of the Legislation Law.[74] This provision would also preclude the State Administration of Taxation that issued Guo Shui Fa [2004] 15 from making the same decision.

Finally, when a rule or regulation is inappropriate, the Legislation Law already provides that the State Council can 'change or revoke inappropriate regulations in departments

---

[72]Ibid.
[73]Ibid.
[74]Ibid.

and local governments'.[75] According to Articles 87 and 88, it is up to the State Council to make these changes, not the State Administration of Taxation.

Moreover, the application noted that the taxation bureau cited and applied the wrong law in the written decision. The decision uses the Tax Administration Law that came into effect on 1 May 2001, but section 1(2) of the decision lists alleged tax evasion from 29 November 2000 to 31 December 2010. This means the taxation bureau's decision and punishment were based on a law that was not in effect from 29 November 2000 to 30 April 2001. In addition, Fake states that Article 84 of the Legislation Law does not make laws retroactive unless the law has 'special provisions for a purpose of better protecting the right and interest with the citizens, legal persons and other organizations', which would not apply in a case of tax evasion.[76] Finally, the same law was cited in section 2(2) on punishment.

The next issue raised by Fake is whether the punishment exceeded the statute of limitations. After first determining that the Law of the People's Republic of China on Administrative Punishments has a statute of limitations of two years, meaning any activity that is not 'discovered' within two years of its commission cannot be punished under this law, Fake noted that the Tax Administration Law has a statute of limitations of five years.[77] Again, relying on a close reading of the law, Fake determined that the this tax case would fall under the two-year statute of limitations, and thus being punished for ten years of tax evasion would be inappropriate.

One of the most critical issues Fake addressed in its application for administrative reconsideration is whether

---

[75]Ibid.
[76]Ibid.
[77]Ibid.

the correct degree of punishment was applied. The law requires that similar actions of similar magnitude should be punished to approximately the same degree. The criteria a court can look at when determining punishment can include 'illegal facts, nature, circumstances and extent of social harm excluding the interference of irrelevant factors; the same kind of administrative violations, that is, illegal facts, nature, circumstances and extent of social harm'.[78]

Fake cited a recent case in which a local taxation bureau fined a real estate company an amount that was roughly half of the taxes it owed. In June 2007 the Beijing Taiyue Real Estate Development Co. Ltd was found to have submitted false tax declarations about its income, meaning it had underpaid its sales tax, education surtax and urban maintenance and construction tax. Fake insisted the case was highly sensitive and also named a 'major tax case' by the State Administration of Taxation, yet the construction company was punished at only half the rate of the unpaid taxes. Fake, in contrast, was punished at a rate between 1.5 times to three times the rate of unpaid taxes, which Fake argued calls into question the appropriateness of the punishment.

Fake admitted there are some situations in which heavier punishment is appropriate, but quoted and dismissed Article 7 of the Several Provisions of Regulating the Free Judging Right of Administrative Penalties in Beijing:

> *'When there is a heavier administrative punishment, the consideration shall be into the following circumstances: (1) acts to cover and destroy illegal evidence or impede law enforcement and etc.; (2) ignore the advice and continue implementation of violations; (3) Offenses resulting in serious*

---

[78]Ibid.

147

consequences; (4) Force [sic], trick, and abet others to commit illegal acts; (5) a major role in joint implementation of the offense; (6) incorrigible, and repeated violations; (7) implementation of the violations in the event of public emergencies; (8) other circumstances which are subject to a heavier punishment.' How can the applicant be subject to the heavier administrative punishment in event of above situations in Article 7 being ruled out?[79]

In its application, Fake's third argument was that the taxation bureau's claim that Fake presented 'illegal facts', facts that contradict evidence presented by the bureau, is based on unclear facts.[80] The taxation bureau announced that much of the accounting information it had on Fake came from the public security department, but the only instance in which this department can be involved in a tax evasion case is when there are fears that a suspect is 'hiding and intentionally destroying accounting vouchers, account books and financial and accounting reports', according to Article 3 of the Criminal Law Amendment. With many of the accounting materials coming from the police, Fake argued the materials were incomplete and unclear.

In addition, Article 3 of Measures for Verification Collection of Enterprise Income Tax says 'If a taxpayer is under one of the following circumstances, tax authorities shall have the power to verify the enterprise income tax: where account books are established, but the accounts are not in order or information on costs, receipt vouchers and expense vouchers are incomplete, making it difficult to check the books.' Fake noted this, saying the taxation bureau should have used 'verification collection' instead of

---

[79]Ibid.
[80]Ibid.

148

'audit collection' in light of the fact that it was 'difficult to check' the studio's accounting books.[81]

Within verification collection, the tax authorities should not have punished Fake because, as the name implies, it is a way first to confirm how much money is owed and then collect it. It is used when 'the taxpayer's account books are not perfect, incomplete information is difficult to audit, or for other reasons is difficult to accurately determine the tax liability. That is, "verification collection" is a collection mode that has to be used by the tax authorities if accurate tax payment information cannot be obtained.'[82] As Fake insisted that it is extremely difficult to determine exactly how much money it owes in unpaid taxes, it would be more appropriate to use verification collection.

Fake cited Articles 4 and 30 of the Administrative Punishments Law and Article, which say that administrative punishments, including any punishments for tax evasion, are determined based on facts. When there are unclear facts about a violation of an administrative order, however, Article 30 specifically forbids punishment. Fake summarized its argument that the taxation bureau had incorrectly punished the studio: 'verification collection' is defined as the appropriate form of tax collection when the facts are not entirely clear, there is incomplete information or the taxation bureau is unable to determine tax liability; and as this is a 'case of unclear illegal facts', it was thus important to use verification collection.[83]

Article 63 of the Tax Administration Law defines tax evasion:

A taxpayer forges, alters, conceals or, without authorization, destroys account books or vouchers

---

[81]Ibid.
[82]Ibid.
[83]Ibid.

for the accounts, or overstates expenses or omits or understates incomes in the account books, or, after being notified by the tax authorities to make tax declaration, refuses to do so or makes false tax declaration, or fails to pay or underpays the amount of tax payable. Where a taxpayer evades tax, the tax authorities shall pursue the payment of the amount of tax he fails to pay or underpays and the surcharge thereon, and he shall also be fined not less than 50 percent but not more than five times the amount of tax he fails to pay or underpays.

Fake alleged the taxation bureau failed to show what actions Fake took that would qualify as tax evasion. Since it also argued that the evidence was unclear, it would be impossible to determine whether Fake violated Article 63, and how much money in taxes went unpaid.[84] Without sufficient evidence, Fake said there was no legal basis for its punishment.

Fake Studio's final argument was that the taxation bureau used the wrong procedures to collect evidence and start an investigation into allegations of tax evasion by the studio. Because of these violations, Fake posited that the punishment against it should be revoked: 'In terms of the respondent in the present case, its law enforcement has committed serious violation of legal procedures and excess of authority or abuse of powers, and thus its penalty decision should of course be revoked according to law.'[85] Relying on the Administrative Reconsideration Law, the Regulation on the Implementation of the Administrative Reconsideration Law and the Rules for Taxation Administrative Reconsideration (No. 21 Decree of

---

[84]Ibid.
[85]Ibid.

the State Administration of Taxation), the taxation bureau's suspected violations preclude it from penalizing Fake.[86]

Fake said the taxation bureau and public security officers violated Article 22(1) of the Tax Audit Regulations when they took Fake's accounting materials from its accounting firm without explaining legal procedure.[87] Article 22 expressly provides for warning before an inspection, 'unless prior notice impedes the inspection'.[88] In addition, Fake argued that no tax inspection notice or tax inspection certificate was issued, as required by Article 59 of the Tax Administration Law and Article 22(2) of the Tax Audit Regulations. Moreover, when police collected the accounting books from Huxin, they never issued a notice for retrieving account book materials or the list of retrieved account book materials, in violation of Article 25 of the Tax Audit Regulations.

One of the final two procedural violations Fake listed in its application was that the taxation bureau failed to return the studio's accounting materials within the three-month and 30-day statutory periods. Article 86 of the Rules for the Implementation of the Law of the People's Republic of China on the Administration of Tax Collection mandates that accounting materials for previous years must be returned within three months of their seizure, and materials for the current year may only be held for 30 days; at the time of Fake's first application for review, the police had not returned any of its account books.[89]

The more serious violation, however, was what Fake termed an illegal penalty hearing.[90] Fake said the taxation

---

[86]Ibid.
[87]Ibid.
[88]Ibid.
[89]Ibid.
[90]Ibid.

bureau failed to provide a public hearing, and by doing so it denied the studio the ability to defend itself properly. Fake cited numerous rules, regulations and laws that mandate a public hearing for tax cases and only allow a private hearing when a third party requests a confidential hearing.[91] Though Fake's hearing was private, the taxation bureau did not provide evidence that a third party requested or needed a confidential hearing to protect its financial interests. In its final appeal for administrative review, Fake noted the lack of original accounting materials, making it impossible to confirm the authenticity of the taxation bureau's evidence:

However, the respondent, only at the beginning, provided the applicant with copies of relevant evidence materials, and such copies did not bear a signature of the applicant for confirmation. Because the respondent did not produce the originals to be checked with the applicant, the applicant is unable to confirm the evidence for authenticity, legitimacy and effectiveness, and moreover, the applicant was substantially deprived of its rights to statement and defence.[92]

Ultimately, however, the first application for administrative reconsideration was unsuccessful. Though Pu Zhiqiang presented strong legal arguments with considerable legal citations, the taxation bureau failed to address many of the legal issues addressed in the first (and subsequent) application. This not only highlights the sharp contrast in training and legal knowledge of lawyers and administrative officials, but also reveals the irrelevance of law within administrative decisions. Fake filed its second application

---

[91]Ibid.
[92]Ibid.

for administrative reconsideration on 18 January 2012, which was similarly rejected.[93]

In its second application, Fake first argued that the taxation bureau committed several procedural errors, including the 'early intervention by the public security department, joint action between the public security and taxation departments, [and] making arrests before auditing', all of which contravened administrative rules and regulations.[94] Fake listed sections of the procedural timeline (see above), documenting the involvement of the police and the arrests that took place prior to the beginning of the tax evasion investigation.

The first set of rules and regulations Fake argued the taxation bureau violated all determined that a taxpayer who evaded taxes would not be criminally punished if he or she paid the back taxes and any late fines issued, and he or she had been administratively punished.[95] Article 201 of the Criminal Law of the People's Republic of China makes an exception and allows for criminal liability if the taxpayer 'has been criminally punished in five years for evading tax payment or has been, twice or more, administratively punished by the tax authorities'. Since this did not apply to the studio, Fake argued that police involvement was premature. In addition, Article 57 of the Notice of the Supreme People's Procuratorate and the Ministry of Public Security on Issuing the Provisions (II) of the Supreme People's Procuratorate and the Ministry of Public Security on the Standards for Filing Criminal Cases under the Jurisdiction of the Public Security Organs for Investigation and Prosecution

---

[93](2011) 'Application for administrative reconsideration, Fake Design Culture Development Ltd, Ai Weiwei, Google+ Account', 18 January; available at: *https://plus.google.com/106372800511710859472/posts*
[94]Ibid.
[95]Ibid.

lists an inclusive number of tax evasion scenarios that could lead to criminal prosecution, but none of them describes Fake's alleged actions.[96] The application argued that any evidence gained from this police investigation would be considered 'illegitimate' and should force the taxation bureau to withdraw its punishment.[97]

In analyzing Article 11 of the Provisions on the Transfer of Suspectable Criminal Cases by Administrative Organs for Law Enforcement, Fake concluded that:

> *if the public security organs have already been involved in the case, then the tax authorities shall withdraw from it; if the tax authorities are handling the case, it implies that the case has not been transferred to the public security department or the conditions for transfer are not met, then the public security department should not be involved in the case. It is not only a procedural mistake for the respondent and the public security organs to join forces in handling a case, it is also a serious confusion of administrative and judicial boundaries.*[98]

Fake reiterated many of the procedural violations it listed in the first application for administrative reconsideration, including that the accounting materials were improperly obtained and not returned within the statutory period, and there was insufficient notice, all of which prevented Fake from adequately defending against charges of tax evasion.

The second application also contested the legal basis used in the written decision for settlement, saying the Beijing Taxation Bureau incorrectly cited Article 5 of the Notification of Beijing Local Taxation Bureau on Definition

---

[96]Ibid.
[97]Ibid.
[98]Ibid.

of Several Policy Business Issues on Enterprise Income Tax in determining that Fake owed over RMB4.7 million in enterprise income tax.[99] The article states that:

> *If in a tax inspection, a company has been found to have hidden income and repayment of the enterprise income tax is required, the method for calculation of the enterprise income tax to be repaid is: the hidden income, minus the turnover tax to be repaid and identifiable undeducted costs and expenses matching this part of income, should be used as the income for repayment of tax, and is multiplied by the enterprise income tax rate of the inspection year to figure out the amount of enterprise income tax to be repaid.*

The problem, said Fake, is that the Beijing Local Taxation Bureau attempted to define 'tax inspection' in this case without the proper authority.[100]

Fake noted that Article 93 of the Tax Administration Law grants the State Council the power to interpret the phrase 'tax inspection'. Fake admitted that interpretation power may also lie with the State Administration of Taxation according to Article 85 of the Rules for the Implementation of the Law of the People's Republic of China on the Administration of Tax Collection, but Fake argued that the Beijing Local Taxation Bureau overstepped its authority by doing so.

Moreover, Fake argued that the power to interpret the 'method for calculating enterprise income tax' lies with either the Ministry of Finance or the State Administration of Taxation, according to Articles 19 and 59 of the Provisional

[99]Ibid.
[100]Ibid.

Regulations of the People's Republic of China on Enterprise Income Tax. Again, Fake alleged that the taxation bureau's interpretation of the phrase went beyond its authority.

The studio's final complaint about the legal basis of the settlement decision is that the Jing Di Shui Qi [2002] No. 526 Document was the incorrect method of determining how much Fake owed in taxes. Not only does Fake argue that the document is in conflict with a higher-level law, but it also notes that 'According to the Legislation Law of the People's Republic of China, Jing Di Shui Qi [2002] No. 526 Document is neither a law, a statute, nor a rule but a regulation of a working department of the local people's government.'[101] What this means is that, according to paragraph 1, Article 7 of the Administrative Reconsideration Law, has the right to an administrative reconsideration in light of the confusing regulation.

As in its first application, the studio claimed the taxation bureau erred in using the 'audit collection' method because there was insufficient information, and thus the 'verification collection' method was more appropriate. Citing the bureau's reliance on incomplete accounting records, Fake said it should have used verification collection.[102] It also noted that the taxation bureau failed to use the audit collection method correctly by not verifying the studio's 'objective costs, expenses, losses and other reasonable expenditures'.[103] Though the bureau says it discovered more than RMB15.8 million in design fees and engineering income that Fake did not claim between 29 November 2000 and 31 December 2010, Fake said 'it is obvious that the respondent has not checked the costs and expenses of the items used

---

[101]Ibid.
[102]Ibid.
[103]Ibid.

156

to identify income'.[104] Instead, Fake claimed the taxation bureau used the audit collection method to come up with a 'ridiculous and peremptory' estimated total enterprise income tax and actual tax paid.

Another contention Fake raised is that the taxation bureau ascribed 'decoration income' to the studio, despite the fact that the studio does not have the construction enterprise qualification certificate necessary to earn decoration income.[105] Because it cannot obtain such income, the money the taxation bureau is calling decoration income cannot be taxed. If the studio were to claim the income, it would need to do so as 'illegal income', for which there is little clarification on how it would be taxed.[106] Though Fake cited Articles 4 and 37 of the Tax Administration Law for guidance, it admits that neither section correctly fits Fake's situation of illegal income. Even if there was a provision that determined how illegal income was to be taxed, Fake noted that Article 65 of the Construction Law vests authority to punish 'an organization which is hired for projects without a certificate of qualification' with the State Council, not with the taxation bureau.

As with the first application for administration review, Pu Zhiqiang and Fake were unsuccessful with the second application. The second and final appeal was rejected on 27 September 2012.

Perhaps inspired by the Al Capone tax evasion case in the United States in 1932,[107] and how the United States handled an infamous gangster and shrewd businessman, in dealing with Ai Weiwei Chinese authorities 'decided to

---

[104]Ibid.
[105]Ibid.
[106]Ibid.
[107]*Capone v. United States*, 56F.2d. 927 (1932).

crush him by resorting to economic measures whose illegality would presumably be less apparent both to its own citizens and to the outside world'.[108]

The Ai Weiwei case exemplifies the difficulties of analyzing Chinese law in Western terms, such as the clear distinction between different categories of law (criminal, administrative, etc.); jurisdiction; and administrative, civil and criminal procedures. The entire contemporary legal system started after the Cultural Revolution, less than four decades ago. China's legal system is still nascent, full of ambiguity, contradictions and inconsistencies. Ai's case started as a criminal case — on suspicion of Article 105 of the Criminal Law's 'inciting to subvert the state power' — but ended up in an administrative law proceeding. During the entire process, particularly after the legal process started, the authorities tried, most of the time awkwardly, to use the law to punish an unapologetic 'maverick',[109] but because of their own incompetence and unfamiliarity with the law, they struggled to cover procedural errors. Ai Weiwei and his lawyers argued his case is full of abuses and utterly lacked fairness: 'at both the administrative and the judicial levels the proceedings against him have been a farce'.[110]

---

[108]Cohen, note 11 above.
[109]See *Global Times* (2011) 'The law will not bend for a maverick', *Global Times*, 6 April; original Chinese version available at: *http://opinion.huanqiu.com/roll/2011-04/1609672.html* ; English translation available at: *http://notesonchina.tumblr.com/post/4387913705/translation-of-the-op-ed-on-ai-wei-wei-in-chinese*
[110]Cohen, note 11 above.

Human Rights in Transnational Business*

I. General Description:

Dr. Julia Ruth-Maria Wetzel's book *Human Rights in Transnational Business: Translating Human Rights Obligations into Effective and Enforceable Business Compliance Procedures after Kiobel v. Royal Dutch Petroleum* consists of nine chapters: Chapter 1 lays out the purpose, structure, and outlook of the thesis; Chapter 2 discusses the situation of the Ogoni people in Nigeria and their relationship with Shell Oil; Chapter 3 examines the history of the Alien Tort Statute and important precedents—*Kiobel* and earlier cases; Chapter 4 discusses the issue of extending human rights obligations to corporate entities; Chapter 5 explores specific multinational frameworks targeting corporate conduct and compliance programs related to human rights; Chapter 6 analyzes the UN Business and Human Rights Agenda, the UN Global Compact, and the UN Guiding Principles; Chapter 7 argues "translating human rights into an enforceable business compliance strategy;" Chapter 8

*This article reviews *Human Rights in Transnational Business: Translating Human Rights Obligations into Effective and Enforceable Business Compliance Procedures after Kiobel v. Royal Dutch Petroleum*, by Julia Ruth-Maria Wetzel, Springer 2015.

offers an outlook of the subject matter; and finally, Chapter 9 summarizes and concludes the investigation.

The structure of the book conforms to principles and requirements of a Ph.D. book in the area of law.

The author has studied and used an appropriate number of bibliographic sources and legal authorities. It is evident that the author has carefully studied and analyzed relevant authorities and resources, with deep understanding of the subject matter and arguments.

II. Importance of the Topic:

The path of international law over the last century has been one of increasing breadth and depth of coverage. Proposing international norms of corporate responsibility for violations of human rights continues the trajectory that the law has taken, but it also represents new challenges for the enterprise. It challenges the state's exclusive prerogative ("sovereignty") to regulate business enterprises by making them a subject of international scrutiny; it makes them entities that have duties to respect human rights.

Globalization has changed the world dramatically. It presents new and complex challenges for the protection of human rights. Economic players, especially multinational companies operating across national borders, have gained unprecedented power and influence across the world. States have a responsibility to protect human rights. However, many are failing to do this, especially when it comes to company operations, whether due to lack of capacity, dependence on the company as an investor, or outright corruption. Companies have lobbied governments to create international investment, trade and tax laws that protect corporate interests. But the same companies

160

frequently argue against any development in international law and standards to protect human rights in the context of business operations.

The legal marketplace also continues to be globalized, and legal professionals must struggle to deal with the challenges presented by this globalization. The development of the law is still behind the reality of globalization, creating even more complications and uncertainties. Corporate human rights responsibility is undoubtedly one of the most daunting challenges legal professionals and jurists face today. As Ms. Wetzel pointed out: *Kiobel* highlights an important emerging issue: if corporations can do just as much harm as states, how does one hold a legal entity responsible if said entity currently has no binding human rights obligations under international law?

The topic of human rights in transnational business is also of enormous importance in jurisprudence, political economics, and sociology.

Ms. Wetzel's book is extremely well researched, thoroughly investigated, and effectively presented. This book is a significant contribution to the area of corporate human rights obligations, as it explores a new path to ensure that by demonstrating human rights compliance is beneficial for multinational corporations and for society, international trade and investment become more sustainable and respectful of human rights.

III. Academic Merits:

This 276-page book has clearly demonstrated Ms. Wetzel's solid academic training, superb scholastic competency, and effective legal argument skills.

The goal of Ms. Wetzel's research is to determine how human rights law can be applied to corporate entities.

She argues that because "insufficient international legal mechanisms exist to bring corporations to justice for their misconduct abroad, an international approach to corporate human rights compliance is needed, to prevent future corporate human rights abuses." As an attorney working at a multinational company dealing with cross-border transactions, I agree with Ms. Wetzel's argument whole-heartedly.

The starting point of her research is *Kiobel v. Royal Dutch Petroleum* and the Alien Tort Statute (ATS). Ms. Wetzel has done a terrific job in analyzing the flaws of the *Kiobel* decision by showing the inconsistencies with previous legal decisions and the court's jurisprudence.

Notwithstanding *Kiobel,* Ms. Wetzel argues, "human rights are, in fact, applicable to corporate entities, because international human rights law is rooted in the liberal commitment to the equal moral worth of each individual, because human rights embody the minimum standards of treatment", and "the origin, aim and purpose of human rights clearly includes corporations in their realm of action."

In the next chapters, Ms. Wetzel analyzes existing international instruments targeting corporate human rights conduct and shows that these "existing international initiatives are insufficient in addressing the underlying problem of corporate human rights accountability because they try to impose a top to bottom approach onto corporations." Therefore, based on the results of her "investigation on the benefits and shortcomings of the existing initiatives," Ms. Wetzel develops a human rights strategy for businesses: "taking into consideration the lessons learnt from *Kiobel* and the fears of corporations with regard to human rights duties," Ms. Wetzel's strategy "will seek to translate human rights obligations for business entities, showing that human rights can be implemented by corporations in a sustainable and business-friendly manner, rather than having states intervene in business activity."

Ms. Wetzel convincingly argues that the strategy "will not only curb the current problem of human rights violations, but will also demonstrate that an effective human rights strategy will increase profit and shareholder value" because the strategy "respects the aim of businesses as profit generators while also paying due respect to the modern understanding of corporations as members of society."

I am hoping that, by publication, Ms. Wetzel's research will reach larger audience, particularly multinational corporations. Adopting Ms. Wetzel's strategy, corporations can tackle their adverse human rights impacts, reduce litigation cost and improve consumer good will.

IV. Questions for further thinking

In Chapter 4, the author pointed out that "corporations are organs of society"; furthermore, some corporations are as powerful as states. An immediate example is Apple. Apple's economic output in 2014 was worth about $87 billion. Just below Apple were Oman at $81 billion, Azerbaijan at $78 billion, and Belarus at $77 billion.

The author insightfully pointed out that "both simple and profound, namely that there is in fact not that much difference between states and transnational corporations" in terms of human rights obligation discussion. I take we can safely presume that in certain aspects transnational corporations function as states.

On the other hand, in *Citizen United v. FEC* 558 U.S. 310 (2010), the US Supreme Court ruled that corporations are persons therefore are entitled to certain constitutional protections.

I am very interested in hearing the author's comments on the concept of "corporate personhood", the relevancy of the concept to the author's arguments, and, if relevant, would the concept of "corporate personhood" strengthen or weaken the author's argument for holding corporations liable for human rights violations and human rights non-compliance?

Why are traditional tort liability laws in different jurisdictions not sufficient for holding transnational corporations liable for damages caused by human rights violations? At the end of Chapter 3, the author listed "foreign individuals who were not granted relief in their home states due to inefficient judicial systems, corruption, or lack of funds." Were these the main obstacles in utilizing traditional tort liability laws? In addition, also at the end of Chapter 3, the author mentioned "Although American citizens may still use the Torture Victims Protection Act (TVPA), this tool seems ill fit to address corporate human rights problems." Could the author please elaborate?

Also note, in a 2007 case against Yahoo! brought by a Chinese and the World Organization for Human Rights USA in a federal court in San Francisco, Yahoo! was sued under both the Alien Torts Statute (28 U.S.C. § 1350) and Torture Victim Protection Act of 1991 (TVPA), 106 Stat. 73 (1992). After unsuccessfully seeking to have the suit dismissed, Yahoo! settled out of court for an undisclosed sum. Could the author please comment on the TVPA and the level of relevancy and sufficiency to address the human rights violations by transnational corporations?

Most corporate compliance program are designed and implemented to laws and regulations in effect, e.g., Export Control, FCPA. They are more reactive than proactive. If there is no urgent legal and regulatory risk, corporations are under no legal obligation to initiate a human rights compliance program. In Chapter 7, the author has listed a number of factors corporations should consider: reputation,

164

brand image, etc. The author has also selected a few examples, such as Yahoo!, Coca- Cola, The Body Shop, and Shell, to illustrate the best practices. Are these best practices built because of specific human rights problems they faced in their business operations, or were they built proactively? If they were reactive and remedial in nature, would that weaken our argument to persuade more corporations to voluntarily translate human rights in their transnational business?

In 2012, Bloomberg News published a series of investigative reports revealing the hidden fortune of Chinese leaders. Chinese authorities retaliated by terminating government purchase of Bloomberg's financial terminals, denying visas to Bloomberg reporters, and blocking access to the companie's website and online services from mainland China, causing considerable financial loss to Bloomberg. In 2013, Bloomberg self-censored another investigative story linking China's wealthiest men to the country's top leaders. (This story was finally published by the *New York Times* earlier this year after the author was forced to leave Bloomberg). Mathew Winkler, Bloomberg's editor-in-chief, said the decision was strategic and compared it to "the self-censorship by foreign news bureaus inside Nazi-era Germany," in order to continue to operate in and report from China.

Recently, Reuters faced a similar situation. Also consider Google, who refused to cooperate with Chinese secret police and withdrew completely from mainland China.

It appears that, for many multi-national companies who have diverse portfolios, options are limited. If operating under an authoritarian regime, a company must either accept the argument that "if the author comes to my country, he must follow my law", or withdraw completely.

At the end of the day, public companies are responsible for their shareholders, not the public. Weighing pros and cons, they are likely to ultimately choose to cooperate with authoritarian regimes for access to market and business profit, rather than hold onto human rights values.

I am interested in hearing the author's comments on the situation Bloomberg and Reuters are facing: when there is an immediate conflict between business branches in an authoritarian market—in this case, China. Does the author publish the news article and suffer financial loss? Or spike the article and continue to sell other services in the authoritarian country? What would the author do if she were a stakeholder at Bloomberg or Reuters?

Thoughts on Business

Good products do not come from a formula

Lu You (陆游, 1125–1210), one of the greatest poets in Chinese history, wrote to his son: "If you want to write a good poem, spend your efforts outside of simply writing the poem." By the same token, if we want to develop a good product, we should make efforts outside of developing the product. That is, we should learn and understand more about the context of the product: the content, the technology, and the target audience. A product, like a good poem, does not come from simply following a formula.

Presumptions are always rebuttable

We tend to understand our customers, our competitors, and ourselves from within the framework of cognition, which is inherently prejudiced. Prejudice may lead to presumptions.

A few examples of prejudicial and stereotypical presumptions: what we do well in the U.S. can be replicated in other countries; customers will switch to our products once launched, even if they are used to other less prestigious products offered by competitors; all lawyers have similar workflows, and all Chinese are good at math.

But any presumption is rebuttable, and innovation comes from creative rebuttal to presumptions.

Don't get lost in translation

We should be more willing to communicate, collaborate, and compromise, because we know how easily language can be manipulated, and how easily information and ideas can get lost in translation, leading to misunderstandings.

Hunger for Knowledge

Hundreds of thousands of Chinese students and young professionals now regularly watch Netease Open Course Channel, where American and British universities offer hundreds of free courses under the Open Course Ware (OCW) initiative. Available courses range from science, technology, and philosophy to art, cultural studies, and even law. Courses offered include Single Variable Calculus (MIT), European Civilization (Yale), Justice (Harvard), and Anthropology (Cambridge).

An army of volunteer translators translates courses into Chinese. Keeping the original English soundtrack, as the audience prefers, Netease's technology team subtitles the videos either in Chinese or bilingually.

A popular vote by the audience determines which courses are translated first. (For example, 82,595 viewers voted to request that Programming Methodology (Stanford) and 105,252 voted that Critical Reasoning for Beginners (Oxford) be translated as soon as possible!)

In Chinese culture, education is of the utmost importance. In their hunger for education, many Chinese will give up even food in order to be able to afford the books and knowledge they crave. The popularity of the Netease Open Course Channel shows just how eager Chinese young people are for Western knowledge, in particular.

Can you think of ways that Thomson Reuters could profitably feed this Chinese hunger for western knowledge?

Legal Market Place Predictions for 2013

The legal marketplace will continue to be globalized, and the legal professionals will have to struggle to deal with the challenges presented by this globalization. It is predicted that the development of the law will lag behind the reality of globalization in the coming year.

International firms will continue to handle multi-national mergers and complex, multi-jurisdictional business transactions; domestic firms will aspire to go international by wading into the water of cross-border transactions, or by dealing with issues related to the acquisition of domestic businesses by foreign investors; and some legal services will continue to be transferred offshore.

The rapid development of technology and the integration of global economic systems will generate more and more legal issues: miscommunication; choice of law; data security and cyber espionage; export control; Foreign Corrupt Practices Act (FCPA); and unprecedented potential human rights violations—Alien Tort Claims Act (ATCA). All these will challenge existing processes and protocols for managing international transactions and enterprises, and will change the way in which we perceive and calculate the benefits of globalization. Furthermore, fundamental tensions among different ideological and political systems will continue to play a larger-than-anticipated role in economic affairs, creating even more complications and uncertainties *intra legem,* legally speaking.

On Global Business*

Question: What does "global business" mean?

Chang Wang: You probably have heard the cliché: "Local is global, global is local." Indeed, understanding the meaning of this cliché would greatly benefit a local company's global aspirations and a multinational company's cross-border operations.

Why has Starbucks succeeded in China, while others haven't? 15 years ago, when Starbucks wanted to open coffee shops in China, few people thought the coffee business would work there, because the Chinese would not easily give up their tea-drinking culture in exchange for a bitter, overpriced drink. But, while 15 years ago, "coffee" meant Nescafe instant coffee to the Chinese, today, in China, "coffee" means Starbucks.

Starbucks now expects China to become its second-largest market by 2014. The company has more than 600 stores in the country and aims to reach 1,500 stores by 2015. This growth strategy involves opening roughly one store per day, *every* day, for three years!

So, how did Starbucks re-educate the world's oldest and largest tea-drinking culture? First of all, they offered the right product; second, they formulated the right message; and third, they used the right method to deliver their message.

Starbucks, fortunately for them, understood that what it had to offer the Chinese was different than what it offers American customers.

---

*This is part of the transcript of a panel discussion on global business strategy and operations at the Carlson School of Management, at the University of Minnesota-Twin Cities. It took place on January 13th, 2015.

In China, the Starbucks message is that Starbucks is the "authentic representative of American leisure culture." In other words, what the Chinese are buying from Starbucks is not simply coffee, but also a piece of American culture. So the price that the Chinese pay for Starbucks coffee includes the price of a sip of exoticism. Which explains why Chinese are paying 24RMB (USD$3.6) for a tall Americano.

Then there's the way that Starbucks delivers its message in China: Starbucks promotes dine-in service by offering comfortable environments and becoming a de facto meeting place for executives and gathering of friends. Inspired by the traditional Chinese tea house, a Starbucks in China spices up the atmosphere with its exotic touch of foreignness.

So what can Thomson Reuters do as we attempt to enter the Chinese market? What product should we sell? And how should we position ourselves? Should we offer local information which, like Chinese tea, is already easily accessible for local professionals? Or, should we provide foreign legal and professional information not now available in this market? Answer: we should offer Westlaw, the premier American legal research service— our Starbucks!

Question: What are the business challenges for a western business in China?

Chang Wang: First, there are the generic challenges we face in many countries, such as developing the right product and delivering the right message, as illustrated earlier in the Starbucks case. Then there are the more China-specific challenges:

Challenge #1: Legal and regulatory compliance, because Chinese society is governed largely by hidden rules, not by the laws on the book. If you do not know and follow the hidden rules, you might get your business and/or yourself in trouble, even if what you do is completely legal.

Challenge #2: Security. Big Brother is watching you and would like to know not only your every move, but what's on your mind and on your hard drive.

Challenge #3: Corruption. Corruption in China is systematic and institutionalized, and there are many gray areas which can potentially trap you. The Foreign Corrupt Practice Act of the United States has very strict rules what we can do and cannot do when doing business outside the United States. We must constantly remind ourselves of these rules when doing business in China.

The last, and probably the most imposing challenge, is the challenge of translation and cultural misunderstanding.

If you speak a second language, you understand the difficulty of translating a concept from one language to another.

In addition, the important role that culture plays in business has been under-appreciated, and the cost of this under-appreciation has been underestimated.

But there are many less obvious cultural nuances which can be vital to the success or failure of a Western business operation in China. It's particularly important, for example, for Thomson Reuters to understand that, in Chinese culture, knowledge is to be paid for, but information is to be shared. So how should we identify and position ourselves in China? Shall we say to the Chinese we are offering information, or shall we say we are offering knowledge?

Question: For several years, your role with Thomson Reuters had you traveling between China and the United States. Tell us a little about being a "dual-country" employee.

Chang Wang: To my American colleagues, I am a Chinese, wholly Chinese, and nothing but Chinese. But, to my Chinese colleagues, I am close to being a "banana": yellow on the outside, but all white inside.

But living as an insider in two cultures gives me vantage points from which to compare. As a result, I take nothing for granted. I am less susceptible to prejudice, because I know how it feels to be discriminated against; I am less willing to accept presumptions, especially when making business decisions, because I know that any presumption is rebuttable when you change your point of view ever so slightly. And, finally, I am more willing to communicate, collaborate, and compromise, because I know how easily language can be manipulated, and how easily information and ideas can get lost in translation, leading to misunderstandings.

In term of my roles, first of all, I assist my supervisor, Rick King, on research, collaborative projects, and communications. I am most fortunate to work on Rick's team. He is a business executive with profound intelligence, superb management skills, and tremendous integrity. In short, he is a wise man with a big heart. He is also a senior leader in the national science and technology communities, bringing prominence to the company. Under his leadership, Thomson Reuters has built strong partnerships with the science and technology communities, universities, and government agencies. We enjoy many benefits that these collaborative relationships have brought to us. I am honored to participate in joint initiatives with the law school, business school, and the international offices at the University of Minnesota, the Minnesota State government, the Supreme Court of Minnesota, the Science Museum, and Minnesota Public Radio.

Second, I serve as a residential expert on legal, regulatory, language, and international project management for the Technology and content teams. I frequently receive requests from different Thomson Reuters organizations to participate in due diligence investigation, product development, content review, cross-border project collaboration and communication, foreign legal research, and language trainings. I honor every request I receive and appreciate the opportunity to work with different teams on interesting and challenging projects. I author internal memos, research papers, and internal blog posts on a wide range of topics from export controls, FCPA compliance, data security, to conducting searches in Chinese, multiple language user interface for our international products, translation, even business norms and travel advisories. For example, I co-authored with Professor David Larson, of Hamline Law School, a recently published article entitled "Preparing to Negotiate in a Globally Diverse Environment: An Examination of Chinese and Jewish Perspectives on Truths and Lies," which I am happy to share with my Thomson Reuters colleagues in China when they are entering into negotiation with Chinese companies. If you read Chinese, I would like to recommend my other publication: *Comparative Cultural Studies*, which reveals frequent misunderstandings that occur during the process of finding commonalities in different cultures.

And thirdly, I serve as liaison between Thomson Reuters and the legal and academic communities, and as a "Good-Will Ambassador" for Westlaw. I am an elected member of the American Law Institute (ALI), the second mainland Chinese ever elected to this institution. I also serve on the Steering Groups of Human Rights Law, China Law, Immigration Law, Legal Education and Specialist Certification Committees at the American Bar Association

(ABA). I am adjunct professor of law at six law schools: two in the US, two in Switzerland, and two in China, where I occasionally teach legal-research courses: researching American law, using Westlaw®; and research in Chinese law using Westlaw China® As you may know, both Westlaw and Westlaw China are premier legal tools developed by Thomson Reuters. My bilingual textbook on legal research will be published by China University of Political Science and Law Press later this year. On the cover page I use the image of the very first print of *The Syllabi*, published by John B. West, on October 21, 1876. These professional and academic accomplishments give me credentials when I promote Westlaw and Thomson Reuters in the legal and academic communities, either by authoring law review articles or by speaking at academic conferences on behalf of Thomson Reuters.

A Behind the Scenes Tour of
Customs and Border Protection*

U.S. Customs and
Border Protection

The Immigration Law Section of Minnesota State Bar Association (MSBA) recently organized a behind-the-scenes tour of Customs and Border Protection (CBP) at the MSP International Airport. As a member of Immigration Law Council of MSBA, and serving as USCIS Liaison for American Bar Association (ABA), I attended the tour with a group of immigration lawyers. We greatly appreciated the opportunity to take an inside look at our borders.

We were greeted by three exceptionally professional and seasoned CBP officers. They guided us through the entire Customs and Border process: initial inspection, secondary inspection, expedited removal issues, I-94 issues, Global Entry Program, Automated Passport Control (APC), upcoming Mobile Passport Control (MPC), FOIA requests and responses, etc.

Three years ago, when I learned from Mr. Rick King, member of the Metropolitan Airports Commission, that

---

*This report covers a 2015 behind-the-scenes tour of Customs and Border Protection (CBP) at the Minneapolis-St. Paul International Airport.

the Global Entry Program had come to MSP, I immediately registered and have enjoyed the benefits ever since. In my view, it is one of the best programs for frequent international travelers. In addition, the Global Entry card is a valid ID issued by a federal agency. As my Minnesota Driver's License is now "non-compliant" with the Department of Homeland Security Standard, I can still use the Global Entry card to travel domestically without a passport.

A dozen Automated Passport Control (APC) Kiosks were installed at MSP. There are six different languages available on the Kiosk: English, French, German, Spanish, Italian, and (surprise!) Gaelic. The officers explained the APC contract started in Ireland. They agreed with us that, considering a large number of Asian visitors and immigrants going through MSP every year, APC interfaces in Chinese or Japanese would be helpful. We were also excited to learn that Mobile Passport Control (MPC) might be at MSP soon, which will allow travelers to "check in" using the MPC app. The MPC app enables a traveler or family to pre-position their biographic information prior to speaking with a CBP officer. The CBP officer is then able to focus on identity verification, admissibility and questioning to determine purpose and intent of travel. The CBP officer spends on average up to three minutes for each traveler, and they are highly skillful in identifying potential threats. The CBP Federal Law Enforcement Training Center is recognized as having one of the most challenging curricula in federal law enforcement. All newly hired CBP Officers learn their basic law enforcement skills by attending the CBP Academy. Each CBP Officer trainee must complete a 19-week resident course of instruction in integrated law, physical training, firearms instruction and driving.

We also toured the newly renovated Passport Control Secondary Room, where travelers are sent for additional screening. Individual interview rooms ensure privacy; onsite bathroom are available as a convenience; a holding cell is available for partial custody; and everything is recorded. Contrary to the common misconception, lawyers are not allowed at port of entry. The officers explained to us that if our clients need professional legal help, they have to wait until the border procedure is completed. If for some reason, the clients/travelers feel their rights are being violated, they can file a complaint, and every single compliant will be dealt with by CBP. In fact, there are very few complaints.

Finally, we were introduced to the Passenger Baggage and Agriculture Inspections area, where baggage is inspected to ensure no contraband, prohibited agricultural items, and items violating Intellectual Property rights would enter the United States. At this point, quite a few international students have to say goodbye to their favorite homemade meat loaf, and to pirated DVDs they had bought on the street. We were also amused to learn that Rolex has a "zero-tolerance" policy toward fake Rolex watches and has registered their trademark with CBP for them to enforce and to confiscate every single fake Rolex.

On a typical day in 2014, Customs and Boarder
Protection (CBP):

- Processed 1,026,234 passengers and pedestrians, including: 293,285 incoming international air passengers and crew; 54,008 passengers and crew on arriving ship/boat; and 678,941 incoming land travelers.

- Conducted 1,333 apprehensions between U.S. ports of entry; arrested 21 wanted criminals and refused admission to 241 inadmissible persons at U.S. ports of entry.

- Discovered 425 pests at U.S. ports of entry and 4,447 materials for quarantine: plant, meat, animal byproduct, and soil.

- Seized: 10,327 pounds of drugs; $650,117 in undeclared or illicit currency; and $3.4 million dollars' worth of products with Intellectual Property Rights violations.

- Identified 548 individuals with suspected national security concerns.

- Intercepted 76 fraudulent documents.

After the tour, the officers kindly answered many
questions from the attorneys. I had only one question:
"How long would you quarantine my dog if I bring it
back from China?"

"As long as you have all the necessary paperwork in
order and the dog is healthy, we normally don't quarantine
dogs. I cannot remember the last time we quarantined a dog."

It was an informative and pleasant experience gaining
insights from behind the scenes, though we are well aware
different people might have completely difference experiences at the port of entry: the gateway of the land of the
free and the home of the brave.

The American Law Institute
89th Annual Meeting*

The American Law Institute is the leading independent organization in the United States producing scholarly work to clarify, modernize, and otherwise improve the law. The Institute drafts, discusses, revises, and publishes Restatements of the Law, model statutes, and principles of law that are enormously influential in the courts and legislatures, as well as in legal scholarship and education. ALI has long been influential internationally and, in recent years, more of its work has become global in scope.

There are 2714 elected members of the ALI; the total membership is 4300, including life, honorary, and ex-officio members.

The 89th Annual Meeting reviewed the following ALI Projects:

- Legal and Economic Principles of World Trade Law

- Model Penal Code: Sentencing

- Principles of Election Law: Dispute Resolution

---

*Chang Wang was elected a member of American Law Institute on March 21, 2012, being the second Chinese national ever elected to the Institute. This report covers the 89th Annual Meeting of the American Law Institute, which took place from May 21st-23rd, 2012 in Washington DC.

- Principles of the Law of Liability Insurance
- Restatement of the Law Third, Employment Law
- Restatement of the Law Third, The U.S. Law of International Commercial Arbitration
- Restatement of the Law Third, Torts: Liability for Economic Harm
- Transnational Insolvency: Principles of Cooperation

"Thomson Reuters Caucus"

Vance Opperman, board member of Thomson Reuters and a sustaining member of the ALI; Tom Leighton, Vice President, Legal Editorial Operations — Content Acquisition,

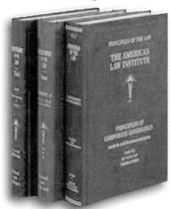

and Jon Olson, Senior Principal Attorney Editor who works on ALI publications at Thomson Reuters, attended the Annual Meeting. As a newly elected member of the ALI, I also attended the meeting for the first time.

Thomson Reuters publishes all the *Restatements of the Law, Principles of the Law, Universal Commercial Code,* and other major ALI publications. Since 1931 Thomson Reuters and the ALI have continuously published and distributed these products through their American Law Institute Publishers partnership.

Restatements (2d, and 3d) and Principles of the Law, published by Thomson Reuters.

Opening Session

The meeting on the 21ˢᵗ began with a report by ALI President Roberta Cooper Ramo and remarks in memory of former Council members the late Nicholas Katzenbach (former attorney general) and the late Louis H. Pollak (US District Court Judge, E. District of Pennsylvania). President Ramo also mentioned the creation of the European Law Institute (ELI) and the potential for collaboration between the ALI and the ELI.

ABA President William. T. (Bill) Robinson III addressed the membership, speaking about the impact of the underfunding of court systems.

The conference was well attended by ALI members from all over the country, as well as some distinguished foreign guests, among them Robert French, the Chief Justice of Australia and a member of the ALI.

New Member Luncheon

On the opening day, the Institute hosted a luncheon for its newest 99 members elected after May 2011. Every new member was seated at a small table with other new members and seasoned members, who were invited to share their knowledge of the Institute and discuss the benefits they derive from participation. Two law professors from Duke University Law School, one senior legal aid attorney, and I were fortunate to sit with President Roberta Cooper Ramo and The Honorable Paul L. Friedman, U.S. District Court for the District of Columbia.

As the President of the American Bar Association from 1995 to 1996, Roberta Ramo was the first woman in history to lead the largest nationwide organization of attorneys. Roberta Ramo serves as the first woman President of The American Law Institute, elected in 2008. Ms. Ramo shared her career development with us, and discussed how, in the different legal employment landscape in the 1960s, female attorneys, even with as brilliant a legal mind as hers, faced challenges.

Judge Paul Friedman was pleased to learn I am from Thomson Reuters. He was the presiding judge who approved the final judgment proposed by the parties in settlement of the $3.4 billion Thomson/West legal publishing merger in 1997. Judge Friedman recounted his opinion in *U.S. v. Thomson Corp.*, 949 F.Supp. 907: the responsibility of the district court and the proper scope of its "public interest" inquiry in a Tunney Act proceeding (15. U.S.C. § 16) is "to compare the complaint filed by the government with the proposed consent decree and determine whether the remedies negotiated between the parties and proposed by the Justice Department clearly and effectively address the anticompetitive harms initially identified." Judge Friedman's only reservation was West's star pagination, the page breaks in the West case reporters. In addressing Judge Friedman's concerns on the pagination issue, Thomson-West proposed free star pagination licenses for small publishers until the legal issue was settled. After detailed review process in which the judge carefully considered comments and arguments from all interested persons on the many issues touched on by the proposed decree, the court concluded the proposed decree was in the "public interest."

I thanked Judge Friedman again for his sound legal opinion. The Judge said the "thank you" reminded him of the appreciation he received from Mr. Dwight Opperman, former CEO of West Publishing, many years later, when they met at a social gathering in California.

Justice John Paul Stevens enters the ALI conference room. © ALI

Justice John Paul Stevens

The highlight of the first day was the remarks by retired Supreme Court Justice John Paul Stevens. He revisited *Bush v. Gore*, 531 U.S. 98, 121 S. Ct. 525, which he said was notable for a "lack of any coherent application of the Equal Protection Clause." In conclusion, he thanked the ALI members for their "efforts to continue to improve the law."

Justice Stevens also answered some questions from the ALI members with a great sense of humor. One member asked: "Did politics play a part of Bush v. Gore?" Answer: "I don't know." Another question: "What do you think about the 8th Amendment?" Answer: "The public will realize death penalty executions are a tremendous waste of resources." When it was asked what Justice Stevens' thoughts were on the Affordable Care Act case, the justice answered he would need to read the briefs first.

Justice Stevens also recommended that all ALI members read *Five Chiefs*, his own Supreme Court memoir.

Justice Stevens received a standing ovation when he entered the room, and received two more standing ovations during and after his remarks. A video-recording of Justice Stevens' remarks is available on the C-Span website.

AALS Reception

Professor Joan Howland, Associate Dean of the University of Minnesota Law School, and I also attended the reception hosted by Association of American Law Schools (AALS) at AALS Headquarters. We also had a chance to meet and greet Professor Mary Kay Kane, Council Member of the ALI and former dean of the University of California Hastings College of Law.

Members' Reception, Smithsonian American Art Museum

The first day concluded with a Members' Reception at the Great Hall at Donald Reynolds Center for American Art and Portraiture, where President and Mrs. Lincoln greeted guests attending the President's second inaugural ball.

Tom Leighton and I had a conversation with Bryan Garner, Editor-in-Chief, *Black's Law Dictionary* and the bestselling book *Making Your Case: The Art of Persuading Judges*, that he co-authored with Justice Antonin Scalia, also published by Thomson Reuters.

We also had a long conversation with Carol Lee, former clerk of Justice John Paul Stevens, who is now in private practice. At the invitation of Jeffrey Lehman, Dean of Peking University School of Transnational Law (PKUSTL), Carol Lee is going to visit the school in Shenzhen City, China to deliver a lecture. In 2009, when PKUSTL was founded, Thomson Reuters was one of the first corporate sponsors of the school.

As a user of WestlawNext, Carol Lee praised WestlawNext. She stated WestlawNext is at least one and a half years ahead of LexisNexis' legal research tools.

Annual Reception and Dinner

The Annual Reception and dinner on the second day featured keynote speaker Nina Totenberg, Legal Affairs Correspondent, National Public Radio. She is the second honorary non-lawyer member of the ALI. The first one is Anthony Lewis, the author of *Gideon's Trumpet* and *Make No Law: The Sullivan Case and the First Amendment.*

Nina Totenberg comments focused on her life-long coverage of the Supreme Court and on the change of the Court, for example, going from no female justices to three on the Court, and the advancement of technology in court filing and reporting.

Eric Holder, Jr., Attorney General of the United States.

Attorney General Eric Holder addresses the ALI members. © ALI

Eric Holder, the United States Attorney General, addressed the Institute on the third day. He thanked the Institute for its tradition of honoring and protecting equal justice under the law through its work. He also acknowledged that a great deal of important work remains to be done, especially in protecting the right to vote. He reminded the members that the founding vision of the Institute has not yet been realized, despite the progress that the organization and its members have made since the Institute was established in 1923.

Attorney General Holder emphasized, among other challenges, changes in the laws governing voter identification in several jurisdictions. While acknowledging the need to protect against voter fraud, he also reminded the Institute of the need to make sure that the franchise is fully available to students, members of the military, and others whose ability to vote has sometimes been made more difficult.

Member's Luncheon, Address by Trevor Potter

The last special event of the 89th Annual Meeting was the member luncheon featuring an address by Trevor Potter, Partner at Caplin & Drysdale. He is the former chairman of the Federal Election Commission and now represents Stephen Colbert and his SuperPAC, "Americans for a Better Tomorrow, Tomorrow."

On Magna Carta and the Rule of Law

*The fundamental concepts of liberty that had
their beginnings in Magna Carta were transplanted
to the American colonies where they were accepted,
refined, and embedded in the instruments of government as well as the thinking of the American
people. Magna Carta provided the basis for the idea
of a higher law, one that could not be altered either
by executive mandate or legislative acts. This
concept, embraced by the leaders of the American
Revolution, is embedded in the supremacy clause
of the United States Constitution. Throughout
American history, the rights associated with Magna
Carta have been regarded as among the most
important guarantees of freedom and fairness.*

*— The American Bar Association:
Magna Carta Commemoration*

Three principles were contained in the Magna Carta:
the rule of law, basic rights, and government by agreement
or contract. These principles have inspired generations of
citizens globally.

As a substantive legal principle, the rule of law refers
to the supremacy of regular as opposed to arbitrary power
and the doctrine that every person is subject to the ordinary
law within the jurisdiction.

Globalization, especially the rapid development of
technology and the integration of global economic systems,
generates more and more legal issues challenging existing
processes and protocols for managing international business transactions and enterprises. Fundamental tensions

among different ideological and political systems also continue to play a larger-than-anticipated role in economic affairs, creating even more complications and uncertainties. It is in this global context that the development of the rule of law is vital in creating a stable and reliable infrastructure for international businesses and free trade.

The rule of law is foundational for economic and social development in emerging countries. It is crucial in building the integrity of the judiciary, delivering justice by providing due process and equal protection, and fostering economic opportunity by ensuring the legitimacy and enforceability of contracts.

In many developing countries which are increasingly being integrated into the world economy, the transition to a market economy has been a major factor in a move toward the rule of law, because a rule of law is important to foreign investors and to economic development. It is also equally important to ensure the development of the rule of law in these countries is not limited to commercial matters but also to enhance prospects for universal values such as constitutional democracy and human rights, thus contributing to a just, orderly and prosperous world.

The legal profession strives to improve legal education within formal university settings as well as to broaden the public's understanding of the law and its role in building a just society governed by the rule of law. Changing the mindset of a country's future legal professionals is one of the surest ways to usher in lasting legal reforms. An educated public that is willing and able to demand that its government act in a fair, transparent and law-based manner is critical to building a society governed by the rule of law.

Legal Information in China[1*]

It is difficult to define the historical and present legal structures and the corresponding legal information systems in China in traditional Western terms. Chinese law was not characterized by fundamental principles of justice and fairness until the beginning of the 20th century, and no uniform legal information system existed until the latter part of that century. Some scholars may plausibly argue that the Confucian moral governance and patriarchal control (mainly through local and family customs) in imperial and modern China offered "alternative solutions" to the Western legal tradition. Others may argue that collecting and revising early penal rules by latter dynasties was a traditional "codification," and that even the sporadic records of arguments and consideration of the courts were a form of "court reporting."[2] Nevertheless, the indisputable fact is that prior to 1979 China never had a stable legal system designed to uphold the rule of law. This void contributed to the abuse of power and official corruption that accompanied ancient Chinese civilization. Historians have pointed out, rather in despair, that traditionally Chinese society was governed by "hidden rules", instead of law, and one of these "hidden rules" was that government has the "right to harm" rather than protect its citizens.[3]

[1*]This article first appeared as a section in "Management of Legal Information in an International Context: A Conundrum of Challenges and Opportunities," co-authored with Joan Howland, Frontiers of Law in China, June 2011, Volume 6, Issue 2, pp 165-179.

[2]Junfan Zhang, 中国法律的传统与近代转型, (The Change of Legal Traditions in Modern China), The Law Press (Beijing), at 234 (1997).

[3]Si Wu, 潜规则: 中国历史中的真实游戏 (Hidden Rules: The Real Game in Chinese History), Fudan University Press (Shanghai), 页码 (2009).

John King Fairbank, a doyen of Sinology in the United States, drew an insightful comparison between Chinese and Western laws when he stated,

> "The concept of law is one of the glories of Western civilization, but in China legalism, although it profoundly influenced the Chinese attitude toward all law, has been a despised term of art for more than two thousand years. This is because the legalist concept of law fell far short of the Roman. Whereas Western law has been conceived of as a human embodiment of some higher order of God or nature, the law of the legalists[4] represented only the ruler's fiat. China developed little or no civil law to protect the citizen; law remained largely administrative and penal, something the people attempted to avoid as much as possible."[5]

Therefore, rather than the "rule of law," the Chinese legal system was basically characterized by the concept of "rule *by* law." As described by Jerome Cohen:

> "Traditional Chinese law was mainly an instrument for enforcing status-oriented Confucian social norms and for bending the will of an unruly populace to achieve the purposes of an authoritarian government. To these ends it provided a complex series of punishments and an elaborate hierarchy of institutions for adjudicating guilt and passing sentence. These institutions relied on orderly but highly

---

[4]"Legalists" here refer to Chinese utilitarian political philosophers during the Warring States Period (475 – 221, B.C.) and after, who advocated that law should be publicly promulgated principles and standards of conduct backed by powerful state coercion, i.e., rule by law. See The Book of HanFeiZi and The Book of Lord Shang.

[5]Fairbank, John King. East Asia: The Great Tradition. (Boston: Houghton Mifflin). at 84 (1960).

repressive procedures that allowed the defendant little opportunity to make a defense."[6]

To put it in other way, in ancient China the government was primarily concerned with ensuring that citizens followed the prescribed rules and directives, and failure to do so always led to appropriate punishment at the "right degree of pain." Those rules and directives detailed the types of activities that were deemed harmful to the government, as well as what actions would be punished and what penalties would be imposed. Thus, "any human act recognized in the law was linked with a punishment."[7] During the first dynasty, the Qin imperial government began to unify penal codes and to publish laws. Subsequent dynasties collected, edited, and revised previous penal codes and promulgated new ones, adding new crimes and punishments.[8] The imperial government maintained a monopoly over the editing and publishing of laws, a tradition that persisted until the 20th century. Following detailed and incontestable directives from the emperor, ministers and legal officials were responsible for crafting, revising, and editing laws. Subsequent to final approval by the emperors and kings, the laws were promulgated, published, and stored in royal libraries. Overall, penal statutes and rules (either scripts or prints) were well preserved, but most operative legal norms in ancient China were not published and were therefore available only to those officials who administered the system. Since the Tang dynasty (618 – 907),

---

[6]Cohen, Jerome Allan. The Criminal Process in the People's Republic of China, 1949–1963: An Introduction. (Cambridge: Harvard University Press). 1968, at 5.
[7]Muhlhahn, Klaus. Criminal Justice in China: A History. (Cambridge: Harvard University Press). 2009, at 14 – 15.
[8]Chen, Weisong, 古代法律文献编纂史略, A Brief History of Ancient Legal Documents Editing 1 Journal of Central China Normal University 39,99 (2000).

statutes were annotated and illustrated, again by appointed government officials. These annotations merged into the code, thereby gaining the effect of the law.[9] The Tang Code became the legislative model for the later Song, Yuan, Ming and Qing dynasties.

It was a tradition in China that courts, including administrative hearing offices, were presided over by magistrates who were appointed officials without any specialized legal training. Court rulings were often arbitrary. And the courts were not obliged to explain to anyone, including the parties to a dispute, the rationale behind its rulings. Court rulings were collected and published at times, but these documented rulings carried no precedential weight.

From 1902 to 1912, the last decade of Late Qing Dynasty (1644 – 1912), there was an unprecedented effort to modernize Chinese law to accommodate social changes under the pressures from foreign powers. Drawing upon the Japanese legal vocabulary and usage, Chinese jurists and officials translated and incorporated considerable amounts of the German Civil Code into the Grand Qing Codex.[10] The government established a legal reform commission, appointed two ministers of "legal revision" (one of whom was Wu Tingfang, the ambassador to the United States), and hired foreign legal experts as consultants.[11] Unfortunately, the Qing Dynasty collapsed before any transformative legal reforms were ready for implementation.

The Republic of China, established in 1912, represented a short-lived period of enlightened legal process which featured a judicial system independent from other branches

---

[9]Yang, Ji, 古代法律文献：中华法制文明的宝库 (Ancient Legal Documents: The Treasure of Chinese Legal Culture, 6 Library Science Studies, at 90 (2002).
[10]See Demei Zhang, 探索与抉择—晚清法律移植研究 (Exploration and Choice: The Transplantation of Laws in Late Qing Dynasty), Qinghua University Press (Beijing), 2003.
[11]Id. 25, 100.

of government. The era was also characterized by the openness throughout Chinese society to foreign influences and Western perspectives on legal thought. In 1915, the American lawyer and missionary Charles W. Rankin established the Comparative Law School of China in Shanghai.[12] Patterned after the American model of legal education, the school devoted a considerable effort to teaching Anglo-American law.[13]

During the same period, China once again used the German civil law as a prototype for legislative reform. Six sets of codes (the constitution, the civil code, the code of civil procedure, the criminal code and code of criminal procedure, the administrative law, and the administrative procedure law) were promulgated as the foundation of a brand new legal system. By the early 1930s, the government had also formalized the procedures through which to publish and preserve court judgments. Many of the cases issued during this period began to have precedential value, especially those involving succession of land, bigamy, and concubinage.[14]

Unfortunately, the Republican China's progress in legal reform came to a halt after 1937 with the Japanese invasion of China and the civil war in 1947-1949. The Chinese Communist Party defeated the Nationalist government in 1949, thus establishing the People's Republic of China (PRC) on the mainland. The Nationalist government reestablished itself in Taiwan as the "Republic of China." The PRC abolished the Nationalist legal system, including the

---

[12]Alison Conner, *The Comparative law School of China*, in *Understanding China's Legal System, Essays in Honor of Jerome Cohen*, ed. by C. Stephen Hsu, New York University Press (New York), at 211 (2003).
[13]Id. at 210.
[14]Priscilla M. F. Laung, *Selected Edition of China Law Reports: 1991- 2004*, People's Court Press & Renmin University Press (Beijing), at 21 (2005).

judiciary, and rescinded the entire existing body of law. The PRC began to construct a "socialist" legal system, drawing heavily on Soviet law.

The PRC's history can be divided into two periods: Mao's era (1949 – 1978) and the era of Deng Xiaoping and his successors (1979 to the present). In terms of the legal system, these two periods share common features but are distinguished by different doctrinal ideologies. Under Mao's leadership, the government took a hostile view toward formalized legal systems. Mao and his party "saw the law as creating constraints upon their power."[15] "The legal system itself was deliberately targeted for attack as being counterrevolutionary, and indeed, the very idea of 'law' was rejected. Legal institutions, such as courts and procuratorates were shut down or paralyzed, law schools were closed, and members of the legal community were forced to shift professions or were sent down to farms to learn from peasants."[16]

Since 1979, Deng Xiaoping and his party instituted an "Open Door" policy which took a utilitarian approach to the reconstruction of social order and the legal system. The law came to be viewed as a useful instrument to support the country's economic growth. Over the past three decades, China has made significant progress in developing a legal system that in many ways is consistent with international norms. Prolific legislative activities and increased emphasis on the implementation and enforcement of law are positive steps toward a stable legal environment.[17]

---

[15]Daniel C. K. Chow, *The Legal System of the People's Republic of China in a Nutshell*, 2nd Ed.(St. Paul: West), at 56 (2009).

[16]Id. at 59.

[17]James M. Zimmerman, *China Law Deskbook: A Legal Guide for Foreign-Invested Enterprises* (2nd Ed)., American Bar Association (Chicago), at 70 (2005).

As noted earlier in this paper, legal publishing in China, as a state-controlled enterprise, has historically been restricted.[18] Before 1979, legal bibliographic systems and legal research methods were primitive. Standardized and advanced techniques for organizing legal information, such as codification, indexing, cataloging, and superseding, were not implemented by legal publishers until the early 1990s.[19] The failure to develop an effective method of organizing information and disseminating legal knowledge can be explained by the long standing and well-established tradition throughout Chinese history that access to information and knowledge is a privilege, not a right.[20]

In addition to the traditional disregard for equal access to information, the lack of technical infrastructure was also responsible for the underdevelopment of a modern legal information system. China had "neither a central government clearinghouse like the United States Government Printing Office for disseminating government information nor a depository library system to have libraries house the government publications and provide public access to them."[21] Government documents, even those with legal implications, could be classified as "state secrets," only available to the officials who executed them. This

---

[18]Even in early 1990s, the State Council promulgated Administration Provisions on Legal Compilation Editing and Publishing (July 29, 1990, effective July 29, 1990), followed by Press and Publication Administration's Notice of the Press and Publication Administration on the Implementation of the State Council's Administrative Provisions on Legal Compilation Editing and Publishing (Dec.22, 1991, effective Dec.22, 1991). These are efforts to regulate legal publishing business.

[19]Joan Liu, & Wei Luo, *A Complete Research Guide to the Laws of the People's Republic of China (PRC)*, http://www.llrx.com/features/prc.htm (last visited)

[20]Imperial China did not fully respect individual rights. Confucianism values order. "The people may be made to follow a path of action, but they may not be made to understand it." (Confucius, 551-479 BC).

[21]Liu & Luo, fn. 36.

again is a unique characteristic that echoes imperial practices. In 2007, the State Council of China promulgated the PRC Regulations for the Disclosure of Government Information.[22] No doubt the Regulations, along with the "Electronic Government Projects" (a set of websites established by central and local governments to transfer some of the government functions online), will contribute to the development of a legal information system in China.

The 1990s witnessed unparalleled economic growth in China driven by vast foreign investment, privatization of commercial and industrial entities, and technological advances. Sir Francis Bacon's dictum "Knowledge is Power"[23] became a motivating force and mantra throughout the country. Demands for more information and more knowledge increased throughout all segments of society. Consequently, the collection, management, and distribution of knowledge came to be viewed as having both social and economic benefits. Legal information in particular was seen as a body of information potentially of high market value.

In 1995, Peking University, the country's oldest and most prestigious university, launched Chinalawinfo, the first online Chinese legal information database. This effort was followed by other technological ventures. "Facilitated with modern technology and aiming to catch up with sophisticated online services, such as Westlaw and LexisNexis, law publishers, online products entrepreneurs, law schools, law firms, and even law enforcement departments, are committing themselves to create comprehensive databases

---

[22]中华人民共和国政府信息公开条例PRC Regulations for the Disclosure of Government Information, State Council, promulgated on April 5, 2007, effective May 1, 2007.
[23]Bacon, Francis, Meditations Sacrae (1597), reported in John Bartlett's Familiar Quotations (15th ed.), at 179 (1980).

and electronic legal services."[24] In 1999, with strong government support, Tsinghua University launched "China National Knowledge Infrastructure," the largest digital value-added information library and a nationwide knowledge sharing platform in China.

Within the last five years, major electronic information providers, including Thomson Reuters, Commerce Clearing Houser, and Reed Elsevier, have developed advanced Chinese legal information services. For example, Thomson Reuters's Westlaw China is an online China law database designed to administer primary sources and key-numbering Chinese legal topics. With their sophisticated legal editing techniques, advanced search engines, and value-added intelligent information business models, these information providers have been and will continue to be a significant reference framework for domestic providers.

Obviously, China is in the period of transition. "Building a legal system is a process that cannot be completed in the span of three decades or even in a generation . . . [therefore] such a fledging system cannot realistically be compared with that of the United States."[25] China's legal "system" differs from that of the United States not only in maturity and sophistication, but also in fundamental values. The "system" being developed does not follow the principle of "rule of law", but rather the "rule by law." In the endeavors to modernize China's legal system and legal information system, Western influences should not be overestimated. Nevertheless, the development of contemporary China's legal system, "like [that of] many other developing nations around the world, has been a process of westernization."[26]

---

[24]Liu & Luo, fn. 36.
[25]Daniel C. K.Chow, *The Legal System of the People's Republic of China in a Nutshell* (2nd Ed.), West (St. Paul), at 61-62 (2009).
[26]Id. at 64.

The same is true for the development of the legal profession, legal education, and legal information systems in contemporary China.

There has been a paradigm shift during the past thirty years. "Concepts such as the rule of law and individual rights are derived from western political traditions and have no equivalents in Chinese history."[27] But the Chinese have long accepted the plausible argument of "Chinese learning for fundamental principles and Western learning for practical application."[28] It is the rationale behind the control over the information and knowledge. Ironically, the standard to evaluate whether China has developed a modern legal system is whether it can be effectively function in the international community by speaking the same kind of legal language universally accepted. The standard to evaluate the level of sophistication of China's legal information system is to reference a resource like Westlaw which offers researchers credible, edited, and annotated information that is knowledge in itself and can be utilized to create further knowledge.

---

[27]Chow, Daniel C. K., fn. 42 at 64.
[28]This expression first appeared in Exhortation to Study, an 1898 publication by late Qing high government official Zhang Zhidong, who was a leading figure in the "Foreign Affairs Movement" but clung to a conservative approach to reform.

When East Meets West*

I feel extremely privileged to be standing here this afternoon addressing such a distinguished audience. I feel as if I'm bringing coals to Newcastle because everybody in this room, I think, knows a great deal about the legal information business and I feel I have a great deal to learn from people here.

So I will adopt if I may this afternoon the well-known traditional Chinese pedagogy of "Pao Zhuan Yin Yu," which means *throw out a piece of brick to attract a piece of jade*, and I think the most productive part of this afternoon may well be in the Q&A session, because I look forward to that interchange.

The concept of incommensurability (having no common standard of measurement) of paradigms is borrowed from philosophy of science. In 1962, the idea that scientific paradigms are incommensurable was popularized by the philosopher Thomas Kuhn in his book *The Structure of Scientific Revolutions*. He argued that the proponents of different paradigms cannot fully appreciate or understand the other's point of view because they are, so to speak, living in different worlds. He gave three reasons: different ideas; different vocabularies; and different experiences. Those cause fundamental problems in communication.

So, how to overcome the difficulties in communication. Kuhn proposed using a neutral language for communication, since the difference occurs prior to the application of language.

*These are Chang Wang's remarks at the Chinese and American Forum on Legal Information and Law Libraries. They were delivered in Beijing in May, 2009.

In this short presentation, I would venture to raise the issue for consideration: can the incommensurability of different paradigms in legal information industry and legal research discipline be reconciled? Particularly when West meets East, the old common law meets the new socialist civil law jurisprudence?

The purpose of my presentation, I suppose, is to attempt to unravel that particular mystery: whether different paradigms are irreconcilable.

It is my best intention, at the end of the day, to offer a solution. I think we all understand the importance of communication and trust. Nevertheless, the solution I am offering is not only based on good faith and tolerance, but also on collaborative efforts to build, to exchange ideas, to share knowledge, and to communicate in a neutral language: the language of the law.

I want to advocate programs in three dimensions:

American Legal Information in English Language for Chinese

A tremendous need exists for English and American legal system information and basic legal research guides. These markets are rapidly growing and merging with the English learning market. Among them, English-language legal education and training is the biggest and safest (least regulated) market, encouraged by Chinese authority. English-language legal material is a traditional business for Thomson West. With the number of Chinese learning English, this market is predicted to grow steadily.

Thousands of English and American law treatises, casebooks, hornbooks and study aids have been translated, annotated or reprinted in Chinese. English-language legal training and translation services are a new business in

China. At least 20 legal English textbooks have been published. In Beijing and Shanghai, specialized legal English training courses are offered to law students and young attorneys.

Chinese Legal Information in English Language for Americans

Some American law schools have co-sponsored Chinese law study programs for American law students and lawyers during the summer with Chinese law schools. Fifty-two Chinese law courses are offered in 40 law schools in the U.S. PRC legal research is a new popular area among legal scholars. More and more studies and law review articles appear about Chinese law and the legal system. Recently the American Bar Association published the second edition of the *China Law Deskbook.*

Sweet & Maxwell, a Thomson legal company, has published more than 30 titles in its "China Law Series." These are staples in law libraries, and the U.S. Thomson Reuters is currently editing a new multi-volume series titled China Law Book for English-speaking legal professionals.

Chinese Legal Information in Chinese for Chinese

Last but certainly not least is the opportunity . . . All of China's legal institutions, including its domestic legal publishing industry, were virtually eliminated during the Cultural Revolution. One result is that there is no entrenched, standard-setting domestic publishing competition in China. A traditional government print publishing function exists alongside many free or low-cost sources of unenhanced legal information on the Web.

Rapid changes to China's legal system (judicial reform, an increase in commercial disputes and the adoption of Western legal structures) have led to the beginnings of a value-added publishing movement.

I want to conclude my presentation with a quotation and a comment:

The quotation is from a PBS documentary on China: "Poised to surpass the United States as the largest economy in the world, yet facing mounting domestic and international pressure for a fair and transparent framework of laws, China is racing to reshape the rules of society."

My comment is this: It is amazing to witness China, this enormous, extremely complicated, complex, and incomprehensible piece of machine manage to maintain its power and balance; it is amazing to see a legal system, a legal information system in the making. I believe the building of the rule of law in China is actually the greatest drama of the 21st century and I feel privileged to witness this and hope one day I can adding a brick to the building. I feel privileged that I'm able to share my observations with all of you because I'm sure all of you will play a role in that particular drama of our lifetimes. You are today's John B. West and Roy Mersky.

China Legal Reviews
2011*

On August 30th, 2011, The Standing Committee of China's National People's Congress (NPC) published the draft and the explanatory notes of proposed amendments to China's Criminal Procedure Law (CPL) on the NPC website, in order to invite suggestions from the public.[1] This is the first time the public has had an opportunity to comment on major criminal procedure legislation before its promulgation, and the public had one month to submit comments by mail or online.[2]

China's current Criminal Procedure Law was promulgated in 1979 and revised in 1996, with eight amendments to it since 1999. In 2004, The NPC Standing Committee's Legal Work Committee proposed making another major revision, but work on the revision has been delayed due to lack of consensus. Finally, in June 2011, the Communist Party's Central Political-Judicial Committee set up the agenda for CPL revision.[3]

There are 99 proposed amendments to the CPL in this revision draft, expanding the number of CPL articles from

---

*This review originally appeared in International Lawyer, Volume 46, "China Law Review 2011," co. with Ying Deng, et. al., 46 Int'l Law. 517 (2012).

[1]Xingshi Susong fa Xiuzhengan (caoan) tiaowen ji caoan shuoming (刑事诉讼法修正案（草案）条文及草案说明) [Amendments to the Criminal Procedure Law of the People's Republic of China (Draft) and Explanatory Notes], available at http://www.npc.gov.cn/npc/xinwen/lfgz/2011-08/30/content_1668503.htm. [hereafter Amendments].

[2]Id.

[3]See Wang Heyan (王和岩), Xingsu fa xiuding zhengqiu yijian: bufen tiaokuan daotui yinfa danyou (刑诉法修订征求意见：部分条款倒退引发担忧) [Amendments to the Criminal Procedure Law Invites Comments: Some Provisions Go Backwards and Cause Concerns], available at http://china.caixin.cn/2011-08-30/100296591.html.

225 to 285. The articles cover seven areas: evidentiary system; compulsory measures; defense system; investigation measures; trial procedures; enforcement provisions; and special procedures.[4]

A. EVIDENCE RULES

The draft proposed new rules against coercing anyone to incriminate themselves, as well as rules to exclude illegal evidence: "the use of torture or extortion to obtain a confession and the use of other illegal means to collect evidence shall be strictly prohibited; no person may be forced to prove his or her own guilt."[5] The proposed evidence amendments[6] incorporate some essential elements of Supreme People's Court of China's 2010 Judicial Interpretation on exclusion of illegal evidence in criminal cases,[7] which was a set of comprehensive rules governing the use of illegal evidence in criminal cases.

Also in the evidence category, the draft of the proposed amendments also suggests improvements in types of proof,[8] standards of proof[9] and protection of witness.[10]

B. CRIMINAL DEFENSE

While Professor Jerome Cohen believes, overall, "the current draft reflects more of a victory for the police and

---

[4]Amendments, Explanatory Notes.
[5]Amendments, (14).
[6]Amendments, (14), (17), (21).
[7]Guanyu banli xingshi anjian paichu feifa zhengju ruogan wenti de guiding (关于办理刑事案件排除非法证据若干问题的规定)[Rules Concerning Questions About Exclusion of Illegal Evidence in Handling Criminal Cases] (released by Supreme People's Court, Supreme People's Procuratorate, Ministry of Public Security, Ministry of State Security, and Ministry of Justice, June 25, 2010), *available at* http://rmfyb.chinacourt.org/paper/html/2010-06/25/content_11353.htm.
[8]Amendments, (12).
[9]Amendments, (16).
[10]Amendments, (15).

their allies among prosecutors and judges than for law professors and defense lawyers," nonetheless, "The draft's attempt to reconcile the CPL with more substantial rights conferred on defense counsel and their clients by the revised Lawyers Law demonstrates the limited success of the criminal bar's strenuous lobbying."[11] In the criminal defense category, the draft confirms lawyers' rights to discuss cases with detained clients before trial, free of jailers' electronic or personal monitoring, it also restricts their ability to "verify" evidence with clients until investigators recommend indictment.[12]

The proposed amendments also encourage and expand the availability of legal aid in criminal proceedings. In the case of life sentence or higher, "the people's court, people's prosecutor's office and public security authority shall also provide legal assistance."[13]

C. SPECIAL PROCEDURES

The draft authorizes more benevolent procedures for alleged juvenile offenders.[14] It also proposes "Provisions on Compulsory Medical Treatment Procedures for Mentally Ill Persons Committing a Violent Act," allowing courts, not police or prosecutors, to order compulsory medical treatment.[15]

D. RESIDENTIAL SURVEILLANCE; SECRET DETENTION; SECRET ARREST

The proposed amendments explicitly authorize secret arrest and detention tactics, which were previously illegal

---

[11]Jerome A. Cohen and Yu Han, *China's Struggle for Criminal Justice*, http://www.usasialaw.org/?p=5928.
[12]Amendments, (3), (6), (7).
[13]Amendments, (4), (95).
[14]Amendments, (95).
[15]Amendments, (98).

but commonly practiced by police and investigators.[16] These "forced disappearances,"[17] as well as the proposed revisions to the CPL, may both be at odds with provisions in current Chinese law that provide for such legal protections as family notification of detainees' whereabouts and access to counsel[18] and international law.[19] The systematic use of arbitrary detention and forced disappearance, and the proposed amendments legalizing these tactics, have received considerable attentions from both academia and media.[20]

- Non-residential residential surveillance:[21] in cases of a crime *suspected* to threaten national security, crimes of terrorist activities and major crimes of bribery, residential surveillance at the domicile may impede the investigation, surveillance can be carried out in a location other than residence.[22]

---

[16]In the first half of 2011, authorities reportedly "disappeared" numerous lawyers and rights activists known for criticizing the Communist Party and for advocating on behalf of politically sensitive causes and groups. *See* generally Congressional-Executive Commission on China Annual Report 2011, *available at* http://www.usasialaw.org/?p=5928.

[17]*Id.*

[18]Press Release, The US Department of State (Aug. 31, 2011), *available at* http://www.state.gov/r/pa/prs/ps/2011/08/171320.htm.

[19]Press Release, The UN Working Group on Enforced or Involuntary Disappearance (April 8, 2011), *available at* http://www.ohchr.org/en/NewsEvents/Pages/DisplayNews.aspx?NewsID=10928&LangID=E.

[20]*See* He Weifang (贺卫方), Zheyang de lifa weibei le zhengfu de chengnuo (这样的立法违背了政府的承诺) [This Kind of Legislation Broke Government's Promise], *available at* http://www.caijing.com.cn/2011-09-02/110839364.html; Donald Clark, *More on proposed revisions to China's Criminal Procedure Law,* http://lawprofessors.typepad.com/china_law_prof_blog/2011/10/more-on-proposed-revisions-to-chinas-criminal-procedure-law.html; Reuters News, *China announces plans to boost secret detention powers,* http://www.reuters.com/article/2011/08/30/us-china-law-detention-idUS-TRE77T2HJ20110830. *Also See* Wang Heyan, *supra.* Online public comments on the Amendments were disproportionally focused on the provisions legalizing secret detention and secret arrest.

[21]"Non-residential residential surveillance" (NRRS) refers to a common practice by Chinese police of locking people up in places other than their residence, but calling it "residential surveillance". *See* Clark, *supra.*

[22]Amendments, (30).

- Secret residential surveillance: where a notice cannot be furnished, or where crimes threatening national security or crimes of terrorist activities are suspected and a notice may impede the investigation, family members of the person under surveillance will not be informed of either the reason for the surveillance or the designated non-residential surveillance site.[23] The six months rule (residential surveillance *may* not exceed six months) remains unchanged.[24]

- Secret detention: where notice cannot be furnished, or when *suspected* crimes involve threats to national security, terrorist activities *or other serious offenses*, and notice may impede the investigation, family members of the person detained will *not* be informed of the reason for detention and place of custody.[25] This provision has been called "Ai Weiwei Clause" by some observers.[26]

- Secret arrest: where a notice cannot be furnished or where crimes threatening national security, crimes of terrorist activities *or other serious crimes* are *suspected* and a notice may impede the investigation", family members of the person arrested will *not* be informed of the reason for arrest and place of custody.[27]

---

[23]*Id.*

[24]Zhonghua renmin gongheguo xingshi susong fa (中华人民共和国刑事诉讼法) [Criminal Procedure Law of the People's Republic of China], art. 58, *available at* http://www.law-lib.com/law/law_view.asp?id=321.

[25]Amendments, (36).

[26]From April 3 to June 22, artist Ai Weiwei was held at a secret location unbeknown to his family and public by Chinese police. The proposed amendment (36) would legalize this kind of secret detention, thus is was called "Ai Weiwei Clause" by some observers. *See* Guo Zhiyuan, *Chance and Challenge for Chinese Criminal Procedure Law Reform, available at* http://www.usasialaw.org/wp-content/uploads/2011/09/20110926-Chance-and-Challenge-for-Chinese-Criminal-Procedure-Law-Reform.pdf

[27]Amendments, (39).

"National security" or "crimes of terrorist activities" are not defined in the draft and are not subject to independent review. Both secret detention and secret arrest provisions include a "catch-all" clause ("or other serious crimes") which was considered by some legal scholars in direct conflict with International Convention on Civil and Political Rights (ICCPR).[28]

The proposed amendments will be discussed and likely passed in March, 2012 during National People's Congress meeting.[29]

2012 – 2013[*]

As Chinese historian Ray Huang researched for his book *1587: A Year of No Significance: The Ming Dynasty in Decline*,[30] he found a fatal problem in Chinese politics: the political structure was premature and the administrative methods never grew to support the structure properly, nor were they based on sensible mathematics. Though the population and economy continued to develop, the administrative system was unable sustain the whole economy. Bureaucrats were working to cope with existing problems while new ones continued to spring forward. Despite the

---

[*]*This section, co-authored with Nathan Madson, originally appeared as the Afterword of* Inside China's Legal System, *Chandos Publishing, 2013.*

[28]*See* He Weifang, *supra*. China has signed have signed International Covenant on Civil and Political Rights on October 5th, 1998, but has not yet ratified the convention. International Covenant on Civil and Political Rights (ICCPR), G.A. res. 2200A (XXI), 21 U.N. GAOR Supp. (No. 16) at 52, U.N. Doc. A/6316 (1966), 999 U.N.T.S. 171, *entered into force* Mar. 23, 1976.

[29]Chen Guangzhong (陈光中), Xinsu fa xiugai zhong de jige zhongdian wenti (刑诉法修改中的几个重点问题) [A Few Important Issues in Revising the Criminal Procedure Law], *available at* http://www.npc.gov.cn/huiyi/lfzt/xsss-fxg/2011-08/24/content_1666933.htm.

[30]Ray Huang (1982) *1587: A Year of No Significance: The Ming Dynasty in Decline.* New Haven, CT: Yale University Press.

fact that the emperor had been very ambitious and the Chinese people very diligent, these individual efforts never really worked out to save the dynasty from decline.

At first glance, 2013, just like any year in the past two decades or so, is a year of no particular significance to China. The CPC, despite political and economic issues, remains firmly in power. Liu Xiaobo, one of two Chinese Nobel Peace laureates, languishes in prison, serving an 11-year sentence. The Tiananmen Square incident of 1989 is still a taboo that cannot be mentioned anywhere in China. Tibet is still burning and the number of monks and civilians who are self-immolating keeps rising, yet Beijing has not changed and shows no sign it plans to change any of its policy in the foreseeable future.[31] There continues to be unrest between the Uyghur and Han populations of Xinjiang. Property prices in Beijing and Shanghai are still sky-high. And blue sky is still a luxury for most Chinese people living in big cities.

Observers like Professor Pei Minxin have argued that China is trapped in a transition from a socialist planned economy to a market economy: 'The market oriented economic policies, pursued in a context of exclusionary politics and predatory practices, make the CPC increasingly resemble a self-serving ruling elite.'[32] Pei has also opined that the 'lack of progress in political reform would be the most important factor in constraining China's development – even more important than economic reform'.[33]

---

[31]Steve Wilson (2013) 'Tibetan monk dies after self-immolation in China', *Daily Telegraph*, 21 July; available at: *www.telegraph.co.uk/news/worldnews/ asia/tibet/10193139/Tibetan-monk-dies-after-self-immolation-in-China.html* (accessed: 8 August 2013).
[32]Pei Minxin (2006) *China's Trapped Transition: The Limits of Developmental Autocracy*. Cambridge, MA: Harvard University Press, p. 8.
[33]Ibid., p. 11.

Paul Krugman is even more pessimistic:

"China is in big trouble. We're not talking about some minor setback along the way, but something more fundamental. The country's whole way of doing business, the economic system that has driven three decades of incredible growth, has reached its limits. You could say that the Chinese model is about to hit its Great Wall, and the only question now is just how bad the crash will be.[34]

Krugman goes on to pose a poignant question: 'China's political regime is remarkable, even given the annals of history, for the hypocrisy of its position: officially it's building the socialist future, in practice it's presiding over a crony capitalist Gilded Age. Where, then, does the regime's legitimacy come from?'[35] We believe there are many different answers.

New president Xi Jinping has used media and propaganda, much like his predecessors, to speak of the 'China dream'. His propaganda storm began in earnest after he became president in 2013, and he referenced the 'China dream' numerous times in his first address to the nation as head of state on 17 March 2013:

"We must make persistent efforts, press ahead with indomitable will, continue to push forward the great cause of socialism with Chinese characteristics, and strive to achieve the Chinese dream of great rejuvenation of the Chinese nation . . . To realise the Chinese road, we must spread the Chinese spirit, which combines the spirit of the

---

[34]Paul Krugman (2013) 'Hitting China's wall', *New York Times*, 18 July; available at: *www.nytimes.com/2013/07/19/opinion/krugman-hitting-chinas-wall. html* (accessed: 8 August 2013).

[35]Paul Krugman (2013) 'How much should we worry about a China shock?', *New York Times*, 20 July; available at: *http://krugman.blogs.nytimes. com/2013/07/20/how-much-should-we-worry-about-a-china-shock/*

nation with patriotism as the core and the spirit of the time with reform and innovation as the core."[36]

Despite President Xi's call for steadfast support of the China dream, he has not specified how to put the dream into practice. One thing is clear, however: this dream is much closer to Mao and farther from the constitutionalism which intellectuals and foreign governments had hoped for. In public speeches Xi tends to elevate the CPC above the nation, and even above the Chinese people. He has tried to clamp down on criticism of Mao: 'To completely negate Mao Tse-tung would lead to the demise of the Chinese Communist Party and to great chaos in China.'[37]

At the same time that the state media have extolled the virtues of the 'China dream', they have also launched a campaign against constitutionalism. Several major party media outlets have written editorials supporting CPC rule by saying that 'Western political concepts like separation of powers are alien and unsuited to China.'[38] Many of the country's intellectuals, however, have been openly advocating for constitutionalism and political reform.[39]

Constitutionalism, which can be defined as the concept of a system of laws and regulations that protect citizens' rights by restraining the government or a political party, has been increasingly ridiculed by the *People's Daily*, a newspaper that is highly supportive of the CPC. One article opines

[36]BBC, 'What does Xi Jinping's China dream mean?', BBC News: available at: *www.bbc.co.uk/news/world-asia-china-22726375* (accessed: 8 August 2013).
[37]Barbara Demick (2013) 'China's Xi more Maoist than reformer thus far', *Los Angeles Times*, 8 June; available at: *http://articles.latimes.com/2013/jun/08/world/la-fg-china-xi-20130608* (accessed: 8 August 2013).
[38]Oiwan Lam (2013) 'China: constitutionalism is for capitalists', *Global Voices*, 27 May; available at: *http://globalvoicesonline.org/2013/05/27/clinging-to-chinese-constitution-is-to-deny-china/* (accessed: 10 August 2013).
[39]Rogier Creeemers (2013) 'The constitutionalism debate in China', 17 July; available at: *www.iconnectblog.com/2013/07/the-constitutionalism-debate-in-china/* (accessed: 10 August 2013).

that the drive for constitutionalism is not inherently Chinese, but rather a sign that Western countries have pushed their values on China and injected them into Chinese society. The editorial went so far as to claim that 'the spread of "constitutional-rule" ideas in China has been fostered by foundations affiliated with US intelligence agencies that aim to overturn socialism'.[40]

Is constitutionalism incommensurable with Chinese communism?

The concept of incommensurability of paradigms is borrowed from the philosophy of science and the philosopher Thomas Kuhn in his book *The Structure of Scientific Revolutions*.[41] He argued that two groups with vastly different paradigms cannot truly understand each other's point of view because they are on two radically different planes. Kuhn suggested that different ideas, vocabularies and experiences all contribute to the inability to see the other group's perspective.

This, of course, raises the question of whether constitutionalism and Chinese communism are incommensurable paradigms. If so, can they ever be reconciled and coexist? If China does adopt constitutionalism, will that mean the end of the CPC as we know it?

If we look at a recent press conference given by US Acting Assistant Secretary of State Uzra Zeya following a conversation on human rights between US and Chinese representatives, we see a split in how the two countries view individual rights. In Zeya's opinion, 'China will be stronger and more stable and more innovative if it represents and

[40]*Want China Times* (2013) *'People's Daily* slams "constitutionalism" as Beidaihe retreat begins', *Want China Times*, 6 August; available at: *www.wantchinatimes.com/news-subclass-cnt.aspx-?id=20130806000072&cid=1101&MainCatID=0* (accessed: 8 August 2013).
[41]Thomas S. Kuhn (1996) *The Structure of Scientific Revolutions*, 3rd edn. Chicago, IL: University of Chicago Press.

respects international human rights norms.'[42] She noted that there continue to be many different incidents the US government has classified as human rights abuses, nearly all of which violated both Chinese law and its international obligations. Yet increasing numbers of individual Chinese citizens are starting publicly to question the CPC.

Though Zeya provided concrete examples of human rights abuses, the Chinese government has noted that the human rights situation is at an all-time high in China.[43] It rejects any claim that things are deteriorating in China, or that it has started to target activists by harassing their relatives. Spokespeople for the government assert that the United States is biased in its criticisms and intentionally distorts the Chinese human rights record.

So, does this mean that constitutionalism and a healthy respect for human rights and Chinese communism are incommensurable? That remains to be seen, at least according to Professor Wang Dong of Peking University School of International Studies, who has said that bilateral talks are an important step toward mutual understanding.[44]

Important Updates

The case involving Bo Xilai is being tried and is near its conclusion. Professor Pei Minxin believes that 'the Bo Xilai affair has exploded several important myths about

---

[42]Uzra Zeya (2013) 'Press conference following US-China human rights dialogue', US Department of State, 2 August; available at: *www.state.gov/j/drl/rls/rm/2013/212667.htm* (accessed: 7 August 2013).

[43]*Washington Post* (2013) 'China says human rights situation is at a historic best, rejects US criticism', *Washington Post*, 2 August; available at: *http://articles.washingtonpost.com/2013-08-02/world/41015432_1_activists-liu-xiao-bo-xu-zhiyong* (accessed: 8 August 2013).

[44]Quoted in ibid.

one-party rule in China'.[45] One of the most striking lessons from Bo's case is that the idea that 'the post-Mao leadership has perfected a system of managing internal conflict and maintaining elite unity' is false.[46] Instead of a rule of law society, the party has chosen to operate by the rule of the jungle: whoever is the most powerful makes the rules. In *A Death in the Lucky Holiday Hotel: Murder, Money, and an Epic Power Struggle in China*, authors Ho Pin and Huang Wengguang not only discussed the killing of Neil Heywood by Bo's wife, a murder that shocked the international community in 2012, but also the 'stunning and unsettling portrait of the different intertwined interest groups and political factions within the Chinese Communist Party's top decision-making body'.[47] As Bo's case and the cases of those closest to him have shown, the top echelon of the CPC is rife with self-interest, corruption and debauchery.

There have also been two recent news stories about judges and lawyers that shed light on the current state of the Chinese legal system. In the first, two judges and an official were caught participating in some unscrupulous activities. In the second, a noted lawyer who has been critical of the government was arrested because of his previous work.

The CPC recently expelled two judges and an official from the Shanghai high court after a businessman collected video evidence of the three allegedly visiting prostitutes.[48]

---

[45]Pei Minxin (2013) 'Bo Xilai's trial exposes truth about China', *Bloomberg News*, 6 August; available at: *www.bloomberg.com/news/2013-08-06/bo-xilai-s-trial-exposes-truth-about-china.html* (accessed: 8 August 2013).
[46]Ibid.
[47]Ho Pin and Huang Wenguang (2013) *A Death in the Lucky Holiday Hotel: Murder, Money, and an Epic Power Struggle in China*. New York: Public Affairs, p. viii.
[48]Jane Perlez (2013) 'Chinese judges disciplined in prostitution scandal after videos circulate online', *New York Times*, 7 August; available at: *www.nytimes.com/2013/08/08/world/asia/chinese-judges-disciplined-for-cavorting-with-prostitutes.html?_r=0* (accessed: 8 August 2013).

The men lost their jobs and are facing discipline after the evidence was turned over to the CPC's internal disciplinary body. The businessman used security camera footage and video he collected after following the judges for a year to compile the incriminating evidence; he believed one of the judges had unfairly ruled against him in a lawsuit, and sought evidence to trap the judge in illegal behavior. The footage was embarrassing and public enough that Han Zheng, the CPC secretary of Shanghai, was forced to denounce the judges publicly and warn other court officials against repeating the behavior:

> "Although this case involved only a few corrupt and dissolute officials, it has shamed the entire judicial and legal system of Shanghai, and, indeed, the entire city itself. . . . Certain judges have spurned law and discipline, forsaken ethics and morality, and behaved with reckless abandon."[49]

The other story involves Xu Zhiyong, a lawyer who has publicly fought corruption and human rights abuses. Xu was arrested on charges of 'assembling a crowd to disrupt order in a public place'.[50] In early August 2013 Xu, wearing a prison uniform, created a video statement in which he said:

> "I encouraged everyone to be a citizen, to proudly and forthrightly be a citizen, to practice their rights as citizens set forth in the constitution and to undertake their responsibilities as citizens; I promoted equal rights in education and allowing children to take the university examination where they have followed their parents to live; I called for

---

[49]Ibid.
[50]BBC (2013) 'China detains activist Xu Zhiyong', BBC News, 17 July; available at: *www.bbc.co.uk/news/world-asia-china-23339401* (accessed: 8 August 2013).

officials to disclose their assets. In these absurd times, those are my three crimes."[51]

Though Xu's arrest may seem to be contrary to China's claims that it is moving closer to a more open and reformed society, Ira Belkin of the US-Asia Law Institute at New York University believes the situation to be 'bizarrely consistent'.[52] Though the government claims to be embracing the rule of law, it is ultimately focused on social stability, yet the CPC has interpreted 'social stability' to mean both a lack of social unrest and also no questioning of the party's authority. When the government determines someone is a 'troublemaker', it will do everything in its power to silence or stop them.

Though the CPC would argue that both these instances are unique and do not represent Chinese society today, they are, to borrow a phrase from Belkin, 'bizarrely consistent'. To remain in control, the party believes it must deter everyone and anyone who questions its actions. At the same time, it will turn a blind eye to abuse by its members; but when that abuse becomes public knowledge, the party will distance itself from its members. What this means is that the CPC continues to remain outside of and above the law. Rather than be held accountable under rule of law and constitutionalism, the party uses the law to maintain its power, reinforcing a rule *by* law system.

Yet 2013 may be a year of significance for China, as all the signs point to either 'the coming collapse of China'[53] or 'when China rules the world'.[54]

---

[51]China Law Prof. Blog (2013) 'Jailhouse statement of Xu Zhiyong', trans. Donald Clarke; available at: *http://lawprofessors.typepad.com/china_law_prof_blog/* (accessed: 8 August 2013).

[52]*The Economist,* 'The rule of law: bizarrely consistent', *The Economist*, 27 July, p. 38.

[53]Gordon G. Chang (2001) *The Coming Collapse of China.* New York: Random House.

[54]Martin Jacques (2009) *When China Rules the World*. New York: Penguin.

2014 – 2015*

2014 Reviews

1. The Chinese Communist Party Pledged to "Governing the Country by Law"

In October, the Communist Party of China (CPC) held the Party's 18th Central Committee's Fourth Plenum session. It should be noted the CPC Congress and its meeting sessions are much more important than the National People's Congress (NPC) and its legislative sessions, because the former sets up the direction and guidelines while the latter merely legitimates the former's policies. At the plenum's closing, the CPC Central Committee issued a communiqué on "comprehensively moving toward ruling the country according to the law." The CPC promised to increase both the accountability and transparency of government and to lessen local authorities' control over the legal system.

With the "socialist legal system with Chinese characteristics", the CPC claims to have built is a "rule by law" system in which the CPC operates outside and above the law. The CPC governs the country by law, yet this is fundamentally different from the "rule of law" as advocated for by the West. The Chinese words "Fa Zhi" (法治) mean rule by law, and "Yi Fa Zhi Guo" (依法治国) means ruling the country according to the law. The fundamental difference between the two is the relationship between the government and law. Rule by law means using the law and the legal system to legitimate the government's actions, creating a situation in which the

---

*This report, co-authored with Nathan Madson, reviews the state of law in China in 2014-2015. It originally appeared in Legal Current on February 18th, 2015.

government is not held legally accountable for its actions. Rule of law, on the other hand, means governing the country according to the laws already in place; the government is required to follow the law just as any ordinary citizen is.

This year was the first time the party made "governing the country by law" the focus of a plenum. The rhetoric of governing the country by law has generated a considerable amount of international attention, but it may be too soon to be overly optimistic. Looking back to December 2003, a "human rights" clause was added to the Chinese Constitution, and yet the last ten years has arguably been one of the most difficult times for the development of human rights in China after 1989.

2. Anti-Corruption Campaign and the Fall of the "New Gang of Four"

In August 2013, former Chongqing Party chief Bo Xilai was sentenced to life imprisonment for his involvement in widespread corruption. 2014 witnessed the fall of the rest of the so-called "New Gang of Four:"

Xu Caihou, Vice Chairman of the Central Military Commission and General of the Chinese People's Liberation Army: Xu was arrested while in the hospital and expelled from the Party. State media supervised by the CPC Propaganda Committee described Xu's alleged crimes as abuse of power, accepting bribes directly or via family members in exchange for promotions, and advancing the interests of those close to him through the powers vested in his office. Xu was a three-star general and one of the top commanders of Chinese army.

Zhou Yongkang is a former Chairman of the CPC Central Political and Law Committee and one of the top nine Party leaders during Hu Jintao presidency. Zhou was arrested and expelled from the Party for corruption and abuse of power. Zhou's fall is particularly significant because the CPC Political and Law Committee supervises China's entire judiciary and domestic security apparatus. All the courts, prosecutors, police, and secret police report to the Committee and, at one point, to Zhou. Zhou was regarded as one of the most powerful individuals in China for a decade, and he was the first Politburo Standing Committee member to be expelled from the party since the fall of the original Gang of Four in 1980 at the conclusion of the Cultural Revolution.

Ling Jihua was Vice Chairman of the National Chinese People's Political Consultative Conference and the head of the United Front Work Department of the Communist Party Central Committee. Ling was put in custody by officers of the CPC Central Disciplinary Committee (commonly known as "Shuanggui" 双规), again on charges of corruption. Ling was the chief of the staff of former President Hu Jintao.

More than 50 senior Party officials at the vice ministerial level or above have been subject to Party disciplinary actions (*shuanggui*) or arrested since 2012, most of them on the charge of "corruption." Through the anti-corruption campaign, Xi Jinping consolidated his supreme authority, eliminated sectarian forces inside the Party, and built personal reputation. The anti-corruption campaign was executed by Wang Qishan, one of the top seven Party leaders and the head of the CPC Central Disciplinary Committee, the quasi-judicial disciplinary body inside the CPC that operates completely outside the criminal justice system.

3. One-Child Policy Loosened

In November 2013, following the Third Plenum of the 18th Central Committee of the Communist Party of China, the government announced its decision to relax the one-child policy, the family planning policy that has controlled how many children may be born to a family without penalty since 1980. Under the new policy, families can have two children if one parent is an only child. In 2014, provinces slowly began to implement this relaxed policy.

4. Hukou System Reform

The Third Plenum of the CPC 18th Party Congress in October 2013 also laid out guidelines to reform the controversial "hukou" (户口) system of household registration that has traditionally inhibited large-scale migration from the country's rural areas into its urban centers. In July 2014, the State Council (the central government) announced that it would reform the hukou system. In December 2014, the Legal Affairs Office, under the State Council, released a draft residence permit regulation for public consultation. This has been a major step toward the abolition of the restrictive hukou system. The new regulations would allow people to obtain the permits necessary to access basic social welfare services in the place of their residence.

5. Anti-Terrorism and the Case of Ilham Tohti

The CPC has been actively fighting against what it has described as Uyghur terrorist elements in the Xinjiang Uyghur Autonomous Region (XUAR). The XUAR is home to one of China's larger minority groups, the Uyghurs, a group of Turkic Muslims who have had a contentious relationship with the Chinese government for decades. Spokespeople in the overseas Uyghur community accuse China of harshly repressing Uyghurs; the government has accused many Uyghurs of terrorism. For example, eight people were recently sentenced to death and five others were sentenced to suspended death sentences on terrorism charges following what some have criticized as unfair trials.

One of the most notable and tragic cases within the past year has been that of Ilham Tohti. Tohti was an economics professor at the Central Nationalities University in Beijing, but was taken into custody on charges of separatism. Government lawyers accused him of fomenting dissent with his lectures and outspoken criticisms of the Chinese government with regard to the administration of XUAR and its treatment of the Uyghurs. His trial was held during a closed-door session in September; his appeal was quickly held in the detention center in which he was being held and at a time in which neither of his lawyers were able to be present. According to his lawyers, this is a violation of Chinese law. Drawing considerable criticism from the international community, Tohti was sentenced to life in prison.

6. Judicial Reform and Corrections of Wrongful Convictions

CPC leaders have also been concerned with the rampant corruption and incompetency of the local courts. "Judicial Reform Measures" and a "Five-Year Plan" were announced in July: The reforms would seek to decrease the influence that local governments have on the court system by changing the way appointments and finances are handled. The measures also established pilot circuit courts to oversee the local courts and a handful of specialized intellectual property courts. The Party realized that to step away from the traditional model of judges as cadres, judges must be professional and accountable.

Furthermore, the Party said it would prevent extorting confessions by torture and prevent miscarriages of justice with a timely correction mechanism. This announcement comes following a series of corruption investigations involving torture that have outraged the public.

The Party also publicized a handful of selected wrongful conviction cases, most notably the Hugeriletu Case. Hugeriletu was executed in 1996, at the age of 18, for a murder he did not commit. These cases were "corrected" as remedial measures to the blatant violation of China's own laws under Zhou Yongkang's watch.

7. Organ Harvesting to Cease

China has vowed to stop harvesting organs from executed prisoners for transplant beginning January 1, 2015, the head of the country's organ donation committee announced.

Human rights groups praised the decision to end the controversial program, which is the country's main source of organs for transplant surgeries. The Chinese government only admitted to harvesting organs from executed prisoners in 2009.

8. Crackdown on Civil Society, Civil Rights Lawyers, and Liberal Intellectuals

The Year of the Fire Horse witnessed an intensified and broadened crackdown on civil society: NGOs, lawyers, journalists, as well as all outspoken "public intellectuals," a title shared by some liberal thinkers and scholars, have all been targeted. Xu Zhiyong, one of the leading figures of the "New Citizens" movement, was sentenced to four years in prison at the beginning of the year for "gathering crowds to disrupt public order." Pu Zhiqiang, the country's most prominent civil rights lawyer, has also been arrested and jailed.

Authorities have significantly increased their use of Criminal Law Article 293 ("undermining public order with provocative and disturbing behaviors") to arrest and charge numerous individuals. The Party has also used the charge in many creative ways, consistent with its overall trend of making the crackdown on political offenses appear apolitical and legitimate.

9. "Martial Law on the Internet"

The Central Internet Security Group was established earlier in the year and has been led by President Xi. The Party leadership believes Internet security and informatization is a strategic issue concerning a country's security and development, as well as people's lives and work. The Great Firewall has enhanced its functions by tightly controlling and censoring social media and carefully filtering "harmful" information. Two hugely popular Chinese websites that provided free subtitles for foreign films and TV series, as well as web streaming services of those foreign shows, were shut down in November. YouTube, Twitter, Facebook, Instagram, and Google are also completely blocked. By the end of 2014, Gmail and Virtual Private Network (VPN) services, two of the last possibilities for educated Chinese to connect to the outside world, were blocked as well. Observers believe the government is determined to make the Chinese Internet a local area network separated from the real Internet.

At the same time, China appears eager to promote its own domestic Internet rules as a model for global regulation. In November, China hosted its own "World Internet Conference" at which the CPC leadership claimed "China is ready to work with other countries to deepen international cooperation, respect sovereignty on the Internet and uphold cyber security." It also formally introduced the concept of "sovereignty on the Internet": not only does China have the right to set up its own rules and regulations for the Internet, but also that an international consensus should be reached to recognize this right.

The New York Times has called this tech crackdown "self-destructive," arguing this will hurt the Chinese economy and create a major rift between China and the rest of the world.

10. Foreign Businesses Facing Unprecedented Legal and Regulatory Problems

Legal, regulatory, and business environments for foreign businesses in China are deteriorating rapidly in China.

GlaxoSmithKline (GSK), Volkswagen, Chrysler, Mead Johnson, Samsung, Johnson & Johnson, and other companies have been hit with multimillion-dollar fines this year. A dozen Japanese auto-parts makers were found guilty of price fixing and received record-breaking fines (USD $201 million). The offices of Microsoft, Daimler, and Qualcomm were raided as part of an investigation of monopolies. Apple was accused of violating state secrecy laws. China is also expanding efforts to rein in what authorities say is tax evasion by foreign companies.

The most representative is the GSK case: a Chinese court in September imposed a fine of nearly $500 million on the British pharmaceutical giant GlaxoSmithKline for bribery; five of the company's managers, including its former top China executive, were convicted of bribery-related charges and received suspended prison sentences. Kickbacks, in which pharmaceutical companies bribe doctors to prescribe their drugs, are a common practice in China, yet domestic pharmaceuticals are not facing similar scrutiny by authorities.

Moreover, foreign businesses have complained they have been targeted disproportionally by opaque antitrust, tax, and state secrecy laws and regulations. For example, The Wall Street Journal recently reported on an investigation by the National Development and Reform Commission into alleged violations of China's antimonopoly statutes by microchip powerhouse Qualcomm. Qualcomm, which makes the microchips that are used in many smartphones, fell under suspicion of the Chinese government because of the way in which it collects royalties on its chips. According to The Wall Street Journal, Qualcomm is expected to pay $975 million in fines and make minor changes with how it collects royalties.

Panasonic and several major Japanese electronics manufacturers have closed their China factories or suspended operations.

2015 Predictions

1. Total financial and tax reform measures announced in 2014 included auditing local government debts (more than 3 trillion USD), reforming budget management, more aggressive tax collection, and reforming state-owned-enterprises. These measures, if implemented, would be instrumental in reshaping China's economy in a healthy way. The State Council is doing a nationwide audit of local debts and imposing debt limits to avoid a potential financial crisis, which could be triggered by local government debts.

2. China's outbound investment will continue to soar, surpassing inbound investment for the first time in the coming year. The Chinese government has significantly loosened the restrictions on outbound investment and Chinese state-owned-enterprises are aggressively acquiring foreign businesses.

3. There will be continued rapid growth of patent filing in China. China patent applications already account for 32.1% of the global total applications.

4. More regulations and measures will be announced to deal with the worsened physical living environment, namely air and water pollution and food safety.

5. The Central Disciplinary Committee of the CPC will continue to drive the anti-corruption campaign and use the extralegal "*shuanggui*" measures to detain and interrogate suspects. The Central Disciplinary Committee may expand its territory outside the CPC to non-Party members.

6. The judicial reform measures announced last year will be implemented. The Supreme People's Court will take some remedial measures to continue to correct the wrongful convictions in the past decade.

7. A series of measures will be implemented by authorities to improve police performance and public approval in the wake of corruption scandals and a string of high-profile wrongful convictions.

8. The Chinese authorities are determined to build an entirely closed network in China, which means continuing to tighten control on the Internet.

9. The government will continue to tighten its control in academia, the arts, and entertainment. Censorship and monitoring of publications and media will be expanded to classrooms. Academics, scholars, and intellectuals will be subject to heightened scrutiny by the authorities.

10. From compliance and licensing to labor and land costs, foreign business will continue to face a complex and unpredictable environment in which to do business in and with China.

2015 – 2016[*]

2015 Reviews

1. Anti- Corruption Campaign

Last year saw its third year of an anti-corruption campaign targeting senior members of the Communist Party of China (CPC): government, military, and state-owned company officials. More than 29,000 Communist Party officials have been investigated and disciplined, including Zhou Yongkang, Chair of the CPC Central Political and Law Committee, Ling Jihua, Chief of Staff to former President Hu Jintao, and Guo Boxiong, Vice-Chairman of the CPC Central Military Commission and one of the top military commanders of the Chinese army.

2. National Security Law

On July 1, 2015, the Standing Committee of National People's Congress promulgated the National Security Law of the People's Republic of China. The law includes an expansive definition of "national security" that outlaws threats to China's government, sovereignty and national unity as well as its economy, society, and cyber and space interests. The new law is troublingly vague and touches nearly every aspect of public life in China.

3. Counter-Terrorism Law

The Standing Committee of National People's Congress passed the Counter-Terrorism Law on December 27, 2015.

---

[*]This report, co-authored with Christopher Luehr, reviews the state of law in China in 2015. It originally appeared in Legal Current on February 10th, 2016.

Critics claim the law employs a recklessly broad definition of terrorism, gives the government new censorship powers and authorizes state access to sensitive commercial data. Notably, the anti-terrorism law also includes a requirement that telecommunication and Internet service providers "shall provide technical interfaces, decryption and other technical support and assistance to public security and state security agencies."

4. End of the One-Child Policy

In October, the CPC reversed its decades-long one-child policy by announcing that all couples are now allowed to have two children. The policy change intends to balance population development and address the challenge of an ageing population. The proposal must be approved by the National People's Congress before it is enacted.

Also, President Xi Jinping announced that China will provide nearly 13 million unregistered citizens, mainly illegally-born second children or "underground children," with household registration permits or "hukou," a crucial document that entitles Chinese citizens to government benefits such as medical insurance and education.

5. Criminal Law Amendment 9

In August, the National People's Congress Standing Committee adopted amendments to the Criminal Law and removed the death penalty for nine crimes, including smuggling weapons, counterfeiting currency and fabricating rumors to mislead others during wartime. The new law adds crimes related to cyber security, enhances protection of citizen's personal information and assigns network security duties to Internet service providers. Counterfeiting passports, social security cards and driver's licenses, organizing cheating on exams and bringing civil litigation based on fabricated facts for illegitimate interests are now listed as crimes under the new law.

The revised law also adds several items intended to crack down on terrorism. Those promoting terrorism and extremism by producing and distributing related materials, releasing information, and inciting terror in-person or through audio, video, or information networks will face more than five years in prison in serious cases. Those who instigate violent terror activities will also face the same punishment.

6. Public Security Reform

The CPC began public security reform in 2015 with a new plan that aims to improve the country's security system by instituting a social credit system that will be set up for citizens based on their ID number. The new plan also states that the system used for international manhunts for those who break the law and the procedures for their repatriation and extradition will be improved.

Most importantly, however, investigators will take life-long responsibility for the cases they investigate. The heightened accountability aims to curb the corruption and abuse of power exposed in recent investigations into the Ministry of Public Security during the Zhou Yongkang era.

7. Crackdown on lawyers and civil rights activists

More than 300 Chinese civil rights lawyers and activists have been targeted by police in an unprecedented nationwide crackdown that began in July. Civil rights lawyers, along with "underground" family churches not registered with the authorities, political dissidents, public liberal intellectuals, and citizen petitioners have been targeted since 2012. As of January 2016, more than 30 lawyers and activists are still in custody and have been charged with criminal offenses.

8. The Case of Pu Zhiqiang

Pu Zhiqiang, the most respected and outspoken civil rights lawyer in China, was taken into custody in May 2014 after he attended a private gathering to commemorate the 1989 Tiananmen tragedy. After 19 months in custody, he was finally charged with "picking quarrels and provoking trouble" and "inciting ethnic hatred," and found guilty after a three-hour "trial" on December 22. Pu was sentenced to a three-year suspended prison sentence and released to "residential surveillance." Pu also will lose his attorney license.

9. The Case of Gao Yu

In April, 2015, Beijing's high court convicted journalist Gao Yu of leaking state secrets and sentenced her to seven years in prison. The authorities accused Gao based on the transmission of an internal document of the Communist Party of China, even though the same document had already been posted online. Eventually Gao's sentence was reduced to five years and she was released on medical parole, but her conviction stands.

10. The Cases of H.K. Booksellers

Five staff members of Causeway Bay Books, an independent bookstore, went missing from October to December 2015 in response to the firm's publication of books highly critical of Chinese leaders. While three of them disappeared from mainland China, one disappeared from Thailand, and another from Hong Kong. Also, two of the staff members are not Chinese citizens: Gui Minhai is a Swedish citizen and Lee Bo is a British citizen. Chinese authorities have admitted they are currently in Chinese custody.

2016 Predictions

1. Anti-corruption Campaign

The Anti-Corruption Campaign will slow down. China's institutionalized corruption and abuse of power are caused by the monopoly of political power and the lack of an independent judiciary. As long as the Communist Party is in total control of all aspect of social life and cannot be held accountable for any wrongdoings, the epidemic corruption cannot be adequately addressed.

2. Cyberspace Sovereignty

Chinese officials recently drafted a new Cybersecurity Law setting out a framework for China's cybersecurity regime and responding to the needs set out in the National Security Law to ensure "safe and controllable" systems and data security. Despite the fact that many internationally popular websites, including YouTube, Facebook, and Twitter remain blocked by the "Great Firewall," more foreign companies are accepting the arguments and demands of the Chinese authority regarding China's "cyber sovereignty" in order to gain access to the large and attractive Chinese market.

3. Outbound Investment

Chinese companies will continue to make foreign investments and acquisitions not only in real estate and manufacturing sectors, but also in the realm of film and media in an expanded employment of "soft power." For example, the Alibaba Group recently acquired The South China Morning

Post; the Wanda Group purchased Hollywood studio Legendary Entertainment; and Visual China Group acquired Corbis. These Chinese "cultural takeover" maneuvers are part of the "Grand Foreign Propaganda" strategy to present foreign audiences with a positive image of China.

4. Borderless Chinese Law Enforcement

Absent pressure and action from foreign powers, the exercise of Chinese police control on perceived dissidents, including non-Chinese nationals, outside of mainland China will continue.

5. Regulating the Financial Market

More regulations will be promulgated to deal with serious financial market issues, including interest rates, RMB devaluation, capital outflows, stock market fluctuation, widespread financial Ponzi schemes, etc. While these measures may provide temporary improvements, they skirt the deeper structural defects of the Chinese financial system.

6. SOEs Reform

Reformation of state-owned-enterprises (SOEs) will continue in an attempt to help stop the decline of the Chinese economy. The change will be slow and the Chinese government and CPC will continue to be heavily involved with these companies, but SOE structure and practice will likely transform in the face of growing economic pressure.

7. Hukou Reform

Household registration permits, or "hukou," policies will relax and allow for greater freedom of movement for residents between rural and urban locations.

8. Patch Measures on Air Quality

Instead of broad and sweeping reforms, the government will continue to employ temporary, but largely insufficient, patch measures to deal with air pollution, food safely, drug safety and hazardous materials.

9. Regulating Foreign NGOs

Greater regulations, including a new law, will be placed on NGOs operating in China, with particular restrictions imposed on foreign NGOs and their employees.

10. Foreign Divestment

Some major foreign-owned companies will begin divesting in China and moving operations outside of the country. This will occur in response to increasing frustrations with unclear laws, inconsistent regulatory interpretation, and rising labor costs.

2016 – 2017[*]

2016 Reviews

1. One-Child Policy Officially Ended

On January 1, 2016, China's notorious one-child policy officially ended. The controversial policy was introduced in 1979 and led to human rights abuses in its implementation and long-ranging, disastrous social consequences in gender

---

*This report, co-authored with Vivian Wu, reviews the state of law in China in 2016. It originally appeared in Legal Current on March 2nd, 2017.

inequality and labor shortages. Although families will still require government-issued birth permits, or face the sanction of forced abortion, couples in China can now request to have two children. But the latest year-end statistics from Chinese media proved no signs of an immediate increase in the birth of newborns. Despite national efforts to increase birthrates, more and more middle-class couples in urban areas expressed no intention to have a second child due to continued cost-of-living increases, a poor outlook for education and medical care resources, and the deterioration of the natural environment.

2. The Establishment of "Jian Cha Wei" and Party Discipline

Last November, the Communist Party of China (CPC) announced the establishment of "Monitoring/Supervisory Commissions" ("Jian Cha Wei") in selected municipalities and provinces, specifically Beijing, Shanxi and Zhejiang. The CPC claimed this move was "an important political reform" aimed at strengthening supervision of administrative, party and government officials. Optimistic observers considered the new commission with its centralized powers might curb corruption and improve transparency with a system similar to the Independent Commission Against Corruption (ICAC) in Hong Kong, perhaps paving the way for political reform. But wary critics criticized that without the authority to supervise the party independently, the measure would merely consolidate CPC's grip of power and extend the longevity of one-party rule.

3. Foreign NGO Law

On April 28 2016, the National People's Congress passed the Law on Administration of Activities of Overseas

Nongovernmental Organizations in the Mainland of China (commonly referred to as the "Overseas NGO Law"). The law was met with wide skepticism and criticism.

The law, which took effect on Jan. 1, will require that international NGOs, foundations and non-profit institutes present in China to register with the government. The new law will impact more than 7,000 organizations that up to this point have been operating in the country without officially-approved registration for decades due to the difficulty of acquiring the license.

With a claim to clean up the gray space and better order overseas organizations' activities, the vague instruction of the new law, particularly measures to be implemented by public security authorities, are a source of concern. Critics describe it as a concrete measure for tightened control through coercive orders. For example, a foreign NGO is required to affiliate with a local state organ before applying for registration, regularly report the source of grants and finance income, and be subject to the supervision of daily activities from the local police, etc. The new law also lists the scope of permitted activities and marks particular business (the rule of law, human rights and labor rights protections, etc.) that may not be tolerated.

4. Cyber Security Law

Despite criticisms, the National People's Congress passed the new Cyber Security Law on November 7, 2016. As the first national law designed to combat hacking, information stealing, cyber fraud, and other crimes on the Internet, it contains articles that require companies and individuals, including foreign entities doing business in China, to provide the Chinese government with potentially sensitive information related to their network infrastructure and software. IT service providers and operators will also be asked to assist with mandatory testing and certification of computer equipment, and cooperate with government investigators by providing full access to their data in the cases that may involve national security and cyber crimes. The law will take effect in June.

5. Nie Shubin Exoneration

In a rare move to correct false and erroneous cases, The Supreme People's Court, the highest court in China, exonerated Nie Shubin, a 20-year-old villager executed by Hebei Higher Court, for raping and murdering a woman in 1995. Ten years after Nie was executed, however, Chinese media disclosed that Henan police had arrested Wang Shujin, a farmer who confessed to the rape and murder of five women in Hebei, including the victim in the Nie Shubin case. Nie's family, with the support of journalists and lawyers, have appealed for a new hearing in Nie's case since 2005, but efforts were hindered by bureaucracy and local protection by court and police authorities. The Supreme People's Court made its exoneration decision in November and supported a request by Nie's family for state compensation, but no further investigation into the responsible parties or examination into allegations of abusive interrogation or negligence by police was allowed.

6. Death of Wei Zexi and a Condemnation of Baidu

In April 2016, Wei Zexi, a 21-year-old student from Shaanxi province, died after receiving a failed experimental treatment for rare cancer at a Beijing hospital.

Before his death in 2014, Wei was diagnosed with synovial sarcoma, and after receiving unsuccessful radiation and chemotherapy treatments, Wei learned of an alternative cancer treatment available at the Second Hospital of the

Beijing Armed Police Corps, a state military-run hospital, on the Chinese search site Baidu. Wei went through four so called "immunotherapy" treatments at the hospital, which cost his family 200,000 Yuan (or $32,116). But all treatments failed, and Wei died two years after his initial diagnosis.

Prior to his death, Wei accused Baidu of promoting false medical information, denouncing the hospital for claiming high success rates for the treatment. Some Beijing journalists read Wei's posts and launched a social media campaign to condemn Baidu and its notorious manipulation of search results driven by commercial payments from illegal medical service providers. Amid critical coverage on state media, The Chinese Internet Administration Bureau also initiated an investigation of Baidu, which led stock prices for the search firm to drop significantly.

7. Lei Yang Case

Lei Yang was a young Beijing-based environmentalist who was found dead in May 2016 while under the custody of Beijing Police in Changping District just hours after he left home for an airport pick up. Witnesses later shared footage with the media and online of Lei in a brutal altercation with five plainclothes police officers who suspected him of soliciting workers for sex at a foot massage parlor. Upon his death, police notified Lei's family that he had died of a heart attack at the police station earlier that night.

The suspicious death of Lei, who was also a father to a newborn and graduate from the renowned Renmin University, trended on social media after his schoolmates publicized the details of his case.

The case also triggered a public outcry by those in the urban middle classes for an investigation into police violence and expanding police powers. In late December

2016, five law enforcement officers involved in the death of Lei Yang were released without trial after being detained for months. Prosecutors found these officers broke the law with an inappropriate use of force, delaying medical care and lying about Lei's death. His widow claimed to accept government compensation (guessed to be a record amount) and dropped litigation amid tremendous pressure. In the end, Lei's supporters regarded the outcome as a failure of political movement.

8. HK Constitution Article 104

In November 2016, China's top legislators adopted an interpretation of Article 104 of the Basic Law of the Hong Kong Special Administrative Region (SAR) by a unanimous vote. The article stipulates: "When assuming office, the chief executive, principal officials, members of the executive council and of the legislative council, judges of courts at all levels and other members of the judiciary in the Hong Kong Special Administrative Region must, in accordance with law, swear to uphold the Basic Law of the Hong Kong Special Administrative Region of the People's Republic of China and swear allegiance to the Hong Kong Special Administrative Region of the People's Republic of China."

This pledge of allegiance is not only the legal content which must be included in the oath prescribed by the Article, but also the legal requirements and preconditions for standing for election. Before assuming office, public officials, including law makers, must make their pledge of allegiance "sincerely and solemnly" and "accurately and completely," and speak these words publically as a legal prerequisite. The interpretation came in response to a controversy that erupted last October after two pro-independence lawmakers in Hong Kong pledged allegiance to a

"Hong Kong nation" and referred to China as "Chee-na," a
derogatory pronunciation of "China" used by the Japanese
during the WWII. The officials also displayed a banner that
read "Hong Kong is not China," an action that escalated
an already-intense political divide in Hong Kong between
pro-democracy forces and Beijing central government.
These two lawmakers were eventually disqualified.

9. Crackdown on Lawyers and Activists, Jiang Tianyong and Others

A crackdown on human rights lawyers and activists
that began in July 2015 reached a peak in 2016, with some
lawyers sentenced to stay behind bars for subversion or
inciting subversion. Among those detained late last year
was Jiang Tianyong, a 45-year-old Christian lawyer, had
been arrested several times before for offering legal aid to
practitioners of Falun Gong, a banned cult in China. Jiang
had also run afoul of authorities for aiding the wives of
lawyers arrested in the so-called "709 Crackdown," which
refers to the date, July 9, 2015, when many human right
activists were arrested, appealing for fair judicial processes
for some 250 lawyers detained nationwide in a sweep by
authorities to rein-in human rights lawyers. Chinese police
confirmed the detention of Jiang in mid-December of last
year, nearly a month after his family reported his disappearance under mysterious circumstances and called for
international attention.

10. Execution of Jia Jinglong

Jia Jinglong, a farmer from Hebei province, was executed after the Supreme Court believed he had murdered

a village party chief with a nail gun. The Jia Jinglong case sparked public outcry, and the man became a symbol of injustice faced by the poor and needy who dared to defy authorities.

The case began when village authorities demolished Jia Jinglong's newly furnished home just 18 days before his wedding to make way for a new development project. Unfortunately, the episode led his fiancée to call off the wedding. Soon after, in February 2015, Jia Jinglong plotted his revenge and vowed to kill the village chief whom he blamed for the destruction of his home and planned marriage.

The Supreme Court reviewed the death penalty ruling leveled by provincial courts and approved the sentence, explaining that Jia Jinglong had used extreme measures that caused severe public fear. The execution was processed secretly amid public outcry and ongoing questions of whether the Chinese judicial system could safeguard basic rights of the lower class.

11. Foreign Investment Laws Revisions

On September 3, 2016, the Standing Committee of the National People's Congress passed the most significant revision of four laws regulating foreign investments in China, namely the Law on Wholly Foreign-Owned Enterprises, the Law on Sino-Foreign Equity Joint Ventures, the Law on Sino-Foreign Contractual Joint Ventures, and the Law on the Protection of Investment of Compatriots from Taiwan ("Revisions"). On the same day, the Ministry of Commerce ("MOFCOM") issued the Interim Measures for Record-Filing Administration for Establishment of and Changes to Foreign-Investment Enterprises ("Record-Filing Draft").

The Revisions and Record-Filing Draft, which took effect one month later in October, lifted previous requirements for administrative approvals on foreign, Hong Kong and Taiwanese investors. Rather, investors setting up ventures in the regulated areas do not need to get approvals and can go through a record filing system at the local regulatory administration. This is a major departure from previous regulations and signals an effort to create a more foreign-friendly business environment.

2017 Predictions

1. China faces the daunting task of controlling a rapid capital outflow to keep the Chinese currency stable, and at the same time creating an investment climate conducive to foreign investment. Investors can expect relaxed bureaucratic procedures and incentives (tax and residency) to further inbound foreign investment.

2. Chinese authority will implement limited police reform to address the widespread public concern over police brutality and abuse of power. The CPC has promised standardized law enforcement procedures to restore public confidence.

3. The CPC will continue its anti-corruption campaign as sentences for life imprisonment without parole and executions may becoming more common in high profile corruption cases.

4. The CPC will tighten its control over the judiciary. In January, Chief Justice Zhou, the head of the Supreme People's Court of China, said in a speech to legal officials in Beijing: "We should resolutely resist erroneous influence from the West: 'constitutional democracy,' 'separation of

powers' and 'independence of the judiciary.'" The legal system will remain an integral part of the CPC administrative system and a tool for the CPC to implement party policies.

5. Since efforts to crackdown on civil rights lawyers and activists began in earnest in July 2015, the campaign aimed to silence and punish civil rights lawyers will continue. The authority views the approach utilized by legal professionals to defend migrant laborers, ethnic and religious minorities, victims of land grabs, and political dissidents as subversive.

6. In the second part of 2017, the 19th National Congress of the Communist Party will be held in Beijing, which is the most important political event in the nation under Xi Jinping administration.

7. The year of 2017 also marks the 60th anniversary of the Anti-Rightist Campaign instigated by Mao Zedong in 1957. The Anti-Rightist Campaign is the largest and one of the most merciless campaigns in China aimed at purging dissent and disobedience. The Anti-Rightist Campaign saw the political persecution of an estimated 550,000 intellectuals.

8. Signs have been surfing that the central authorities are making extreme efforts to maintain the stability of its control over the increasingly divided Chinese society amid intensified political environment and slow down GDP growth.

Book Reviews

Legal Research in American Law, by Chang Wang, China University of Political Science and Law Press, 2014.

First Bilingual Legal Research Book Published in China[*]

China University of Political Science and Law Press, a leading legal publisher in China, just published a bilingual (English and Chinese) legal research textbook based on West's Analysis of American Law/Key Number System and WestlawNext. This 700-page textbook is the first bilingual textbook of legal research in American law. The author, Chang Wang, is the Chief Research and Academic Officer at Thomson Reuters. He is a graduate of the University of Minnesota Law School, where he "found and read the law," and as such, he dedicated the book to the school (and to Thomson Reuters). Wang is the second Chinese national ever elected to the prestigious American Law Institute (ALI) and holds associate and adjunct professorships at six universities in the U.S., China, Italy, and Switzerland.

Rick King, chief operating officer, Technology, at Thomson Reuters, and Joan Howland, Roger F. Noreen professor of Law and associate dean for Information & Technology at the University of Minnesota Law School, authored forewords. Fred Gordon, former editor-in-chief, U.S. Legal Publications of Thomson Reuters, authored an important introduction.

---

*This book review, authored by Susan Martin, first appeared on Legal Current on September 9, 2014. © Thomson Reuters

The book consists of three parts:

1) A monograph on legal research in American law.

2) Annotated materials of selected U.S. legal documents: primary authorities such as the U.S. Constitution, Constitution of Minnesota, federal statute, federal regulations, federal procedural rules, leading U.S. Supreme Court cases, as well as representative secondary authorities such as American Jurisprudence, Corpus Juris Secundum, Black's Law Dictionary, Key Number Digest, and USCA (most of them are Thomson Reuters proprietary information and available on WestlawNext).

3) Legal Information Tools and Reports: United States Code, Federal Judicial Circuits and Federal District Courts, National Reporter System, West Outline of the Law, West Key Number System, U.S. Supreme Court Review, Minnesota Supreme Court Review, American Law Institute, and the history of West Publishing.

This is the companion book to an upper-level law school course, "Legal Research in American Law: The Westlaw Approach," taught by Wang at top law schools in the U.S., China, and Europe. His lectures and training sessions on WestlawNext have also been viewed widely online on Chaoxing Academic Videos, a premier online learning provider in China. Simultaneously to the publication of the textbook, Erya Education, another leading online learning platform, launched a 36-hour WestlawNext training course taught by Wang.

Upon the launching of Wang's online course and the publication of the textbook, Che Hu, head of the Legal business of Thomson Reuters Global Growth and Operations, China, said: "Legal research is the foundation of the study of law, and Chang Wang's online course is one of the best I have seen for this important topic. This online course and textbook will also help Chinese law students better understand how to use Westlaw and strengthen Thomson Reuters market position in academic institutions and beyond."

Dean Joan Howland praised the book: "Comprehensive in scope and concise in presentation, Chang Wang's book is an invaluable addition to the broader body of literature on legal research in American law. One of the many strengths of this book is the roadmap it provides lawyers and students of how to develop an efficient research strategy that ensures a comprehensive, cost-effective result. This book provides lawyers, faculty, and students with the foundation and tools needed to not simply succeed, but to excel."

The book is ranked number five on Amazon China's best-selling foreign law books list and has been adopted by a number of top law schools in China as the official text-book on legal research.

"With my lectures and this new volume, Thomson Reuters offers Chinese legal professionals and law students a comprehensive overview of the American legal information and the best way to find the law," said Wang. "I firmly believe, under the wise leadership of Mr. David Liu and Mr. Che Hu, Thomson Reuters China Legal business will see more fruitful and productive collaborations with Chinese judiciary and the legal community in the coming days."

Inside China's Legal System: A New Legal Treatise on Chinese Law*

Thomson Reuters recently received international acknowledgement for a legal treatise on Chinese law authored by two employees. The 350-page volume — *Inside China's Legal System* — is a comprehensive overview of the Chinese legal system. The book is co-authored by Chang Wang, chief research and academic officer, and Nathan Madson, who previously worked for Findlaw until August 2014, when he was admitted with a full scholarship to New York University as a PhD candidate in Anthropology.

The book has been adopted by a number of law schools in the US and in Europe — the University of Minnesota, William Mitchell College of Law, the University of Bern, the University of Lucerne, and the University of Vienna — as the official textbook on Chinese law. The book has also received rave reviews on Amazon and Barnes & Noble.

The book discusses the development of legal discourse and the ever increasing influence of Western jurisprudence in contemporary China through comparative law. It begins with a study of the legal traditions and core assumptions underlying the current role of law in China, followed by a comparative analysis of the respective legal conventions and beliefs in China and the West. The book examines Western, especially American, influences in specific areas of Chinese

---

*This book review, authored by Susan Martin, first appeared on Legal Current on January 7, 2015. © Thomson Reuters

law, and the role US jurisprudence has played and could play in the "modernization" of the Chinese legal system. Attention is paid to cross-cultural misunderstandings and misinterpretations, as well as the interaction between culture and law.

There are three main parts to the book:

1) Historical views: Starting with the competing schools of legal thought — Confucianism and Legalism — the authors move from the legal systems of imperial China to the Republic of China and finally the People's Republic of China. Part I ends with a discussion of the growing influence the West has had on China's current legal structure.

2) The players: Individuals, governmental bodies and bureaucracies that have a prominent role in China's legal system are examined. It is not just laws that compose the legal system of the PRC, but also the courts and judges who explain what the laws mean. Moreover, lawyers, police and the secret police all play an important role in China's legal system.

3) Case studies: Civil, criminal and administrative laws are described through case studies. In addition to describing important selections from these three bodies of law, the authors look at how the laws have been implemented. Though China is not a common law system, and thus does not follow case precedent, the case studies still give the reader a broader understanding of the Chinese legal system than she would gain by solely reading statutes.

"In the case of China, the facts, studies and research support two extremes: the imminent collapse of the CPC and the PRC as a whole, or that the PRC will one day take the leading role in the global economy and serve as a pre-eminent world power," said Wang and Madson. "Yet there is also empirical evidence and sound analyses that support a variety of other outcomes."

Wang and Madson continued: "This book, however, offers the reader a look inside the Chinese legal system, from its innermost workings to the larger themes surrounding the rule of law. While we hope to provide as complete a picture of the legal system as possible, the best that any legal scholar or scholar of China can do is present the facts and an interpretation of those facts. We hope that this book helps us to understand China and ourselves a little better."

First Chinese-Language Book About Minnesota Published by Thomson Reuters[*]

New Tales of the Twin Cities: The History, Law, and Culture of Minnesota, the first Chinese-language book about Minnesota, was just published by Thomson Reuters. The book was authored by Chang Wang, chief research and academic officer at Thomson Reuters and an attorney. Wang is a native of Beijing, a graduate of the University of Minnesota Law School, and a recipient of the "China 100 Distinguished Chinese Alumni Award" from the University of Minnesota.

Throughout this book, Wang intends to give Chinese residents, students, and visitors a comprehensive overview and in-depth analysis of Minnesota's history, law, and culture. Rick King, COO, Technology at Thomson Reuters and a transplant to Minnesota, as well as Fred Gordon, editor-in-chief emeritus of US Legal Publications at Thomson Reuters and a native Minnesotan, authored forewords and shared their insights.

---

*This book review, authored by Susan Martin, first appeared on Legal Current on November 25, 2014. © Thomson Reuters

Starting with a 30-page brief history of Minnesota, Wang wrote about a wide range of topics such as Minnesota's judicial system, Minnesota Supreme Court cases, West Publishing, the University of Minnesota, immigrants in Minnesota, science and technology in Minnesota, and the "Best of the Twin Cities." He also divulges his top 10 Minnesota pleasures, a list of charming and simple activities easily taken for granted by native Minnesotans: browsing used bookstores, walking around the Cities' lakes, listening to Minnesota Public Radio, and watching a Twins game at Target Field, among others.

The book is dedicated "To all the early settlers of the Land of 10,000 Lakes, and to all the strong, good-looking, and above-average Minnesotans who live there today." A special tribute to Minnesotan author Garrison Keillor and A Prairie Home Companion.

This book was also selected as one of the "Books: Winter Reading" by *Minnesota Magazine*.

First bilingual US Constitutional Law textbook by Chang Wang published in China[*]

In January, 2017, China University of Political Science and Law Press, a leading legal publisher in China, published a bilingual (English and Chinese) U.S. Constitutional Law textbook based on West's Analysis of American Law/Key Number System. "Constitutional Law: Lectures, Cases, and

---

[*]This book review, authored by Elaine Dunn, was originally published in the May, 2017 issue of *China Insight*. © Thomson Reuters

Resources" is a two-volume, 1200-page text and the first bilingual textbook of U.S. Constitutional law. The author, Chang Wang, is a regular contributor to China Insight and chief researcher at Thomson Reuters.

"Constitutional Law" is a sequel to the first bilingual legal research book on American law — "Legal Research in American Law," also authored by Wang and published by China University of Political Science and Law Press in 2014.

The new book on U.S. constitutional law is dedicated to "Chinese lawyers," while "Legal Research in American Law" is dedicated to "The University of Minnesota and Thomson Reuters," where the author "found and read the law."

Dr. Peter Warwick, executive vice president and chief people officer of Thomson Reuters authored a foreword on Magna Carta and the rule of law. Warwick analyzed the influence of Magna Carta and pointed out that the Magna Carta provided the basis for the very idea of the rule of law.

Constitutional Law: Lectures, Cases, and Resources, by Chang Wang, China University of Political Science and Law Press, 2016.

Vance Opperman, president of West Publishing Company (1993-1996) and member of the board of directors, Thomson Reuters and lead independent director, authored an introductory foreword for the book. Opperman is a prominent supporter of the rule of law and a stellar representative of the legendary West Publishing. Opperman's introduction relates to the development of the Key Number System and the common law development of the decisional law in the United States.

This book is another fruit of the strategic partnership between Thomson Reuters, who provides professionals with the intelligence, technology and human expertise they need to find trusted answers, and China University of Political Science and Law (CUPL), the world's largest law university in terms of enrollment. The Thomson Reuters–CUPL strategic partnership was initiated in 2007 during CUPL's official visit to Thomson Reuters, when Chinese Congressman Xu Xianming, president of CUPL, and Rick King, executive vice president and chief information officer of Thomson Reuters agreed on the partnership to promote global rule of law and cross-cultural legal information sharing.

Upon the publication of the book, King commented: "China and Constitutional Law? These two topics collide in a legal thriller by a Thomson Reuters man."

Wang's new book consists of three parts: 1) Wang's 25 lectures on constitutional law; 2) Annotated case briefs of 39 U.S. Supreme Court cases; 3) Resources to research and study U.S. Constitutional Law: Key Number System: 92 Constitutional Law; Constitutional Law Research Guide; Constitutional Law Glossary; bibliographies of Scholastic Books in English Language on constitutional law and scholastic books in Chinese Language on constitutional lawas well as a list of films and documentaries about Constitutional Law.

The book also includes Chinese translations of Magna Carta and the U. S. Constitution, and, for the first time, translations of the Constitution of the Commonwealth of Massachusetts (the oldest constitution in the U.S.) and the Constitution of the State of Minnesota.

In the book, Wang pointed out: "The story of West Publishing parallels the story of American law, and these two stories have become one, inspiring jurists and citizens globally. It is amazing to read the story of the law—from

Magna Carta to the U.S. Constitution to the Key Number System — and to learn how the American law has become the role model of the legal systems of so many countries in the world."

Thomas S. Kim, managing director, Thomson Reuters China, welcomes the publication. "This first bilingual textbook on U.S. Constitutional Law based on West's Key Number System will help Chinese lawyers and law students better understand the principles of governance in the United States and reinforce Thomson Reuters thought leadership in Chinese academic and legal communities. Thomson Reuters is committed to contributing to the ongoing development of the rule of law in China. Our legal products and services provide trusted answers to legal professionals, and meet the needs of a growing nation and its ever more complex economic and social realities." Kim said.

Chang Wang (second from right) and his students presented a copy of Constitutional Law: Lectures, Cases, and Resources to Chief Justice Lorie Gildea of the Supreme Court of Minnesota (center, seated).

The Luckiest Generations in the U.S. and in China: the Baby Boomers and the Generation '89*

Rick King and Chang Wang

(China Insight Editor's Note) Both Rick King and Chang Wang consider themselves lucky, and the luckiness is generational. King, a "baby boomer" who was born in California and grew up in Massachusetts, believes overall, his generation is better off than his parents' and his children's; Wang, originally from Beijing, belongs to "Generation '89" in China, even believes his generation is the luckiest in Chinese history since 1842.

China Insight invites King and Wang to author a conversational style essay to compare the lives and the key characteristics of the "baby boomers" in the U.S. and the "Generation '89" in China.

Defining Generations

King: I am part of the so-called baby-boomer generation, born between the end of WWII and up to around 1964. Coming out of the war and being born in the 1950s, the boomers experienced no world war, a booming economy, and the industrialization of the United States, which was pretty significant at the time. People had come back

---

*This four-part series of conversations first appeared in the April–August issues of *China Insight*. The first of this four-part series defines who the boomer and Generation '89 are in the U.S. and China respectively. The subsequent parts will describe, contrast and compare the various economic and societal factors that impact and shape the two groups in their respective countries.

from the war; companies were expanding, and the
wartime footing turned into a really robust economy for
quite a while. It's a large group of people seeing rapid
expansion of housing, and of suburbs containing housing
and schools.

As a child, you were rarely alone. It seemed that the
world was geared toward children, spurred by parents
who had been gone during the wartime. The parents'
time was a lot tougher because they were the children of
the war and children of the depression. They tended to
be conservative and frugal, but our generation began to
experience a lot bigger world, though not the broadest part
of the world.

During the early 50s, the Korean War occurred,
although it was not a war in the sense of WWII. It was
more of what the historians called a "policing activity."
From the United States' point of view, the United States
was trying to prevent the
spread of certain lifestyle,
ideology, and governmen-
tal form, similar to that of
the Soviet Union and with
which we did not agree.
So the Korean War was
different, in that we were

not all involved in the war. This kind of war was "police
action," and it was quite limited, so that the whole U.S.
economy was not thrown behind it. The Korean Conflict
was unpopular in some areas because of the "police
action" nature. Even people coming from the war did
not show the same commitment as we had seen in WWI
and WWII.

One defining moment for my group was the Vietnam
War, which, again, was not a war that involved everybody

and did not throw the whole economy behind it. It was worse than the Korean War in the sense that the whole country was not fully behind the people who participated in the war, as evidenced by widespread social unrest. That unrest was very prevalent when I went to high school. By the time I went to college, the draft had ended and the war had ended. But the Vietnam War was a very defining moment in my middle school and high school years.

Then why, given these events, making things good for my generation? Because even though the country was in conflicts, not the entire country was involved in the conflicts. To most people, it was a booming economy that invited participation. You were not much impacted by those wars. You saw the news, but not everybody was participating in the wars. For some, it was a time of some stability; of course, for those in the war, it was not a good time at all. But there were many ways for people to defer their commitment to the war. I was too young then. I had a draft card, but I was not selected to go. When I went to college, the war was pretty much done. The focus of my generation was on the big growing country. Despite all those conflicts, we did not have all these terrorist organizations around at that time.

When I think about my son and daughter, who are in their early 30s, for them and their children, the world has a whole new set of conflicts, totally different from those before. Somewhere between my generation and my children's' generation, people have had to learn new ways to get on an airplane. They have to worry about terrorists who do not hesitate to take the life of children. It is a whole different level of conflict. Guerrilla warfare is potentially in everybody's neighborhood now. The generations after mine learnt that through 9/11. My son was in his late teens at that time. When you think about something like that, if you

compare the levels of security of their generation and mine,
they've had to deal with a very different world. My parents'
generation was involved in WWII, and my kids are involved
in the world full of these scary entities entirely dedicated to
the destruction of the United States, simply because they
do not agree with our ideology. The fear and lack of safety
that the younger generation and their children are experiencing are radically different from what my generation
experienced. Looking at generations between the WWII
and terrorism as we know it today, overall my generation
was much secured. My generation fought two wars half the
world away, but my children are fighting a "war" in their
own towns and cities.

Wang: It makes perfect sense to me to compare generations with the level of security and the sense of security.
FDR proposed four fundamental freedoms that people
"everywhere in the world" ought to enjoy: freedom of
speech; freedom of worship; freedom from want; and freedom from fear.

Now let's look at China: Modern China started in 1842,
the end of the First Opium War. Since then, almost every
single generation witnessed war, famine, natural disaster,
political terror, one after another, enduring endless misery
and suffering.

There is one exception, however, that is the generation
of people born in the urban areas of China between 1962
and 1972—the "Generation '89." This generation was born
at the right time, in the right place, and was provided with
opportunities to thrive and prosper.

We were named "Generation '89" for the time we went
to college: before, during, or after 1989, the end of a short-
lived "Golden Age" of 1980s. The Tiananmen tragedy in
1989 represented the closing of the "Cultural Renaissance"
and political tolerance in China. So my generation has this

shared value system of the 1980s and shared traumatic experience in 1989. Nevertheless, my generation has not experienced war and famine. We cannot say with absolute certainty that there will be no war or famine in our lifetime, particularly in light of the political instability and the environmental crisis in mainland China.

Because of the "Hukou" (Residency Permit) system in China, we have to admit that the lucky ones are mostly from the urban areas of China. Rural residents have far less opportunities than their urban counterparts do. This is a man-made caste system sanctioning discrimination

Tiananmen Square, Beijing, 1989

and exploitation, but I am glad to see Chinese authority is reforming it.

Our generation was born after the Great Famine (1959 – 1961) caused by Mao's disastrous political and economic policy that killed at least 37 million innocent farmers, elders and children. During our childhoods, we had very limited resources — but we didn't starve to death, thanks to food and cloth vouchers issued to urban residents.

A 50 grams grain voucher issued in 1986 by Beijing Municipal Government

Our generation also was born before the implementation of the One Child Policy in 1979. So our

generation has siblings; I have a sister. Almost everybody
in this generation I know has siblings. The One Child Policy
also has caused devastating effects in China, I am very glad
it is over.

Overall, from early education to middle-age healthcare,
in almost all the important life stages our generation, life
has treated us well, and we are extremely grateful.

Education

King: Many people coming
back from the war — the parents
of the "baby boomers" were educated thanks to the G.I. Bill. After
that, the "baby boomers" and their
parents needed to figure out how
to fund a college education. At that
time, our technical high schools
were very strong in skill-build-
ing. Guidance counselors in your
school steered you into a technical
career, meaning you would learn
to be a professional carpenter,
plumber, or other trade worker. Or you would go on to college based on their assessment of your aptitude and interests. Cost of college tuition hadn't exploded yet, but were
already significant. But our parents were ready to sacrifice
to send us to college to make the future better for us.

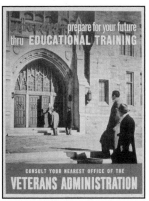

A poster of the G.I. Bill after
the WWII

This was a time that certain government grants started
to show up, to help with educational expenses. There were
need-based grants: e.g., Pell Grants and Stafford Grants,
to help people who did not have the means to pay for a
college education. Universities with strong academic programs also began their own grants. The price of university

continued to escalade during our time. It was a time people were clearly routed toward a career aspiration: either college or the trades. For my children's generation: the expansion of the colleges and schools — two year degrees and four year degrees in college — continued to a great extent, making colleges more and more accessible, but also more unaffordable.

So when you look at school and education, I might say we lived in a good time, though probably not the best time, but definitely better than my children's generation. The G.I. Bill actually continued after the Korean Conflict, still pretty significant.

For my parents' generation, educationally, very few people did anything outside the United States. The United States was a big booming market itself with plenty of opportunities, so people were very much focused on the U.S. My generation began to think about a semester abroad, but most people who did that were in international finance, international relations, or related fields, working for a foreign degree or foreign language. But, generally speaking, my generation was not encouraged to study aboard. The expansion of the United States was so big that people did not spend much time outside. However, for my children's generation, it would be almost unheard of for someone to finish college without at least a semester abroad. These days, living and traveling experiences in foreign countries before graduation are the norm, not the exception. It was a good time, but it was a little late because the global market had already evolved considerably with the expansion of possibilities outside the U.S. A lot of my generation was not trained globally to become the leader of global enterprises. They have to learn on the job and learn to know the rest of the world along the way.

Education-wise, my generation was probably not in the best spot, but counting pluses and minuses and considering the accessibility of college for my generation, the result was very positive.

Wang: Generation'89 did not participate, fortunately, in the Cultural Revolution (1966 -1976) and the "Down to the Countryside Movement" (1968-1978). The Cultural Revolution destroyed China's arts, culture and education. In 1968, Mao declared certain privileged urban youth would be sent to mountainous areas or farming villages to learn from the workers and farmers there. In total, approximately 17 million youth were sent to rural areas as a result of the movement. Many fresh high school graduates, who became known as the *zhiqing* ("Educated Youth," 知青) in China and the "Sent-down" or "Rusticated Youth" abroad, were forced out of the cities and effectively exiled to remote areas of China. Some commentators pity these people, many of whom lost the opportunity to ever attend college. This generation is now in charge of China's political and economic policies. Their overall hostility to the modern principles

One of the freshmen classes at Tsinghua University in Beijing, 1978

of governance and economy probably could be explained by their early experience in the countryside.

China's education system was completely shut down during Mao's Cultural Revolution—and a whole generation before us did not receive education. In 1977, Chinese colleges reopened, so everybody in my generation could have the chance to go to college should they decide to. Most received at least a college education. Graduate school and professional degrees were very popular for my generation. Study abroad was allowed and was common.

From the late 1970s to early 1990s, Chinese universities were basically tuition-free, and with subsidy and scholarship. However, when I decided to study abroad after graduating from Peking University Graduate School, I had to return the college tuition and graduate school tuition, totaling 22,000RMB (2,660 USD) to the Ministry of Education in 2000.

China's higher education became commercialized in 1993, so for the generation after us, almost everybody needs to pay for college.

Employment

King: For my parents' generation, the economy was booming, jobs were readily available. Not everybody was fully employed, but people worked their way out of that. For my generation, the economy was still pretty strong so there weren't a lot of people who did not find a job when they graduated. Generally speaking, the economy was very positive. I actually think it was a good time for jobs.

I grew up in Massachusetts, went to school there, then to college in Vermont, and taught in Vermont for a while, volunteering for a couple of years before that. There were not a lot of desirable job openings in teaching: I wanted to coach and teach in a small school district, which did not have a lot of openings. But then there was a math-teacher opening, and I took it.

Wang: In the 1980s and early 1990s, Chinese universities and colleges took care of job assignments after students' graduation. So a lot of people in my generation did not need to make a lot of effort to search for jobs when they graduated from college.

For the generation after us who went to college after the mid-1990s, job market became very competitive. The unemployment rate skyrocketed, even for college graduates.

If you decide to study abroad, then there will be a different story. I am also very fortunate in that scenario — landing a job with Thomson Reuters.

Housing

King: My generation witnessed a big housing boom. There were lots of differently priced houses. There were not as many different ways to finance a house as today,

Levittown, Long Island, early 1950s

but home ownership was preferred. People would start with an apartment, and then try to buy a house. The only involvement of the government would be certain types of loans, depending on where you lived, there were types of programs to help people with different levels of income.

For many people of my generation, seeing housing prices decline in certain areas was a shock because, in most of our lifetime, housing prices always went up. Buying a house was considered to be "the biggest and most secure investment."

In general, for my generation, housing was booming and purchasing a house was considered a saving tool.

Wang: For my generation, the first residence after you became married was normally a small flat provided by the employer—normally a state-owned-enterprise or government entity. Very few of this kind of flat had an individual bathroom or kitchen, but at least they offered a minimal level of privacy, and it was almost free. You only paid nominal electricity and water charges. As your rank improved, you qualified for a larger flat.

In 1998, commercialization of real estate officially began in China. If you had a flat rented from your employer, you paid a one-time fee to purchase the flat. Since 1998, housing prices increased at least 20 times. So during the process, you most likely had sold your first flat, purchased at least one large apartment, and built a lot of equity, perhaps even bought a few investment properties. Again, this is only true for urban residents. The housing bubble will burst sooner or later, but most of my generation has already cashed in their profits.

I was in graduate school in 1998 so I was not qualified for a flat—I probably missed one of the biggest investment opportunities offered to my generation.

Economy and Childbearing

King: The parents of my generation were frugal. Normally, a family had only one car. But, three to five kids in a family was pretty normal, generally speaking. When we were growing up, we did not go out to eat, didn't go to the movies, and didn't go on vacations. Any entertainment was very rare. As a family, we had modest means. My parents had their children early in their lives. My mother became a grandmother at 48. Most of the older baby boomers had their children earlier, the younger baby boomers had their children late and there was a split within the generation.

My wife and I had our children pretty early, our son at 24 and had our daughter at 28. My parents believed it was right to have kids early. The size of the family also shrank from my parents' generation to my generation: we had two. We did not consider three. We decided to spend more time with the kids and take the economic factor of childbearing into account. That is differ-ent from my parents' generation, because they would just adjust everything to accom-modate more children. A lot of people in my generation had kids almost at the same time, and things were geared toward that.

Lines of cars at the gas station during the Oil Embargo

Economy was good, but one example of the negative was the Oil Embargo (1973-1974) during my college years. We were seeing service station selling gas for a very limited number of hours per day, maybe 2-3 hours/day; there were lines of cars at the pumps. It was the first time in my life we experienced the semblance of "rationing" of any com-modity. It had seemed that the United States had plenty of everything. That was a wake-up call that resources were not unlimited in some areas.

Wang: My parents' generation had large families. My father had eight siblings and my mother had three brothers. My grandparents experienced war and famine constantly, but somehow managed to endure and raise their children for a better future.

My parents' generation normally had two children per family, three maximum. They received a complete educa-tion in spite of the Great Famine. The parents of Generation

'89 went to college after the Communists took over in 1949, but had completed school before the Cultural Revolution started in 1966. Normally they had their children during the Cultural Revolution.

For my generation born from early 1960s to early 1970s, when we wanted kids, only one child was allowed. But many people in this generation got away from the One Child Policy by paying the fine or going abroad. The notorious One Child Policy officially ended this year, so the future generation will be allowed to have two kids in China. When you think that it is up to the Communist Party to decide how many kids you can have, it is quite counter-intuitive.

For all the generation before us, resources were scarce. It is impossible to imagine the tremendous hardship and suffering my grandparents and parents endured. My generation is the first generation in modern Chinese history to enjoy abundance of the commodity and consumerism, at the cost of total destruction of the environment.

Environment

King: There was very little care taken of the environment before my generation. My generation began to pay close attention to it. When I was growing up, the Environmental Protection Agency came into existence. People began to be more concerned with the environment, the water, the air, and other natural resources. We began to hear about things about "global warming." We had some accidents at nuclear power plants. All these things happened during my generation and my kids' generation.

My generation is more accepting the environmental
issues from a scientific and technological perspective,
trusting the government to be on the ball concerning those
things. But sometimes it turned out the government wasn't
on the ball concerning these things. Sometimes you see
regulators come in and be overly aggressive regarding
the environment.

On the other hand, my kids' generation growing up
and seeing environmental problems became immediately
distrustful of the government. For example, they might say
"don't trust the government even if they say the water is
good." Sadly, we are seeing this played out today in Flint,
Michigan. Even in the state of Minnesota, we see some failures of the water testing.

My generation continues in great part, not in total, to put
more trust and faith in the government regarding environmental issues. As things go on, there is a lot of distrust of
the government by my children's generation.

Wang: From late 1970s to early 1990s, food and drug
safety, as well as water and air quality, were not issues.
Food was precious but organic, medicine was cheap and
effective, the sky was blue, and rivers were clear.

Today in China: food safety issues are everywhere. You
probably have heard of the recycled cooking oil and tainted
baby formula scandals. Unfortunately, they are norms. The
recycled and poisonous cooking oil industry is controlled
by the elite families of the ruling Party and account for at
least 10 percent of all China's cooking oil, according to the
Chinese FDA. The drugs are no better: fake or ineffective
drugs occupy most of China's pharmaceutical market. Two
directors of Chinese FDA were convicted—one was executed—for selling drug licenses to unqualified manufacturers. But the problem goes on.

As for water today: the Chinese government reported 43 percent of state-monitored rivers are so polluted they're unsuitable for human contact; at least 60 percent of all rivers are seriously polluted and almost every single river is polluted.

China's hazardous smog is also notorious: during one interview, a 6-year old Chinese girl told the reporter that she had never seen a star at night.

Healthcare

King: For my generation, healthcare is at the whim of the employer. That was also true for my parents' generation. There was very little regulation so we have explosive issues of healthcare costs. That the United States chose to make healthcare a benefit from the company where you work is problematic. My father worked for one company for his whole career, even though the company was acquired by another company; but the healthcare stayed. That is very rare indeed for my generation. Healthcare follows the job, so if you change the job, your healthcare dramatically changes. Healthcare issues continue to be a part of the national discussion. I believe that we received good medical attention when we were growing up; it was a good period of time.

Wang: My generation has healthcare benefit—if you are in the public sector in China, or have health insurance —if you are in the private sector. The government promises a pension, too.

China's healthcare industry is for-profit, so if you don't have coverage, they won't even admit you into the ER. I witnessed patients who were sent back home to die because they could not pay at the hospital. Now the Chinese government promises minimal healthcare benefit covering most citizens. We will see.

Value system

King: My parents' generation has some of the finest ethics and values, many of which were passed on to my generation. My generation got corrupted in many respects by material things. There are many people in my generation who are actually responsible for the financial problems that hurt the banking and housing industry so badly in recent years. We saw a lot of organizations go down because of that. It's sad to admit, but many people responsible for that disaster are members of my generation.

My kids' generation has a different set of values. They tend to be more skeptical toward large institutions, such as government and banks. That's why Google is valued by its corporate motto of "Do no evil," which resonates with the young people who work there.

My generation had the freedom to define our own value system: we could be simultaneously nationalistic in supporting our country, but also against the war in Vietnam. That was a freedom given to my generation that my parents' generation did not have. Unfortunately, some people of my generation took that freedom to an excess, e.g., creating the banking crisis. My generation took the freedom and made a good decision to be good and involved citizens —that was a big strength of our time.

Wang: My generation is both conservative and progressive. We are conservative because we received a complete education, filled with traditional arts and culture, literature and history. We are progressive because we grew up in the 1980s, which was marked by its idealism, openness, forwardness, westernization, academic freedom, cultural renaissance and religious tolerance.

My parents' generation was educated to be atheists by the Communist propaganda. On the contrary, most

The Lama Buddhist Temple in Beijing

members of my generation are either religious or spiritual. There are many Tibetan Buddhists and Christians in my generation. Arts and culture are valued by my generation: we like museums and galleries more than bars and nightclubs; poets and artists are treated like heroes. We value diversity and inclusion, and despise discrimination and exploitation in any form.

We have a simple value system and we believe there is a clear distinction between what is right and what is wrong: freedom of speech is right, censorship is wrong; helping people in need is right, turning away refugees fleeing from war is wrong; freedom of worship is right, and religious persecution is wrong.

Global Citizenship

Wang: 1980s was the most open and creative period in contemporary Chinese history. Thousands and thousands of western books were reprinted or translated into Chinese western philosophy studied, and western art exhibited. We had the opportunities to familiarize ourselves with Freud, Einstein, Solzhenitsyn, Max Webber, Marc Chagall, Wassily Kandinsky, Thomas Mann, Hanna Arendt, Karl Popper, Jean- Paul Sartre, Albert Camus, George Orwell, Michel Foucault, Marcel Duchamp, Italo Calvino, Umberto Eco, Ingmar Bergman, Luis Buñuel,

Eugene O'Neill, Hemingway, F. Scott Fitzgerald, Yasunari
Kawabata, and Yoko Ono.

My generation is well-connected to the outside world,
particularly during the information boom. The Internet
came to China in 1994, and we were able to connect to it
without restrictions. China's "Gold Shield Project" or the
Great Fire Wall, was implemented in 2000 and isolated
China from the rest of the world.

My generation also benefited
tremendously from studying abroad,
some ultimately returned to China,
but many stayed on overseas.

King: The world opened up
during my generation. Most of us
had an education that brought us a
glimpse of the world as very young
kids. It was not a global education,
but as we entered high school,
the world opened up considerably. For example, the Oil
Embargo made us realize that somebody in another part of
the world could suddenly impact our household.

My generation also became more curious, and we had
the freedom to explore those curiosities by experiencing
more. The world indeed became smaller or as Thomas
Friedman said, "the world is flat." It also became more
necessary to be a global citizen, just to be more effective
citizens of our country. At the beginning of our generation,
people might just think about the United States versus being
a citizen of the world; but we are more and more aware
that the United States is just one country in the world and
our job is to be collaborative and work with people all over
the world.

Historical incidents of the baby boomers' birth years in the United States: 1946–1964

1946 President Truman proclaims end of World War II; the first general-purpose electronic computer is unveiled at the University of Pennsylvania.

1947 The first practical electronic transistor is demonstrated at Bell Laboratories.

1948 The first tape recorder is sold; the US Supreme Court rules that religious instruction in public schools is unconstitutional.

1949 President Truman establishes rocket test range at Cape Canaveral, Florida; President Truman increases minimum wage from 40 cents to 75 cents.

1950 Korean War begins; the first TV remote control is marketed.

1951 Direct-dial coast-to-coast telephone service begins in the U.S.; first regularly scheduled transatlantic flights begin operation.

1952 A mechanical heart is used for first time in a human patient in Detroit; the U.S. successfully tests a hydrogen bomb.

1953 The CIA helps overthrow the government of Mohammed Mossadegh in Iran; Korean War ends.

1954 The first shopping mall opens in Southfield, Michigan; the first mass vaccination of children against polio begins in Pittsburgh, Pennsylvania; the first microbiology laboratory opens in the U.S.

1955 The first electric power generated from atomic energy is sold commercially; Vietnam War begins.

1956 The first transatlantic telephone cable goes into operation; videotape is used for the first time on television; IBM introduces the first computer disk storage unit.

1957 President Eisenhower orders U.S. troops to desegregate schools in Little Rock, Arkansas; the Ford Motor Company introduces the Edsel car; Toyota begins exporting vehicles to the U.S.

1958 The first successful American satellite, Explorer 1, is launched into orbit; the U.S. Army launches the Explorer 3 satellite; CBS Labs announce stereophonic records.

1959 Congress passes a bill authorizing food stamps for poor Americans; Pan Am begins regular passenger flights around the world.

1960 John F. Kennedy becomes the 35th President of the United States; Vietnam War escalates.

1961 Astronaut Alan Shepard becomes the first American in space; TWA shows the first in-flight movie.

1962 President John F. Kennedy begins blockade of Cuba; astronaut John Glenn is first American to orbit Earth; the first Wal-Mart and K-Mart stores open.

1963 Reverend Martin Luther King Jr. delivers his "I Have a Dream" speech on the steps of the Lincoln Memorial in the District of Columbia; President John F. Kennedy is assassinated in Dallas, Texas.

1964 Civil Rights Act of 1964 passes in the U.S. Senate 73-27; Dr. Martin Luther King is awarded The Nobel Peace Prize; NASA launches its first Orbital Geophysical Observatory (OGO-1).

Historical incidents of the Generation '89 birth years in China: 1962-1972

1962 China begins to recover from the three years Great Famine (1959–1961); Sino-India Border Conflict.

1963 The Communist Party of China begins "Five-Anti" campaign and "Socialist Education Movement",

1964 China conducts its first successful nuclear test.

1965 Chinese scientists synthesizes crystalline bovine insulin, a bioactive protein.

1966 Mao and the Communist Party of China start the "Great Proletarian Cultural Revolution"; "The Destruction of the Four Olds" campaign destroys most of traditional culture in China; "Red Terror" (mass killings and tortures) by the Red Guards took place in urban areas.

1967 Mass killings (including Hunan Daoxian Massacre) and turmoil spreads throughout China; China's first hydrogen bomb test successful; China's judiciary and public security system collapses; British Legations in Beijing is attacked by red mob.

1968 The Communist Party of China purges 70 percent of its senior members, including President Liu Shaoqi; "Down to the Countryside Movement" begins, and millions of urban youth are sent to rural areas to work.

1969 Sino-Soviet Border Conflict.

1970 Communist Party of China starts three-year long "One Strike-Three Anti" campaign, causing over a quarter-million wrongful convictions; China launches its first satellite.

1971 Lin Biao, China's second-in-command, dies after a failed coup d'état against Mao; The People's Republic of China (mainland) replaces The Republic of China (Taiwan) as the permanent member of the United Nations Security Council.

1972 Richard Nixon visits China; The U.S. and China jointly issue Shanghai Communiqué; China and UK issue joint communiqué concerning upgraded diplomatic relations; Japanese Prime Minister visits China and Japan and China issue Joint Statement.

Desert Island Choices: the Baby Boomers and the Generation '89*

Rick King and Chang Wang

(China Insight Editor's Note) "Desert Island Discs" is a talk show radio program, broadcast on BBC Radio 4 since 1942. Each week a guest, called a "castaway" during the program, is asked to choose eight recordings (usually, but not always, music) a book, and a luxury item that they would take if they were to be cast away on a desert island, while discussing their lives and the reasons for their choices.

Below are choices by Rick King, a "baby boomer" of the U.S., and Chang Wang, a member of China's "Generation '89."

China Insight: Imagine you were stranded on a desert island for an indefinite period of time, at least a decade, and you could bring only a handful of items with you. Assume that your basic human needs of food, water, and shelter have been taken care of, but you will be incommunicado: no telephone, newspaper, or internet access.

You can bring only three books with you. These are the books you have read, but that you would read again and again on the desert island. What books would you bring with you? Also, please briefly explain why you chose these books.

Rick King: Obviously, there are a lot of choices: one of the books that I will bring would be either a dictionary

---

*This is an interview with Rick King and Chang Wang, following their articles on being a "baby boomer" and part of "Generation '89," respectively. It originally appeared in *China Insight's* July/August 2016 issue.

or thesaurus. I am not sure which, but probably the most comprehensive dictionary one could have because one of the things I had always wanted to do is to learn every word in the English language. A dictionary or a thesaurus would provide ongoing stimulation of my mind.

If you want to learn a foreign language, you can do that by yourself with a book, but I do not think that is really the best way to learn a foreign language.

I would also bring the World Almanac, because I read those and do not ever get a chance to go into the details. Now, presumbly, I will have a lot of time to read.

Ian Fleming's James Bond books

The third book will be enjoyable and fun, so the things that I think about would be, if permitted, a series of books by the same author. I might pick all 14 James Bond books written by Ian Fleming. I might pick all the books Jane Austen wrote. Or . . . I might pick poetry I like, such as Byron's.

There is an equal amount of enjoyment reading those books. I like to read about the fascinating things: the details of the election, or about who was Secretary of State during the 1790s. I do not know why it fascinates me, but it does.

Chang Wang: All of my choices are multiple-volume sets. The first one would be The Complete Tang Poems (全唐詩), the largest collection of Tang poetry, containing some 49,000 lyric poems by more than 2,200 poets, representing the highest achievement of Chinese literature. Tang Poetry is poetry written in or around the time of, or

in the characteristic style of, China's Tang Dynasty
(618 – 907).

The second set would be The Great Treasury of Sutras
(大藏經), the total body of Buddhist literature deemed
canonical in Chinese Buddhism.

The third set would be the
Supreme Court Reporter published
by Thomson Reuters. The Supreme
Court Reporter Bound Volume set
is a federal caselaw reporter series
in West's® National Reporter
System. This set covers opinions
and decisions from 1882-to-date-is-
sued by the United States Supreme

Supreme Court Reporter,
published by Thomson
Reuters

Court. Cases published in this product series are enhanced
with headnotes, Key Numbers, and synopses prepared by
Thomson Reuters' highly trained attorney-editors.

Even on a desert island alone, I would be extremely
happy and busy with traditional Tang poetry, Buddhist
teachings and American law.

China Insight: You can bring three music albums,
either in a traditional Walkman or in digital format, both
playable on a solar-power-based device. What albums
would you bring?

Rick King: I would start with either some Queen or the
complete collection of ABBA. I have to have one collection
that would be on the fun and stupid side, something you
are going to listen to all alone. So, you are going to see me
singing in the shower. I think I'd probably pick ABBA.

In addition, I'm going to have Tchaikovsky, the Russian
composer. However, I love Strauss as well; but I think I'll
just say Tchaikovsky.

Finally, I think I should have a deep collection here. So
I'm going to go with all the Rolling Stones.

I'm going to have fun and fantasy in the ABBA; I'm going to have the serious and relaxing music of Tchaikovsky, and I'm going to have the classic rock and roll of my lifetime: the Rolling Stones.

Pyotr Ilyich Tchaikovsky (1840 –1893)

Chang Wang: I will have Tchaikovsky for sure. We Chinese have an immediate affinity and empathy with Slavic music, like that of Tchaikovsky, Rachmaninoff, Shostakovich and Dvořák. We normally do not need any explanation or background information to understand what the music is about. In my opinion, Tchaikovsky is the most beautiful; his melody is from another universe. But Tchaikovsky is so sad; there is a deep sense of despair and suffering. Just listen to "Pathétique;" you feel the pain.

So I will need some balance. That will be Mozart. We know the "Mozart Effect," scientific research results indicating that listening to Mozart's music may induce a short-term improvement on the performance of certain kinds of mental tasks. For me, Mozart simply brings happiness.

Last but not the least, I will have *The Butterfly Lovers*, a violin concerto (梁祝小提琴协奏曲). It is one of the most famous modern works of Chinese music. It is an orchestral adaptation of an ancient legend, the Butterfly Lovers. Written for the western style orchestra, it features a solo violin played using some Chinese techniques.

The Butterfly Lovers, a violin concerto

278

China Insight: You can bring three personal or luxury items that are meaningful to you. They must be inanimate and of no use in escaping the island or allowing communication from outside. What would your choices be?

Rick King: Since I am surrounded by water, I would pick a boat. I understand I cannot escape as stipulated. However, I would enjoy just rowing around the island. No motor. Just a rowboat. I could circle the island. I would figure out the way to fish, to swim and exercise. I think a rowboat might be fun.

I do like the idea of a game of some sort. I have always wanted to play chess better so I could play that with myself. So one of the items would be a chess set, but then I think I could possibly trade the chessboard for a knife. With the knife I could make a chessboard, and a lot of other things. I think the knife would be very handy. So that would be another thing I would bring.

I realize I cannot communicate with the outside world, but the rule did not say the outside world could not communicate with me, so I would take a solar-powered radio. I can get either BBC or NPR on it and listen to what's going on in the rest of the world.

First you take time to adjust to the new environment, even if the basic human needs have been taken care of. In the beginning, you do not have enough time to think about anything else, but that will change after you have all the basics covered, and you will start focusing on what the rest of your stay on the island will be like. Then you begin to think about the regular things of the day. That's when I think I would use the radio.

Chang Wang: I am not a handy person so I am hoping there will be a cave I can take refuge in and there are plenty of fruits I can pick from the trees or from the ground.

My other choices are the strategy game of Go, calligraphy brush, and zither, the three key instruments of the four arts (四藝) of the Chinese literati, the traditional scholar. The four arts were the four main accomplishments required of the Chinese gentleman scholar. They are qin (the guqin, a stringed instrument. 琴), qi (Go, 棋), shu (Chinese calligraphy, 書) and hua (Chinese painting, 畫).

I have always wanted to polish and improve my four arts skills, so with all the time I have on the desert island, I shall finally be able to do that.

China Insight: Last, you can bring the ghosts of three persons in history to keep you company. You will have long and constant conversations with them on the desert island, so they are presumably persons whose companionship you would enjoy for a very long time. Who would you like them to be?

Thomas Jefferson

Rick King: The rule is that they must be deceased. So I think that, historically, I would probably have Thomas Jefferson (1743 – 1826) and Queen Elizabeth I of England (1533 – 1603). With these two, I could explore elements of history.

And I think I'd also have my grandfather, who was a doctor. Then I could explore elements of the family, beyond what is already known to me.

Chang Wang: I would also like to have my late grand-father Zhou Po, a World War II veteran, war correspondent, and senior reporter for a Chinese newspaper. I would like to learn from him everything about his life, his time and our family history.

I would also like to have the companion of Maestro Hong Yi (弘一, or Li Shutong 李叔同, 1880–1942), a master painter, musician, drama-tist, calligrapher, seal cutter, poet, and Buddhist monk.

Last, but not the least, I would like to have Professor Fang Lizhi (方励之, 1936 – 2012), a Chinese astrophysicist, an icon of liberal intellectual-ism, and my neighbor in the 1980s.

Hong Yi (Li Shutong)

China Insight: Where were you born, and where did you grow up?

Rick King: I was born in California and grew up in Massachusetts. I went to college and graduate school in Vermont.

Chang Wang: I was born and grew up in Beijing, China, went to college and graduate school in Beijing, and came to the U.S. in 2000 for my second graduate degree and law school.

Doing Business with China and the Chinese People:
A Conversation on Cultural Challenges*

Chang Wang and Joe Pearman

Parallel Universes

Pearman: I recently read a commentary by Dr. Christopher Ford, a senior fellow at the Hudson Institute, which claims that, compared to the rest of the world, China lives in a "parallel universe of competing facts and historical claims." Dr. Ford explained that "the Chinese and non-Chinese participants [of a defense conference] seemed to start from radically different starting points on the most basic matters of fact (e.g., who started the Korean War, or whether or not Japanese history textbooks acknowledge that country's invasion of China in the 1930s)." In addition, from his own experience in negotiating with the Chinese, Ford said that the Chinese are "quite comfortable telling non-Chinese what their various governments' intentions are. We were told, for instance, 'The United States wishes to 'contain' China and obstruct its rise.'" As a native of China who lives in the U.S., do you feel we are living in two parallel universes?

Wang: The commentary you mentioned perfectly illustrates the most difficult aspect of doing business with China and the Chinese people: cultural communication. Not only

---

*This is Chang Wang and Joe Pearman's series of articles about doing business *with* China, as opposed to *in* it. They originally appeared in the January – May 2015 issues of *China Insight*.

do some concepts simply not exist in another language, but also the context of that particular concept is unknown to the other cultures. When dealing with many cultures, but especially with the Chinese, there is a constant need for "cultural translation" to contextualize concepts and events, such as the Chinese military stating that America started the Korean War.

I also hope this commentary will illustrate the truth of an old adage: "I don't know what I don't know." It's reminiscent of what Gore Vital said: "What he knew he knew well. Unfortunately what he did not know he did not suspect existed." In a language, either your mother tongue or a foreign language, if you don't know the word, it does not "exist," but once you learn the word, it appears everywhere. The word simply defines a concept for which you did not yet have a name.

People don't realize that the "parallel universes" exist, so they don't recognize the massive potential for communication difficulty in every interaction between China and the rest of the world, especially the United States, and the need for "cultural translators." Perhaps if we come to a fuller understanding of these parallel universes, we will be able to understand each other's respective perspectives. Frankly, however, I think there are many roadblocks to true understanding. In fact, I find it hard to believe that outside of a small field of Sinologists and "America experts," people on either side will ever truly comprehend each other.

Pearman: Well, there's no reason to lose hope completely. For instance, China might have a separate narrative of history and politics, but every year there's more trade and more exchange between our two countries. For instance, every year, more Chinese students come to study at colleges and universities across the United States. These are some of the most politically active places in this country; I'd say it would be almost impossible for them not to go back to China with a greater understanding of the freedoms and advantages of democracy. And, for that matter, when people from other countries do business in China, they expose the Chinese to new industrial practices and ethical standards. That's got to have a positive effect in the long run.

Wang: I wouldn't be too hasty to believe that being educated in a democracy makes one a democrat; more than one foreign national with anti-American values has defended tyranny or religious extremism with a perfect Midwestern accent on CNN. And I'd also caution against believing that businesses will change China. Remember Professor Jonathan Spence's masterpiece "To Change China: Western Advisers in China." The Chinese eagerly accept Western technical advice, but always cling stead-fastly to Chinese "values": first Confucianism, and later Maoism. Chinese call this principle "Chinese learning for fundamental principles and Western learning for practical-ities." Rather than changing China, most Western advisers are changed *by* China, such as the devout Jesuit monks who got caught up playing Ming and Qing dynasty court politics. Indeed, I would submit that today a business *in* China must adapt to Chinese rules or leave. For instance, Google was forced to withdraw after it would not cooperate with Chinese censorship.

But let's start with the unique universe the Chinese inhabit. For instance, recently I received a request from a Chinese colleague to comment on a document entitled "The Secret Ten Commandments of the CIA in Undermining China," a list popular on the Chinese Internet. It is not only popular with and commonly regarded as authentic by most of the Chinese people; it is quoted frequently by the Chinese government, even the military. It is supposed to be a list of things the CIA, and the U.S. government will do to encourage the fall of the Chinese government. I quote:

1. Destroy their belief in assiduous working. Induce their youth with materials, make them scorn their original education, especially the communism [sic] ideology, and encourage sexual promiscuity, superficial honor.

2. Spread our lifestyle through all media including films, books, television, radios and religion.

3. Distract them from ccp [sic] propaganda. Make them focus on sports, pleasure, games, criminal films, etc.

4. Divide the people into hostile groups by constantly harping on controversial matters of no importance.

5. Destroy the people's faith in their natural leaders by holding the latter up to contempt, ridicule and obloquy . . .

I was amused by this malicious fabrication and took the time to examine the list and write back to my Chinese colleague, telling him there was no way on earth this document was authored by the CIA and in fact, there was no way it was authored by an English-speaker. I am no fan of the Agency and am personally appalled by the Torture Memo. But it is abundantly clear that this document was put together by a Chinese-speaking individual with a strong belief in the conspiracy theory. Nevertheless, the Chinese authorities took it very seriously, and this reminds us again we are living in two "parallel universes."

Pearman: That list seems strikingly familiar. I read that in the 1960s there was a book called "The Naked Communist," and it contained 45 things the Communists in America were supposed to do to allow takeover by the USSR. Conveniently enough, both of these "lists" make it clear that anyone who criticizes the government is a foreign agent, and anyone who lives in a way that differs from the mainstream is a saboteur of some kind or another. I think you can argue that's the root of many conspiracy theories: people seek to justify a certain bias or prejudice by constructing a narrative that gels with it. They don't need proof *per se*, as these beliefs are self-justified truth to them, so the conspiracy theory *must*, by extension, be true.

Wang: That's precisely what I found — the new list is a replica of the old list, with sides switched. I agree with you that conspiracy theories are constructed to justify a belief, and that's borne out in our example. The Chinese believe they were the victims of Western imperialism and there has always been the intention of the West to encroach, undermine and "contain" China. As Professor Perry Link argued: "China is still living in the syndrome of being the victim, and we don't know when that

A corner of the Yuanmingyuan Ruins in Beijing. In their day, these gardens were some of the most magnificent in the world.

syndrome will finally be cured. It's going to take a while." The preamble to the Constitution of the People's Republic of China narrates the history of what is known as "The Hundred Years of Humiliation," which goes from 1841, the start of the first Opium War (the Opium Wars were two conflicts in the mid-1800s where Britain and France forced the Qing Dynasty to allow them to sell opium, a forerunner of heroin, in China) to 1949, when Mao declared the founding of the People's Republic. We are taught in school that during those Hundred Years, China was raped and pillaged both by a decadent elite and by the West. This is shown in "The Burning of Yuanmingyuan," a popular 1980s film, which depicts the looting and destruction of a series of magnificent pleasure gardens by the British and French during the Second Opium War. In school, our teachers showed it again and again, as part of the "patriotic education" curriculum, to remind us of all the terrible things foreigners had done to us.

A corner of the Yuanmingyuan Ruins in Beijing. In their day, these gardens were some of the most magnificent in the world.

Pearman: From the Chinese perspective, were foreign invasion and forced trade the main reasons for the fall of Imperial China, or was it the civil war and the famines? And weren't the Qing Dynasty and its successors extremely despotic and corrupt in their own right?

Wang: Maybe they were, but we Chinese believe that no matter how crazy and brutal our leaders are, that's our internal affair. That logic could lead to a bizarre question: would it be more acceptable to be killed by a fellow Chinese than to be killed by a Japanese, or to be exploited by Americans? One Chinese person killing another may be a regrettably normal part of life in China, but death or injury from a foreigner is a stain on the whole nation's honor.

Chinese citizens are reminded of how we were a semi-colonized, exploited backwater in the 1800s and early 1900s. We are taught that after a great struggle, the Party managed to drive the exploitative capitalists and imperialists from China, but that they will come back if they ever have the opportunity. That's why many Chinese citizens today believe the United States seeks to "contain" China in the Pacific, to prevent its rise to power. And since the U.S. seeks to contain China, the CIA's secret list must be real. And since the CIA's secret list is real, the U.S. seeks to contain China. It's exactly the sort of circular reasoning you described: this truth is self-evident, so it requires no proof.

Pearman: Moving on from parallel universes to the overall theme of cultural communication, I've heard there are three "taboos" in China, three topics that one should never bring up in conversation, either among Chinese or between Chinese and foreigners. They are Taiwan, the Tiananmen Square tragedy of 1989 and Tibet.

Wang: You're right about the existence of these taboos, but before we go on, I would like to clarify something. The Chinese people are not satisfied with the status quo in their country. They dislike corruption and abuse of power in the government. However, at the same time, it is true that they believe much of the propaganda the government puts out, or the "core values" as the government purports to embody. And this brings about the three T's. I would advise everyone who plans to do business with China and the Chinese people to make a short study of each of these three issues. You are advised not to argue with your host or visitors, of course, but each one provides important insight on a facet of China.

I submit that if you understand the history of the relationship between Taiwan and the mainland, you understand China's past. As you know, after Mao Zedong's Communist forces won the Civil War, the government of Chiang Kai-Shek fled to the island of Taiwan, which continued to call itself the Republic of China. Nowadays, China asserts that Taiwan is a run-away child that should be brought back to its "home," the People's Republic of China, while conservatives in the Taiwanese government assert that the Republic of China is the legitimate government, if not all of China, at least the island of Taiwan. It's also important to note that while the mainland is still a one-party state, Taiwan is now a multi-party representative democracy. A full understanding of the so-called "Taiwan issue" would be vastly beneficial to understand modern Chinese history, as much of it is defined by the interplay between Taiwan and the mainland.

The Tiananmen Square of 1989 was the tragic end of an era of semi-liberal politics that had defined China in the 1980s, and the intellectual revival in the mainland engendered by that era. I think it's the key to understanding the China of today. Before Tiananmen, the Chinese government had been experimenting with limited political reform as well as economic reform. We also had a very short-lived renaissance of academic freedom and culture in the 1980s. After Tiananmen, the door to political reform was slammed shut, while economic reform was manipulated to benefit a handful of "red elites," the oligarchy, at the expenses of environmental and social welfare. So now you have a country where there are more than 100 billionaires but no general elections, a country where everything is a business and yet the power of the state is absolute. It's an immense contradiction, and one that can only be understood with a study of contemporary history before and after Tiananmen.

And if Tiananmen explains the China of today, Tibet provides a sobering glimpse of the future. Ethnic moderates have tried to conciliate with the authorities, but the government is determined to use a hard-line approach to maintain stability. The future of the ethnic issue is not only indicative of the future of Chinese society, but will itself greatly impact and shape the future of Chinese society, particularly in the ethnic regions which make up near a half of the mainland.

The Chinese authorities have no intention of ending up like the Soviet Union's Communists; they will not to make Gorbachev's "mistake" of reconciliation.

Pearman: May we say the future, overall, is not a terribly pleasant prospect. So it's hardly surprising you're discouraged from bringing these things up. They all challenge the nationalist narrative of the authority, and it seems to me that this nationalism is the basis of the "parallel universes."

Wang: You could argue, I think, that nationalism is the underlying cause and the "parallel universes" are just a symptom. Another "symptom" is the resentment I mentioned earlier that's tied to the colonial actions of the "Hundred Years of Humiliation." When you don't remember how touchy the Chinese can be about being treated as equals, the results can be disastrous.

I would like to share a real story to illustrate this point. There was a multinational firm that decided to develop a local product for China. It hired local Chinese employees, most of whom did not speak English well, and brought in supervisors from the U.S. and the U.K. who spoke no Chinese. The supervisors had to sign off on all the work the Chinese did, which led to a somewhat inefficient situation. Say a Chinese employee wrote a report detailing his progress on a certain task. This report had to be translated to English, where it would be read by a supervisor. The supervisor would issue instructions, which then had to be translated back to Chinese. It was a massive time sink, and I don't think it's surprising that the Chinese came to find the communication with their supervisors laborious. They could have done the work on their own, and the foreigners seemed to be there because the company believed that their international experience in other countries would be valuable to Chinese product development.

After six months, the supervisors had to transfer back to their home country for income tax purposes. A representative from Human Resources, another non-Chinese, addressed the Chinese employees at a town hall-style meeting. The HR representative firmly believed these Chinese were heartbroken seeing their foreign colleagues leaving: "I know you feel lost, like orphans," she said. "I know you don't know what to do without your colleagues. But don't worry! They will continue to communicate with you and instruct you via Skype. You are not abandoned!"

Bear in mind that this woman was not acting with malice; she really wanted to reassure the Chinese employees. But there was a fundamental misunderstanding: she had no idea how offensive her words would be to her audience. She thought the foreign workers were *helping* the Chinese, but the Chinese felt like they were being treated like ignorant laborers, or second-class citizen in a multinational company.

Pearman: It makes me wince to hear that story. But I will say that woman's words would have been offensive no matter whom she was addressing. Anybody would resent the implications of that talk. So while I can understand why her words were so egregious to the Chinese, I would say that's not exclusively a cultural problem. If anything, it's more about not understanding how an organization actually functions, or a simply lack of civility.

Wang: Perhaps. But that's hardly the only misunderstanding I've witnessed over the years. Although I will say that because of the effective propaganda machine and the narrative of national humiliation, the Chinese are quite sensitive to perceived disrespect and are suspicious of the intentions of foreigners. Meanwhile, look at the other side of the aisle: thanks to the legacy of the "Chinese Exclusion

Act" and the Cold War, Americans are also making a similar mistake by assuming the "bad" intent of the Chinese. And that leads us to the next part of this discussion, which will appear in next month's China Insight.

They eat puppies, don't they?

Pearman: When some Americans talk about the Chinese, their attitude is close to "they eat puppies, don't they?" That actually is the title of a political satire about the U.S.-China relationship by Christopher Buckley, and it does a great job of expressing ignorance combined with mild, slightly disgusted apprehension.

Wang: The novel is very entertaining and I highly recommend it. I can share with you several occasions I witnessed, where the communication broke down, the message was lost, and the intents misinterpreted, largely due to the difficulty of cultural translation. For instance, once I was at an occasion where a Chinese judge hosted an American judge at a banquet. The final course was soup—*dog* soup! The American judge was appalled, but finally tasted it, reluctantly of course. Afterwards, he confided to me that he was sure it was his Chinese host testing his commitment to working with the Chinese. If he didn't drink the soup, this American judge thought, the Chinese judge would have concluded the American was not serious about collaboration.

I had to tell the judge that it was definitely not a test. Dog soup is very popular, sadly, in the Chinese judge's home province of Guizhou; the man was simply serving him a local delicacy and trying to please the American dignitary!

This rather grotesque incident underlines another one of the cultural challenges in doing business with China and the Chinese: the Americans' prejudice and stereotypes about the Chinese. Make no mistake, I don't eat puppies and I condemn those who do. But during cultural communication, it is ill-advised for Americans to start by assuming bad intent and being suspicious of the motives of the Chinese. Some of them, unfortunately, enter into business expecting enmity, when in fact the reverse is true. Although the Chinese aren't fond of the American government due to the CCP's propaganda, they're quite enthusiastic about American culture and individual Americans.

Pearman: In that way, I think you could say they're quite like the American people themselves. Polls indicate that the majority of the American people are not confident in the administration and the Congress, but we truly believe in ourselves and our peers.

Wang: Certainly. You see, in the 1980s, China was introduced to American culture for the first time, and a large part of that was in the form of sitcoms. We "met" Americans on TV, in a sense. They were warm-hearted, outgoing, optimistic and ingenious, and that's the impression many Chinese still have of them. So don't be surprised if a Chinese business partner might resent Washington mightily but still be extremely friendly to you as an individual. It's one of the contradictions you have to get used to in dealing with the Chinese. Yet again and again, people from the United States —and the West in general, for that matter—assume the worst about the Chinese.

Pearman: I remember reading an account by an American journalist who visited Iran. He was obviously from the States, and so when he went to observe an anti-American rally, he was more than a little nervous. Throughout the rally, people would break off chanting "Death to the Great Satan!" in order to approach him and enquire solicitously if he was enjoying his visit to Iran! I think you can see an innate decency and friendliness in most people from any culture that will shine through if you let it.

Wang: I agree. But too often people assume the worst. Once I was part of a group of faculty at a major Chinese university that welcomed a group of American professors. The chancellor of the university, who spoke some English, thoughtfully started his welcome in English. The group of teachers arrived, and the chancellor moved to greet the American dean.

"You are such a pretty dean." he said with a smile.

The Americans were, as I'm sure you can imagine, aghast. The dean, with her poker face firmly in place, replied "What?"

"You are such a pretty dean," the chancellor repeated.

Now I'm sure all of the Americans were certain they were witnessing some form of sexual harassment. But the chancellor had no thought of that. What he was *trying* to say was something along the lines of "It is my honor and privilege to welcome such an elegant and accomplished senior professor to my school." And he was trying to say it in English, as a courtesy to the Americans. But instead, the discussions started off on a very awkward footing, because the cordial message was lost in cultural translation.

Pearman: I'd say that's true in any culture. For instance, I've studied German for several years. Suppose someone who did not speak any or only a little German was in charge of a high school group from the U.S. touring Germany. A sensible phrase to learn would be something like "I am the leader," so you could inform authority figures you were the person to talk to. Now, if you worked purely out of a dictionary, you might come up with the phrase "Ich bin der Führer." This is technically correct. But unfortunately, the word *Führer* has been under something of a cloud since 1945, as it was the word that referred to *Hitler* as leader of Germany. That's why someone with more knowledge of German would say "Ich bin der Leiter." They mean the same thing, but one carries such negative baggage. Sometimes when we deal with a foreigner speaking our native language, we forget that they might not understand all the nuances.

Wang: That brings to mind one more example of cultural miscommunication, and I have to say I think it's the best yet. Once, a Chinese businessman hosted an American businessman I knew in China. After a long day of working out commercial agreements, the Chinese businessman invited the American out for dinner. And of course, as a good host, he wanted to do more than simply go to a restaurant. He wanted to show his guest something interesting and uniquely Chinese. You may have seen pictures of Deng Xiaoping, China's leader from the late 1970s to the early 1990s, attending a rodeo in Texas and sporting a cowboy hat with his Mao suit. Well, this Chinese businessman sought to give his guest a similarly fascinating experience. So he booked them a table at a "Cultural Revolution restaurant."

Pearman: Oh dear. I do hope that "Cultural Revolution restaurants" aren't at all related to the Cultural Revolution that led to a decade of bloodshed and slaughter in the name of loyalty to Chairman Mao and Communist purity?

Wang: They are, indeed! At a Cultural Revolution restaurant, you sit on simple wooden benches and eat a plain, traditional Chinese meal. The walls are plastered with old-style propaganda posters, and an actor dressed in the uniform of a Red Guard, one of Chairman Mao's

teenage supporters, reads quotations from Mao's "Little Red Book." After dinner is served (and a sizeable amount of alcohol is consumed), you sing along to old Red Guard marching songs.

"Red Classic," a Cultural Revolution theme restaurant in Beijing.

Pearman: That's grotesque! It's like Ted Koppel said in his documentary film, "The People's Republic of Capitalism": "If some German entrepreneur had opened a beer garden on the outskirts of München, dressed an actor up in an old SS uniform, and then had him read excerpts from Hitler's "Mein Kampf" into a microphone while a couple of hundred nostalgic Germans chowed down on bratwurst and sauerbraten, if that had happened . . . well, it wouldn't! It couldn't!" Why would the Chinese pay homage to one of the most destructive and violent events in their history, when thousands were killed and millions persecuted for what George Orwell would have called "thought-crime?"

Wang: My businessman friend had a similar reaction. Indeed, he was at first repulsed, and then, as the evening wore on and more drinks were consumed, and the "revolutionary fervor" grew, he began to get distinctly nervous!

He failed to understand two things. First, China commercializes everything these days, including its own history. Many younger people see a "Cultural Revolution restaurant"

296

as simply an interesting evening, a day in the life of their forefathers. They don't know about the vast casualties of the Cultural Revolution, of the hardships, because these things have been suppressed.

But how can older people who remember the Cultural Revolution go to these restaurants, you may ask? Well, for those Chinese people in their 60s right now, the Cultural Revolution was the time of their adolescence. It was the only time in their lives many of them had complete "freedom," as Red Guards who dropped out of school, roamed the countryside, and "fought" for Mao. It was also "the best years of their lives"—when they could first smoke and drink, when they had their first loves. So, when they look back on the Cultural Revolution, they see it a little differently than you or I.

But all in all, the poor businessman's attempt to show his partner an interesting part of Chinese "culture" was a rather abject failure.

Cultural Competence

Wang: These stories all illustrate certain aspects of cultural misunderstanding, and illuminate the need for "cultural translation" and contextualization. The lack of understanding between Chinese and Americans continues to frustrate businesspeople on both sides of the Pacific and is one of the biggest unexpected challenges that faces anyone who attempts to business in China or with the Chinese.

Pearman: We've talked *cultural* challenges in general; would you mind giving our readers a brief rundown on some of the more concrete problems they might face in attempting to do business in or with China?

Wang: Certainly, and there are plenty. First, there are the generic challenges faced in many countries, such as developing the right product and delivering the right message. Then there are the more China-specific challenges.

The first challenge is legal and regulatory compliance. This isn't as simple as following the printed laws, because Chinese society is governed largely by "hidden rules," codes of conduct and behavior many would describe as institutionalized corruption. Ignore them at your peril, for if you do not know and follow the hidden rules, you might get your business and or yourself in trouble, even when your business is completely legal.

The second challenge is security. To put it simply, Big Brother is watching you and would like to know not only your every move, but what's on your mind and on your hard drive. The surveillance state is ever-present in China, and not always well-disposed to foreign businesses.

The third challenge is corruption. Corruption in China is systematic and institutionalized, as mentioned above, and there are many gray areas which can potentially trap you. The Foreign Corrupt Practice Act of the United States has very strict rules about what businesses can do and cannot do when doing business outside the United States, and it is vital to remind oneself of these rules when doing business in China.

Pearman: However, you could say that understanding these challenges is simply part of cultural translation and contextualization.

Wang: Certainly. The last — and probably the most imposing — challenge is the challenge of translation and cultural misunderstanding. If you can conquer this challenge, the other challenges should be easier to deal with.

If you speak a second language, you understand the difficulty of translating a concept from one language to another. And if you can't communicate a concept to a business partner properly, problems ensue. I feel the important role that culture plays in business in general has been under-appreciated — and the cost of this under-appreciation has been underestimated. For instance, in China, you should not give people the gift of a clock, which means "I will attend your funeral;" nor should you write business correspondence in red ink, which means "I am done with you;" and, during a business meeting, if the Chinese host asks "would you like a cup of tea?" it means "there is nothing more I want to say, and it's time for you to leave." Not understanding the import of any one of these seemingly innocent actions, and countless others, has the potential of damaging relationships between business people irreparably.

And there are many less obvious cultural nuances which can be vital to the success or failure of a Western business operation in China. It's particularly important, for example, for an information services company to understand that, in Chinese culture, knowledge is to be paid for, but information is to be shared. So how should a company identify and position itself in China? Should it say to the Chinese that it offers information, or *knowledge*?

There are small nuances and major differences, and you have to learn to navigate them all. I would say one of the biggest differences is American and Chinese business culture. I remember hearing a Chinese businessman once say: "American businesses do things right. Chinese businesses do the right thing." In my experience, many U.S. firms get locked into a very rigid, bureaucratic decision-making structure, and they have trouble innovating — which Americans used to do the best. In Thomas Friedman's words when he addressed the innovative Chinese economy: "That used to be us." On the other hand, Chinese businesses *have* to innovate, as their market is constantly shifting and changing. And that can produce cultural conflicts when you try to work between organizations.

Pearman: I agree that U.S. companies should be mindful of not falling into a stagnating routine, but I don't believe we're consciously counter-innovative here in the States. I would say that we have standard protocols and procedures because the U.S. is a very mature market: we have fully defined commercial and contract laws, an apolitical regulatory system, etc. Of course, you can't assume that these things will follow you when you do business abroad.

I've often been struck by how much China's economy resembles America's economy at the turn of the 20th century, the era between, say, 1880 and 1910. I think that's what Thomas Friedman was alluding to. There's a tremendous amount of creative, freewheeling innovation, but there are also abysmal safety standards, little worker protection, and plenty of monopolies and cronyism. So I might submit to that Chinese businessmen you mentioned that Chinese firms have to innovate so much because they can never be sure of the ground under their feet: what happens if a local official takes a dislike to them, or a bigger company wants them crushed?

Wang: Of course there's plenty of truth to that, but I just wanted to point out that global operations, international business transactions, and cross-border project management all require a certain level of cultural competence. This cultural competence not only refers to an ability to interact effectively with people of different cultures and socio-economic backgrounds, but also a conscious awareness of "we don't know what we don't know:" the existence of another universe. And the existence of that other universe means that a company that can usually work from a formula in developing products needs to innovate.

One good example is Starbucks, which is everywhere in China now. But before Starbucks, coffee in China meant instant coffee. Everyone, especially people with enough disposable income to afford Starbucks, drank tea. A conventional firm, following the protocol of market research and strategic planning, would have analyzed consumer wants and desires and decided to enter the Chinese tea market, since most of the Chinese people drink tea. After all, why would the Chinese want to give up tea for a bitter and overpriced drink? It would make much more conventional business sense to be a tea retailer.

Pearman: Well, but that sounds about as smart as selling cigars to Cubans. An American firm wouldn't know anything about the tea market. You have to convince customers they want something new, rather than break into an existing market.

Wang: Precisely. What does Starbucks know about tea? Do they understand how and where teas are made? Do they know how many different teas there are? Do they know which teas are the "top 10 Chinese teas," and the cultural connotations associated with each brand? For example, what is the difference between Long Jing, Bi Luo Chun, Mao Jian, and Wu Long? Why do people drink one kind of tea before dinner, and another kind after? Why do people in Fujian province drink Da Hong Pao, a special black tea, while people in Hangzhou city drink Long Jing, or Dragon Well, a local green tea? And why can tea leaves picked before the Qing Ming Festival in early April sell for five times more than tea leaves picked after the festival? Starbucks could have hired a dozen researchers to write a dozen treatises apiece on tea, and they still wouldn't have understood it like the Chinese.

But Starbucks was smart. In its research, the company found out that the Chinese market loves luxury goods

301

and they launched a marketing campaign that portrayed Starbucks as the epitome of chic. Starbucks was portrayed as "an authentic representation of American leisure culture." It became an upscale venue for informal executive meetings and friendly get-togethers, in some ways replacing the traditional tea-house. Starbucks was new, trendy, and just a little exotic. Their coffees sold like hotcakes. Now, China is Starbucks' second-largest market, and its coffee is a status symbol in all the major cities. By 2015, there will be 1500 Starbucks stores in China. The people at Starbucks did their homework and they *innovated* in China. And they succeeded.

Pearman: That reminds me of the story of Häagen-Dazs ice cream. They cater to the luxury market, like Starbucks, and they have special products for the Chinese market. For those of our readers who don't know, during the Mid-Autumn Festival, it's traditional to give moon cake pastries to friends, family, and business associates. The thing is, many people disliked the way they taste. Häagen-Dazs now sells a premium ice cream version of the moon cake, which is seen as an upscale alternative to the traditional moon cake.

Wang: Starbucks and Häagen-Dazs both had cultural competence; it showed in how they could recognize and penetrate the Chinese luxury goods market. And yet this cultural competence is so often undervalued. We have long ago recognized that history did not "end" after Communism fell, and yet it sometimes seems businesses are living in Fukuyama's utopia of a perfectly liberal-capitalist globe. Businesses rely too much on formulas, convinced that in the 21st century, countries are more alike than different; what has worked in one place must work in another.

Let me ask you something: if someone had done business successfully in Italy, would they automatically be qualified to do business in Japan?

Pearman: Absolutely not. It's a whole different culture with a different set of rules, for that matter, it's a whole different *language*!

Wang: Absolutely, but many firms don't recognize this, and they apply it to their business models. If a certain strategy has been successfully implemented to create and sell a product in Italy, *voilà*, it's international and will work in Japan! Or China. But you need cultural competence to develop a good business plan, and that competence is tremendously country-specific.

Pearman: You know, in the mid-1800s in China, California was viewed as "Gum Shan," the "Gold Mountain," someplace to get rich quickly and easily. No one knew of the hardships and pitfalls waiting in the gold fields. And now I feel that China has become "Gum Shan" to those companies who approach it confident in their ability to make money with an "international" strategy.

Wang: There are so many pitfalls, as we both know. For starters, China and the United States exist in, as Ford said, "parallel universes." We've seen there can be miscommunication on both sides, such as when the Chinese are ultra-sensitive of their own feeling of victimhood, and when Americans are led by prejudice instead of knowledge and trust. And we understand that there is really no such thing as a uniform "international" business model. Doing business with China and the Chinese people requires cultural competence, which is deceptively simple but exquisitely profound.

Pearman: If you ask me, cultural competence starts with two things: awareness and humility. Specifically, you have to be aware that "you don't know what you don't know" and be open to learning, as well as a willingness to trust in people's good intentions. You also have to be humble, to accept that many Western ideas will not change China, and must be changed by China in order to work properly. However, cultural competence will mean that you have something valuable to bring to the table. If you remember those two things, humility and awareness, there's a good chance that you and the Chinese can achieve success together.

Wang: Indeed. I hope this conversation has been illuminating and helpful for our readers. Remember that we Chinese may live in parallel universes, but we don't eat puppies. And if a business develops an understanding of China and the Chinese people, it may well find there is some gold in the Gum Shan.

Hidden Rules

Wang: In cross-border communication, you have to guard against not only mistranslation, but also misinterpretation. For instance, if you go to the Supreme Court of Minnesota, you will see a mural of Confucius and his disciples titled "The Recording of the Precedents." In it, they are making records of past legal proceedings to guide future rulings. If you go to the United States Supreme Court, you also will find Confucius on the top of the "Eastern Pediment," sharing space with Moses and Solon, who are chosen to represent the lawgivers of three great civilizations: Judea, China and Athens. But Confucius was adamantly against the public proclamations of the laws; he did not *like* laws. He believed that if a society's rulers were virtuous and moral; their subjects would emulate them, obviating the need for laws. The practice of creating and publishing laws, then punishing people for violating them, would just encourage people to do whatever they could to avoid punishment. According to Confucius, it was better to craft a code and keep it secret from ordinary citizens.

Top of the eastern pediment, the Supreme Court of the United States

Doing so would allow those who enforced the code to use some moral judgment and discretion in applying it. But why then should the Westerners believe Confucius was a great lawgiver and even recorded precedents?

Pearman: I think it has to do with the popular image and perception of Confucius. Westerners imagine Confucius as a withered wise man with a long beard, handing out sage advice to his disciples. And in the West, the idea of "lawgiver" is a natural outgrowth from the idea of "teacher." A teacher explains the ways to live and conduct oneself properly; a lawgiver codifies these teachings into rules for a civilization.

Wang: Exactly. People start with a popular image (which is erroneous, by the way), and then extrapolate from it based on how things work in *their* society. More often than not, of course, they're quite wrong.

For starters, Confucius was not a passive individual. He was a firm believer in exercise and fitness; maintaining good physical health was one of the marks of a "true gentleman." And he didn't wait around for students to come

305

to him; he publicized his ideals vigorously and was a great orator. So in the end, he typified someone who taught by example and personal inspiration—which is how he felt society should be led.

Chow Yun-fat's new interpretation of Confucius is historically accurate.

Confucianism is not the only part of China that's misunderstood by many Americans. Indeed, I think a lot of people who come to China have the mindset that China is simply an undeveloped United States with no minimum wage. What I mean by that is that they're unprepared for many of the things they will face in doing business. For instance, it is commonly accepted that China is a Confucian society under Communist rule, or China is a Communist regime with Confucian values. But Chinese like Professor Wu Si, a leading historian and intellectual, would tell you that China is actually a society governed by "hidden rules." It's something of a shadow code, a parallel system of practices that aren't publicly acknowledged, but everybody knows except the outsiders. One must understand and obey these rules to do business with China and the Chinese. And more than that, this system informs a great deal of the unofficial governing philosophy of China. The system of "hidden rules" dates back thousands of years, though it's only been named and even partially acknowledged in the last decade-and-a-half.

Pearman: How did these hidden rules come to be?

Wang: Maybe it all started with Confucianism. As I said earlier, Confucius taught that the legal code should not be widely known or understood. Hence, in Imperial China, knowledge of the law was reserved for officials. Only the officials were allowed to know the laws, because they were considered the "parents" of society. Confucius believed that if the officials knew the laws, they would guide people down a righteous path by example, use compassion and flexibility to correct them, and cultivate an atmosphere of virtue.

Pearman: So in essence, the officials had complete control over the people they administered, and those people had no way of knowing what rights they might have or if an official were doing anything wrong. I have a feeling that didn't turn out very well.

Wang: It didn't. Without a publicized law code, you see, there was no way to guard against abuses. And if Chinese officials were parents, they were the sort of parents who would lose their children today. Part of the ideology of being a "parent official" meant that the official-and the government as a whole—automatically *knew better* than the people they governed, and were allowed to hurt them —in order to help them. Of course, this was in the name of protecting and teaching them. They saw no need to take the considerations of the people they governed into account; do parents let a toddler tell them what sort of groceries to buy?

Pearman: Paternalism at its most condescending, in other words. And I'm sure that none of those officials missed out on the chance to line their own pockets.

Wang: Rampant corruption was attendant to the system. Low-level officials exploited the peasants and merchants; higher-level officials demanded "gifts" from their inferiors. If you didn't play the game, you never got anywhere, and you were likely to be forced from your job, or worse. The Ming and Qing dynasties tried to eradicate this corruption, but they were unsuccessful, because corruption is embedded within the system. One of the "hidden rules" is that corruption is permitted as long as you are loyal to the system. But the King/Party has total discretion to use corruption to punish/discipline you if you lose their trust.

Pearman: I take it that mass executions of the Imperial bureaucrats would have been too steep a price to pay.

Wang: Moreover, there was no guarantee that whomever they selected to replace them would not simply return to corruption. The sad truth of the matter is, not even the upheavals of the 20th century have disrupted the basic ideas of "hidden rules." It was in 1999 that historian Wu Si coined the term "hidden rules," but they are far from history.

Pearman: Hidden rules developed because of the lack of a publicized legal code. Are you saying that having a widely known set of laws hasn't helped?

Wang: It has helped, but less than you might think. I'll give you an example. The salaries of many civil servants in China are quite low. Yet plenty of candidates are always available to fill them. Many do this because they approach the job the same way officials did when they purchased positions in the Imperial system. The job is simply the key to wealth and power.

Pearman: So the law can say what it likes, but the idea of a "parent official" is too ingrained in the culture to be erased overnight?

Wang: Sadly, this appears to be the case. Many at even the highest levels of government still feel that having a position of power entitles them to enrich themselves at the cost of society. Only recently, Zhou Yongkang, former head of the entire security and the judiciary, was arrested on charges of corruption. It turned out that he was not only extremely corrupt on a personal basis; he was the "godfather" of the biggest organized crime organization in the world.

Pearman: I'm curious . . . does that sense of personal entitlement bleed over into other aspects of government?

Wang: Absolutely! Consider another aspect of the "parent official." Parents, unfortunately, often feel as if their child has no right to keep secrets from them; they have no right to privacy. In China, the government, despite all laws and protestations to the contrary, essentially believes that its citizens have no right to any privacy. The government should be able to know everything about them whenever it wants.

Pearman: That's fascinating, and more than a little terrifying. It is an interesting contrast with the American system: here, the government is seen as potentially intrusive and subject to checks, whereas in China, government intrusion is a "good" thing — the government knows best and has only your best interest at heart.

Wang: Yes. There's also an unfortunate corollary: anyone who agitates for the right of privacy *must* be suspect.

Pearman: Because why would you want to hide things from your "parents?"

Wang: Precisely.

Guanxi, 關係

Wang: Moving on to another facet of "hidden rules," you may have heard of the case of GlaxoSmithKline. GSK, as it's commonly called, is a British pharmaceutical company. Its China branch is now facing a serious problem. In order to boost revenues, some of their senior managers in China engaged in some questionable practices, including bribing government officials who regulate the healthcare industry, paying kickbacks to doctors for prescribing GSK drugs, and arranging vacations for doctors and officials.

Pearman: I take it there's more to this story than a corrupt branch of big pharma getting their just desserts?

Wang: Well, GSK's China team made an interesting argument. According to them, they were simply playing the game according to Chinese rules. *Every* pharmaceutical company in China bribes doctors and officials. It's not talked about, but an absolute prerequisite for doing business: yet another "hidden rule." In fact, GSK was less open about it than most Chinese firms, who openly hand over cash to doctors.

And I'd argue that GSK is less morally reprehensible than a lot of the Chinese companies for another reason: *their drugs actually work*. Many Chinese companies behave like the villain in "The Third Man," selling defective drugs that don't help or actively harm the people to which they're administered.

Pearman: This begs the question: why did the government single out GSK to punish? If they were just playing the game, and behaving better than most, why did they deserve punishment?

Wang: Closely entwined with "hidden rules" is something called the "double standard." Officials feel perfectly entitled to both engage in corruption and prosecute people for being corrupt. In a way, this ties back to the presumed benevolence of "parent official." A "parent official" may choose to let a citizen do something in return for a bribe, or they make take the bribe and not help the citizen or even arrest them. But imply that *they* did anything wrong and you'd get a blank stare. After all, they're a *parent*. Parents can't be judged by the same standard as children.

Pearman: It strikes me that there could be another facet to the persecution of GSK. I remember reading that back when Mexico was run as a one-party state, drug trafficking was much less violent than it is today. Drug traffickers would simply pay their bribes to an official and move their products to the U.S.A.; no muss, no fuss. But every so often, the government would arrest a major drug trafficker. It wasn't because they forgot to pay or because they'd gotten rebellious. *It was just to show that they could.* In other words, it was a reminder that the government, not the traffickers, or in this case, GSK, held the upper hand in the relationship.

Wang: Precisely: *It was just to show that they could.* And the most amusing thing is every time a scandal came out, any time a high official got busted, you will hear the propaganda machine praise the authority and assure the people that this just shows how determined the government is on anti-corruption.

Pearman: This is kind of insulting. They underestimate the intelligence of the people.

Wang: You may also have heard that the JP Morgan Chase case is in some hot water right now. Apparently, they hired several Chinese nationals as full-time employees and consultants. Turned out that many of them are members of the "red nobility," or the princelings, and their positions were merely sinecures. JP Morgan is now under investigation by the U.S. government for violating the Foreign Corrupt Practices Act (FCPA).

Pearman: For those readers who may not be familiar with the term, the "red nobility" consists of the families of the oldest Communist Party leaders: the descendants of those who marched with Mao. Since the arrival of capitalism to China, I know that the red nobility has leveraged its

311

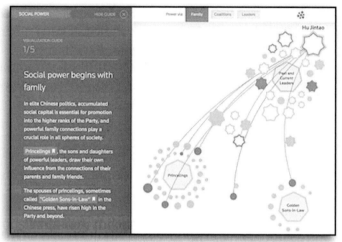

An illustration produced by Reuters "Connected China" shows extensive networks of Chinese leaders. © Thomson Reuters

status to become extremely rich. The "princelings" are a specific subset of individuals—the lineal descendants of the original leaders. Many of them are seen as spoiled brats, enjoying the vast benefits their position brings without providing anything in return.

Wang: And so they get no-show positions so that JP Morgan can operate in China. If you have the right ancestors, finding a job is never that difficult.

Pearman: I'm reminded of the "legacy" programs at the Ivy League schools. If you had an ancestor who went to Harvard, Princeton or Yale, you don't have to be nearly as smart as the rest of the applicants to get in.

I understand this kind of connection plays a major role in Chinese society, too. Would you agree?

Wang: I agree wholeheartedly. The system you just alluded to is known as "guanxi," and it's one of the most misunderstood aspects of doing business with China. There was a book titled "Guanxi" about Microsoft's operations in

China, and a handful of business books have been written that mention "guanxi," but very few of them ever understand the true meaning of the term.

At its basis, "guanxi" is about connections. The problem of Western thinking on this issue is that when they hear "connections," they think "networking," and since they know everything about networking, they assume they understand *guanxi*. In fact, if you replace "gaunxi" with "networking," you would've lost "guanxi."

There are three key features of "guanxi" that I'd like to address. But first, a definition. "Guanxi" describes the basic dynamic in personalized networks of influence, and is a central idea in Chinese society. There are three key features about "guanxi," which are not apparent to outsiders:

1) "Guanxi" cannot be transferred.

2) "Guanxi" *must* be understood within the context of a strictly hierarchal and somewhat opaque system, and,

3) "Guanxi" is a double-edged sword.

When I say "guanxi" cannot be transferred, I mean it in the following way. Suppose you make a contact in the Chinese business community, and this contact introduces you to a Chinese official. Now, in the Western sense of networking, you might assume that you can approach this official for help in the future. This is not true in China. Any contact with this official needs to be handled through your original contact in the business community. Many businesspeople assume they can build "guanxi" with people they've just met. The reality is that the links of "guanxi" are only established over years, if ever, and by trying to force them, you will alienate everyone.

I'd like to preface my second point by stating that there is not a single unified "guanxi system" in China. It's not possible to simply start at the bottom and work your way to the top. There are thousands, if not millions, of different circles of connections. Some of them overlap, but many do not.

Pearman: So, for instance, could you say that a migrant worker has no idea how the factory bosses make the connections that enable them to get permits and supplies, and the factory bosses in turn have no idea where or how the connections are made that bring multinational businesses into China?

Wang: Yes, precisely. "Guanxi" tends to be divided by hierarchy. And even if you've gained access to a certain group, you need to understand the hierarchy within that group.

For instance, I once witnessed the catastrophic effects of failing to understand hierarchy as it relates to *guanxi*. A man I knew in New York hosted a banquet for a Chinese trade delegation. He had business he wanted to do in China, and he was trying hard to build "guanxi." He took each delegate's business card—with two hands, like all the business etiquette books say—and proffered his own, again in the approved two-handed fashion.

Having read the cards, he zeroed in on the delegate who was (apparently) the highest-ranking. As it happened, this man spoke English, and the host plied him with conversation and attention. And by the time we reached the dessert course, he was pushing hard to get the approval he needed for his projects in China. That was another thing he'd read, you see: all business in China is done at the dinner table.

But the official the man was speaking to never gave him a straight answer. And the dinner ended without the man making any progress. Still, he was confident that, all things considered, he'd built some good "guanxi."

In fact, that was the end of his deal.

Why he was finished has to do with the opacity of the Chinese system. The host of the dinner had read all of the

314

business cards and assumed that actual power was vested in the man who was ostensibly the highest ranking — partly because the English translation of their titles. The man with real power had an unassuming title and didn't speak a word of English; he'd been left alone to stew all through the dinner while the host lavished attention on his *de facto* subordinate. The powerful man was eager to connect with Americans but he felt vulnerable and embarrassed after the dinner.

My third point about "guanxi" is that possessing it incurs risk. The CPC is constantly racked with power struggles, big or small. Whenever an official goes down, foreigners with whom he'd built "guanxi" tend to be hit with a wave of corruption charges. Being tied to someone has risks as well as rewards.

Pearman: So any time you build "guanxi" with someone, you're backing a horse, and the trick is to pick winners — or at least, bigger winners than your losers.

Wang: Exactly.

Ti-yong, 体用

Pearman: I'd like to ask you about something I read in the news: On Jan. 30, Minister of Education Yuan Guiren spoke at a conference on ideology and propaganda in higher education, saying it was necessary "to strengthen control over the use of original-edition [i.e., not processed and censored by the party] Western materials. We must by no means allow materials that propagate Western values into our classrooms; it is absolutely forbidden for all kinds of speech that attacks and slanders the Party's leadership and blackens socialism to appear in university classrooms; it is absolutely forbidden to have all kinds of speech that violates the Constitution and the law spread in university classrooms; it is absolutely forbidden for teachers to complain and vent in the classroom and to transmit all kinds of harmful moods to students."

What I found interesting about this speech was the fact that Mr. Yuan did not know or had chosen to forget that his country is run on a Chinese interpretation of a "Western value": namely, Maoist Marx-Leninism (for the given value of Lenin as a European).

Portraits of Lenin and Stalin on the Tiananmen Square in Beijing. Their portraits, as well as portraits of Karl Marx and Frederic Engels, were normally displayed during the most important holidays in China. The practice lasted until the 1990s.

Wang: I understand your confusion. This incident reminds me of a time when a group of Chinese government officials came to the University of Minnesota to receive training on public administration and public policy. Before the course began, they coolly informed the professor, "We are coming here to see how you are doing things, but we will never adopt a Western-style government system." And by "Western-style" they meant "democratic."

Pearman: Well, what on Earth is the point of studying administration and policy in a Western college if you don't support democracy?

316

Wang: I believe they were trying to find out if Western-style methods of administration were more efficient than the ones they were using. China, you see, has become very good at using bits and pieces of the Western system to support the maintenance of the authority of the Party. It's something that Chinese have been doing ever since the 1860s, and it's best explained by a vital concept called the "ti-yong" dichotomy.

I'll explain that more fully in a moment. But first, think back to when Nixon opened China in 1972. Nixon, guided by Kissinger, assumed that he was setting China on the road to democracy. More contact with the West would increase democracy's allure, make the forces of liberalization harder to resist. Bill Clinton, encouraged by the capitalist reforms and mild liberalizations of Deng Xiaoping, made this same assumption when he normalized trade relations with China.

What these smart men failed to take into account was the "ti-yong" dichotomy. The "ti-yong dichotomy" is best explained this way: China can use practical Western ideas, such as jet fighters or stock markets. But the guiding principles of China, its "ti," will always stay Chinese, untouched by Western influence. In the 1860s when this philosophy was developed, "ti" meant the Imperial system and Confucianism. After a brief interlude of comparative intellectual freedom during the reign of the Republic of China, when "Mr. Democracy and Mr. Science" were introduced to the nation by Dr. Sun Yat-Sen, "ti" was re-established as Marxism, and later, Maoism.

The "ti-yong" dichotomy was introduced after China suffered a crushing defeat in the First Sino-Japanese War, its antiquated armed forces thoroughly outclassed by the Western-trained Japanese. Though there was general agreement that China could learn a lot from the West on how to strengthen itself, there was very little agreement on how to learn, how much to learn and how fast the learning could be implemented. The concern was that China should not lose its uniqueness and traditional values as it tried to craft widespread reforms and fundamental changes throughout the country.

China sought to emulate the Meiji Restoration that had strengthened Japan through modernization. Similar to the Meiji restoration, the Chinese Foreign Affairs Movement was an attempt to extract Western knowledge to bolster Chinese power. The principle of the movement was articulated by Zhang Zhidong (張之洞), who in 1898 published "Exhortation to Study." In it, he insisted on a method of relatively conservative reform, summarized in the phrase "Chinese learning for fundamental principles, or *ti*, and Western learning for practical application, or *yong*."

After seeing Japan's great successes, China sought to bring in technical experts, engineers and manufacturers to acquire the knowledge to recreate and adapt Western weapons and machines. Many in China believed that the West's power came from its deadly and effective arms and warships. Thus, Imperial officials hired experts to build the ships, munitions, and other weapons they believed would give China the capacity to become a great military power. What they failed to realize was that the Meiji Restoration also had been founded on building an efficient bureaucracy and a parliamentary monarchy with a Constitution. Neither of these were introduced in China, nor were there educational reforms or a loosening of social classes. And from then on, China's absolute rulers, though willing to accept Western guns, science and economics, have turned their back on political freedoms. It's notable that when Deng Xiaoping decided to rebuild China after Mao's death, he did so with 'four modernizations' taken from the West: agriculture, industry, national defense, and science and technology. Some political activists also declared the need for a 'fifth modernization'—democracy—but this was not accepted by the CPC.

Pearman: And yet, as we have said, Marxism remains a Western idea.

Wang: That's why we need this conversation. Perhaps if people understood the contradictions in their own philosophy, they would be more open to change of all kinds.

Additional resources

Pearman: Now that this series is coming to the end, I hope that we've helped people gain a better understanding of China. For continued learning, what are some books or movies you would recommend that cover the complexity of doing business with China?

Wang: Start with Xi Jinping's **"Governance of China,"** the one Mark Zuckerberg is reading and asking his senior staff to read! What a nice gesture for Zuckerberg to make nice with the upper echelons of Beijing! But I am still not sure a dark brown nose would convince Beijing to unblock Facebook.

But seriously, for general historical and cultural content: Jonathan Spence, Orville Schell, Perry Link, and Minxin Pei are all quite relevant to today's China. If your time is limited, I have a few specific titles to recommend:

Evan Osnos's "Age of Ambition: Chasing Fortune, Truth, and Faith in the New China" paints a "riveting and troubling portrait of a people in a state of extreme anxiety about their identity, values and future." It's a very accurate portrait of contemporary China and the Chinese people, though I would just argue that instead of an "Age of Ambition," China finds itself in an "Age of Anxiety."

319

An earlier book (published in 2012) that remains relevant is "The Party: The Secret World of China's Communist Rulers" by Richard McGregor. The Economist review says (and I agree) "this is a marvelous and finely written study of how China is really run, and how its strange but successful system of Leninist capitalism really works."

For the Bo Xilai scandal, which lit up the system's corruption and power struggles with a spotlight, I'd recommend "Death at the Lucky Holiday Hotel: Murder, Money, and an Epic Power Struggle in China," by Pin Ho.

For snippets of Chinese life that reveal parts of a broader whole, I'd recommend "Postcards from Tomorrow Square: Reports from China" by James Fallows, "Country Driving: A Journey from Farm to Factory" by Peter Hessler, and "China in Ten Words," by Yu Hua.

Chinese translation of *1984*

Pearman: I read Yu Hua's book. He takes a unique approach to explaining China, studying the connotations of 10 words such as "leader" (Mao's impact and legacy) and "bambooze" (the massive copyright infringement at the center of China's freewheeling economy) to explain the nation. It's a great piece, and I agree it's very helpful. But are there any fictions that capture the Chinese experience?

Wang: It pains me to say this, but George Orwell for the realities of daily life, and Kafka for the state of mind.

Pearman: What about documentaries or movies?

Wang: There are several I'd recommend. "From Mao to Mozart: Isaac Stern in China" covers the experiences of Isaac Stern, an American violin virtuoso and conductor who was invited to tour China in 1979 and again 20 years later. It's a beautiful film that shows the joy of music and China's tentative recovery from the ravages of the Cultural Revolution.

Ted Koppel's "The People's Republic of Capitalism" is a more down-to-earth film, focused on the gritty, gilded realities of modern China. The British Channel 4 documentary "China: Triumph and Turmoil," produced by Niall Ferguson, is also worth watching.

There's also one fictional film I'd like to recommend. It's called "The Story of Qiu Ju," about a pregnant woman trying to find justice for her injured husband in the labyrinth of Chinese bureaucracy. It's terrific. It is the most accurate picture of the Chinese legal system I have ever seen.

Perman: In your view, are there any books and films about China that are not accurate and potentially misleading?

Wang: I would not recommend the popular business etiquette books about China. They teach people how to receive business cards but not how to communicate.

I would *not* recommend Henry Kissinger's "On China." Kissinger and President Nixon believed they "opened" China to the West. I would argue that in fact, America was "opened" by Mao. By allowing the visit, Mao showed that he was still in control of China, and it was such a stunning success that he managed to stay in power for four more years. Otherwise, the ravages of the Cultural Revolution and the Lin Biao incident in 1971 might well have seen him deposed.

And finally, I do not recommend the Richard Gere's masterpiece "Red Corner," in which an American businessman finds himself in what is apparently an alternate universe iteration of China, where a foreigner accused of murder can team up with a Chinese lawyer to prove his innocence. Richard Gere is a great actor, but everything about China in that film was so wrong!

Perman: So, in closing, what is the most important piece of advice you can offer to anyone who wants to do business with China and the Chinese people?

Wang: "Do the right thing," not "do things right."

Chinese Law for Swiss Students*

A brief look at the legal system of a country that's difficult to understand

NZZ: Professor Wang, why does it make sense for Swiss students, to care about such a brief look at Chinese law?

Chang Wang: The first reason is walking through the streets of Lucerne, right under our noses: the streams of tourists from China grow year by year, and these people spend a lot of money. Here in Switzerland, people should at least have an idea of who they are and from what circumstances they come.

Besides, China is too large and too important for global economics and politics to be ignored. It makes sense to assume that that country will win greater significance and influence. There are also good arguments to be made that in the coming years, China will undergo processes of huge changes, which will also have a big influence on global business and politics. In any case, one should have at least a little understanding of that enormous country. I appreciate it very much, that Professor Alexander Morawa of the University of Lucerne understands China's importance, and is inclined to listen to the arguments of both sides.

---

*This is an interview with Chang Wang by Anna Chudozilov, reporter from Neue Zürcher Zeitung (New Journal of Zurich) on the subject of his teachings on Chinese law and history in Switzerland. The interview's original German version appeared in NZZ Campus on June 10th, 2011. The English version was translated from German by Janice Anderson.

NZZ: What knowledge of Chinese law would you like to convey to the Swiss students?

Chang Wang: In my presentation, of course I focus on the current legal system, but I also try to provide a few facts from the 4000-year-old history of this country. Because one can hardly understand Chinese law without knowing the historical connections. The students should learn the different paradigms and patterns of discourse of law in China and learn to analyze the legal system from a comparative viewpoint. In the instruction, I also value having the students get to know the traditional societal role of the law in China. A further crucial point lies in the understanding of the relationships of China with western countries and the efforts to introduce western legal models into China.

I share with students how the abstract norms of daily life work themselves out. So, for example, access to information in China is a privilege, not a right. Last year when Chinese human rights activist Liu Xiaobo was granted the Nobel peace prize, each time that foreign TV programs, which one could see in some hotels, mentioned the Nobel peace prize, they would be interrupted. It's also important for me to convey, that a rule of law, as we in the west know it, simply does not exist. It's not that there are no laws. The Chinese legal system is, rather, if you will, very flexible: if one wants to achieve a certain result, one simply creates a corresponding law.

NZZ: European universities try to have good relations with Chinese colleges in order to make possible foreign stays for their students. What should one pay attention to, when one is interested in a foreign semester in China?

Chang Wang: The Chinese college system is very young, the difference between colleges is immense. In the field of law, there's only been an actual collegiate education for about 30 years. That's why there's also a dearth of qualified teaching staff. While in the meantime there are colleges that can handle international students, the college system as a whole is massively underfunded. To be sure, this situation is improving. In any case, you can assume from that, that their home university pays attention to this in their selection of partner colleges. One must also not forget that the demands on students in China and Europe are very different. In Europe there is clearly more value laid on having students learn to formulate independent questions and to development their own solutions.

NZZ: What else must one pay attention to when one plans an exchange in China?

Chang Wang: On the one hand, the Chinese are very hospitable people and always make an effort to make a good impression. He who just stays a short time in the country, will therefore hardly get anything from the "other" China that those on longer stays get to know. On the other hand, there are good reasons not to stay too long. When one stays longer in China, one must begin to live according to the rules of the system. It can be difficult to understand this.

When, for example, you need a medical treatment in a clinic, nothing goes without the so-called "red envelope." This can also be yellow, but must contain the correct financial amount for care personnel and doctors, which one must hand over at the right moment. A second, weightier reason, which speaks against a longer stay in China, is the enormous environmental pollution and questions of food safety. He who stays too long and eats the wrong things, will get sick.

If you go to China, you need three lists: one with the tourist sights, one with tips about which foods one must try and last but not least, a list of things that you may, under no circumstances, eat.

NZZ: *What films would you like to watch to understand China?*

Chang Wang: There are many. Here two good ones and one not-so-good one.

The Story of Qiu Ju: The film tells the story of a woman from a small provincial place in Northwest China, whose husband was kicked in the groin by the town chairman. Qui decides not the let the matter rest until the chairman asks her husband's pardon. Because he refuses, she takes the case from one administrative authority to the next until she gets to the highest court in Beijing. As a viewer, one experiences the great difference between city and country of that time. The film takes place at the beginning of the 90's. A lot has changed since then. And yet it conveys a very striking impression of China's kafkaesque legal system of that time.

The Last Emperor: The history of the last emperor of China is closely tied to the history of the country in the first half of the 20th century. The film, winner of nine Oscars, tells the life of Pu Yis, who, as a 12-year-old in 1908, was declared emperor. When in 1911 the republic of China was proclaimed, he was deposed. Later the Japanese installed him as emperor of Manchukuo, but he was again deposed just a few years later by soviet troops. He dies suddenly in 1967 as a simple gardener. The film relays by means of an example of a very unusual person the life of very simple people in China in the last century.

Red Corner: The 1997 film shows well how US Americans imagine the Chinese legal system. It is purely arbitrary that he who remains stubborn and proves innocence, finally goes free. In reality, the western businessman, who in the film was accused of the murder of a woman, would probably be condemned to a draconian punishment. As a foreigner, of course he wouldn't serve a sentence. Often foreigners are simply expelled from the country shortly after the verdict; for the system, it's important to save face under all circumstances. On the contrary, the country wants to avoid trouble due to arrested foreigners.

Chinesisches Recht für Schweizer Studierende

Zum dritten Mal besuchte im September 2011 der chinesische Rechtsprofessor Chang Wang die Universität Luzern. Dort Studierenden einen Einblick in das chinesische Recht und die Geschichte seines Landes. NZZ Campus hat nachgefragt, warum Schweizer Studierende für chinesisches Recht interessieren sollten.

Professor Wang, warum ist es sinnvoll für Schweizer Studierende, sich um einen noch so kleinen Einblick in chinesisches Recht zu bemühen?

Der erste Grund spaziert direkt vor unseren Nasen durch die Strassen Luzerns: Die Touristenströme aus China wachsen von Jahr zu Jahr, und diese Menschen Geld aus. Sie sollten hier in der Schweiz wenigstens eine Ahnung haben, wer sie sind und aus welchen Verhältnissen sie kommen.

Zudem ist China zu gross und zu wichtig für die globale Wirtschaft und Politik, als dass man es ignorieren könnte. Es gibt gute Gründe davon auszugehen, weiter an Bedeutung und Einfluss gewinnen wird. Es gibt auch gute Argumente dafür, dass China in den kommenden Jahren riesige Veränderungsprozesses wird, die auch einen grossen Einfluss auf die globale Wirtschaft und Politik haben werden. So oder so sollte man versuchen, das riesige Land wenigstens verstehen. Ich schätze es sehr, dass Professor Alexander Morawa von der Universität Luzern die Wichtigkeit von China versteht und gewillt ist, Argumente anzuhören.

Welches Wissen über chinesisches Recht möchten Sie Schweizer Studierenden vermitteln?

In meiner Veranstaltung fokussiere ich zwar auf das aktuelle Rechtssystem, versuche aber auch einige Eckdaten der 4000-jährigen Geschichte des Landes Denn chinesisches Recht kann man, ohne die historischen Zusammenhänge zu kennen, kaum verstehen. Die Studierenden sollen die unterschiedlichen Diskurs-Muster des Rechts in China kennenlernen und das Rechtssystem aus komparativer Sicht analysieren. Im Unterricht lege ich auch viel Wert darauf, die traditionelle gesellschaftliche Rolle des Rechts in China kennenlernen. Ein weiterer Schwerpunkt liegt auf dem Verständnis des Verhältnisses von China Ländern und den Bemühungen, westliche Rechtsmodelle in China einzuführen.

Ich vermittle den Studierenden, wie sich abstrakte Normen auf das Alltagsleben auswirken. So ist beispielsweise der Zugang zu Informationen in China kein Recht. Als letztes Jahr der chinesische Menschenrechtler Liu Xiaobo den Friedensnobelpreis verliehen bekam, wurde das Programm von ausländischen Fernsehsendern, die man in manchen Hotel durchaus zu sehen bekommt, jedes Mal unterbrochen, wenn der Friedensnobelpreis erwähnt wurde. Wichtig vermitteln, dass eine Rechtsstaatlichkeit, wie wir sie im Westen kennen, schlicht nicht existiert. Es ist nicht so, dass es keine Gesetze gibt. Das chinesische aber — wenn man so will — sehr flexibel: Will man ein bestimmtes Ergebnis erhalten, schafft man einfach ein entsprechendes Gesetz.

Europäische Universitäten bemühen sich um gute Beziehungen zu chinesischen Hochschulen, um ihren Studierenden dort Auslandaufenthalte Was gilt es zu beachten, wenn man sich für ein Auslandsemester in China interessiert?

Das chinesische Hochschulsystem ist sehr jung, die Unterschiede zwischen den Hochschulen sind immens. Im Bereich Recht existiert eine eigentliche Hochschulausbildung erst seit rund 30 Jahren. Deshalb besteht auch ein Mangel an gut qualifizierten Lehrpersonen. Während es inzwischen Hochschulen gibt, die international können, ist das Hochschulsystem als ganzes massiv unterfinanziert. Diese Situation verbessert sich allerdings laufend. Sie können jedenfalls davon ausgehen, Heimuniversität dies bei der Wahl der Partnerhochschulen beachtet. Man darf auch nicht vergessen, dass die Anforderungen an Studierende in China und unterschiedlich sind. In Europa wird deutlich mehr Wert darauf gelegt, dass Studierende lernen, selbständig Fragestell-ungen anzugehen und eigene Lösungen entwickeln.

Was muss man noch beachten, wenn man einen Austausch in China plant?

Einerseits sind Chinesen sehr gastfreundliche Menschen und stets darum bemüht, einen guten Eindruck zu machen. Wer sich nur kurz im Land aufhält, etwas vom «anderen» China mitbekommen, das Kurzaufenthalter kennen lernen. Anderseits gibt es gute Gründe, nicht zu lange zu bleiben. Wenn sie sich aufhalten, müssen sie anfangen, nach den Regeln des Systems zu leben. Diese zu verstehen, kann sehr schwer sein.

Wenn sie beispielsweise eine medizinische Behandlung in einem Spital benötigen, geht nichts ohne sogenannte «rote Couverts». Diese können auch gelb die richtigen Geldbeträge enthalten für Pflegepersonal und Ärzte, denen man die Umschläge im richtigen Moment zu übergeben hat. Ein zweiter, gewichtiger gegen einen längeren Aufenthalt in China spricht, ist die enorme Umweltverschmutzung und Fragen der Lebensmittelsicherheit. Wer zu lange bleibt und isst, wird krank.

Wenn sie nach China kommen, brauchen sie drei Listen: Eine mit den Sehenswürdigkeiten, eine mit Tipps, welche Speisen man unbedingt probieren sollte, least eine Liste der Dinge, die sie unter keinen Umständen essen dürfen.

Filmtipps von Prof. Wang

Chang Wang bindet in seine Veranstaltungen immer wieder auch Filme ein. Hier zwei Tipps und eine Warnung.

The Story of Qiu Ju

Kommentar Chang Wang: "Der Film erzählt die Geschichte einer Frau aus einem kleinen Provinznest im Nordwesten Chinas, deren Ehemann vom Dorfvorsitzenden zwischen die Beine getreten wird. Qiu Ju beschliesst, die Sache nicht eher zu ruhen lassen, bis sich der Dorfvorsitzende bei ihrem Mann entschuldigt. Da zieht sie den Fall von Behörde zu Behörde bis zum obersten Gerichtshof von Peking. Als Zuschauer erlebt man so auch die damals schon grossen Unterschiede Stadt und Land mit. Der Film spielt Anfang der 1980er Jahre, vieles hat sich seither verändert. Und doch vermittelt er einen sehr treffenden Eindruck vom kafkaesken Rechtssystem Chinas."

The Last Emperor

Kommentar Chang Wang: "Die Geschichte des letzten Kaisers von China ist eng mit der Geschichte des Landes in der ersten Hälfte des 20. Jahrhunderts neun Oscars ausgezeichnete Film erzählt über das Leben Pu Yis, der als Zweijähriger 1908 zum Kaiser Chinas erklärt wird. Als 1911 die Republik China wird er ein erstes Mal abgesetzt. Später wird er von den Japanern als Kaiser von Mandschukuo eingesetzt, nur wenige Jahre später aber wieder von sowjetischen abgesetzt. Er stirbt schliesslich 1967 als einfacher Gärtner. Der Film erzählt am Beispiel eines sehr ungewöhnlichen Menschen auch viel über das Leben Menschen im China des vergangenen Jahrhunderts."

Red Corner

Kommentar Chang Wang: "Der Film aus dem Jahr 1997 zeigt schön, wie sich US-Amerikaner das chinesische Rechtssystem vorstellen. Es sei zwar voller hartnäckig bleibt und die Unschuld beweist, kommt schliesslich frei. In Wirklichkeit wäre der westliche Geschäftsmann, der in dem Film des Mordes an beschuldigt wird, sehr wahrscheinlich zu einer drakonischen Strafe verurteilt worden. Als Ausländer müsste er diese allerdings wohl nicht absitzen. Ausländer kurz nach dem Urteil einfach aus dem Land ausgewiesen: Für das System ist es wichtig, unter allen Umständen das Gesicht zu wahren. Ärger wegen inhaftierten Ausländern will das Land hingegen vermeiden."

Teaching American Law in Switzerland

In the last week of September 2011, I visited Lucerne, Switzerland and co-taught a week-long law course at the University of Lucerne Faculty of Law, where I have taught condensed Chinese-law and American-law courses annually since 2009. This year, Professor Joan Howland, associate dean for information and technology of the University of Minnesota Law School, joined me to co-teach a course, "American Law Fundamentals: Globalization and Artistic Interpretations."

We used Hollywood films to teach some fundamental concepts of American law, because we believe that artistic representations of American law in 20th century American films offer unique visual and emotional perspectives on the context in which the legal order operates — and serve as a valuable supplement to the case method and blackletter laws. This interdisciplinary approach not only engaged students in a more visual and emotional way to understand and discuss legal concepts, but also provided the broader context of humanities and arts in which legal discourse evolves.

Twenty-eight students—from Switzerland, Austria, Luxembourg, Germany, and Canada—took this class. All had good English skills and, as you can imagine, class discussions were vibrant.

The eight films we used in our teaching—and the subject matter covered in each—were:

- The Paper Chase: Legal Education

- A Civil Action: Civil Procedure (Rule 11); Environmental Torts

- The Insider: Corporations (Corporate Liability)

- The Devil and Daniel Webster: Contract and Jury Trial

- The People v. Larry Flynt: The First Amendment

- Reversal of Fortune: Criminal Law and Criminal Procedure (Search and Seizure)

- My Cousin Vinny: Evidence (Expert Testimony)

- . . . And Justice for All: Criminal Justice System in the U.S.

Fred Gordon, recently retired Editor-in-Chief, Legal Editorial Operations, was the guest speaker in our first class. He spoke about the forms of legal information, and about the contributions that Thomson Reuters/West makes to the legal research enterprise. Fred and his wife Karen were enjoying their "Grand Tour" of Europe and, by pure serendipity, our paths crossed in Lucerne. His speech was very well received. The official legal research tool for our class is, of course, Westlaw®.

Both Dean Howland and I are impressed by the students' enthusiasm for American law, and by their depth of understanding of it.

Students' final grades will be based on a take-home exam. Four exam questions are below. What would your answers be?

- In the case "Hustler Magazine v. Falwell", the United States Supreme Court stated that a "bedrock principle" of the First Amendment is the protection of ideas that are "offensive or disagreeable." Larry Flynt has personified the battle to protect offensive speech. Flynt said: "If the First Amendment will protect a scumbag like me, then it will protect all of you. Because I'm the worst." Do you agree or disagree with Larry Flynt's statement? Why?

• In this course, you have been exposed to competing views on the American criminal justice system. Do you think that the American criminal justice system is a fundamentally fair system with a few of miscarriages of justice, or is the American criminal system fundamentally flawed?

• The U.S. Supreme Court is the highest court in the land, the final arbiter of federal law. Like all federal judges, Supreme Court justices are appointed for life. But the Supreme Court has made many mistakes in the past, most infamously the Dred Scott decision in 1857. Recently Erin Chemerinsky, a leading Constitutional law scholar, concluded that the role of the Supreme Court in American history is largely a "failure" and urged reform. One key reform proposal would be to limit justices to 18-year terms. Do you agree or disagree?

• The presumption of innocence is a legal right of the accused in a criminal proceeding. The burden of proof is on the prosecutor, who is required to prove the guilt of the accused beyond a reasonable doubt. "The evidence upon which a jury is justified in returning a verdict of guilty must be sufficient to produce a conviction of guilt, to the exclusion of all reasonable doubt." Although most courts refuse to attach numbers to the phrase "beyond a reasonable doubt," some people believe it means 90%, 95%, or even 99% confidence that the accused did the crime. What do you think about this standard?

Living within Parallel Universes*

Minnesota Lawyer published featured article on the "Immigrant Attorneys Among Us" Panel. © Minnesota Lawyer

Webber: You are a native of Beijing. Why did you decide to come to the United States to study and work?

Wang: I grew up in a scientific and technological family and community in Beijing. Both my parents are senior scientists at Chinese Academy of Sciences. I was born and

---

*In January, 2016, Minnesota State Bar Association (MSBA) Section of Immigration Law hosted the Second Annual "Immigrant Attorneys Among Us — Successes and Challenges of Our Colleagues Who Were Born Outside the U.S.," a panel discussion and a continuing legal education program. Chang Wang is a member of the Immigration Council at MSBA and served as a panelist at the program. The panel was moderated by Robert Webber, chair of MSBA Section of Immigration Law. This is Webber's conversation with Wang About his journey from Chinese graduate student to his career at Thomson Reuters and in immigration law. This interview first appeared in February and March issues of *China Insight*.

raised in the Zhong-guan-cun neighborhood, the "Silicon Valley" of China — the home of thousands of high-tech companies, research institutions, and dozens of top Chinese universities and technical colleges. I attended Renmin University Middle School and High School; I then went to Beijing Film Academy for my undergraduate studies, receiving a Bachelor in Fine Arts degree in filmmaking. In 1997, I went to Peking University for graduate studies, where I received an M.A. in comparative literature and cultural studies. Renmin University High School, Beijing Film Academy and Peking University are arguably three of the most liberal schools and universities in China. For nearly two years, between college and graduate school, I worked as an editor and correspondent for "Science Times," a major Chinese newspaper. In 2000, right after I graduated from Peking University Graduate School, I came to the United States and enrolled in the art history graduate program at the University of Illinois at Urbana-Champaign.

My generation is the so-called "Post-89" generation: born at the end of the "Cultural Revolution" but before the "One-Child Policy." We grew up witnessing China's cultural renaissance in the 1980s and had high hopes for a constitutional democracy in China — only to have our hopes crushed in 1989 in Tiananmen Square. We went to college after 1989 and were suffocated in the Post-Tiananmen "white terror" ideology purge and intellectual mediocrity. The authorities rewarded conformity and punished integrity. We had three options: shut up and accept all the lies; speak up and go to prison; or leave.

Many of us decided to leave.

Webber: Looking at your resume, it appears you had been trained in arts and literature for 10 years, awarded with three degrees, but you switched your career by attending law school. What's the story behind this change?

Wang: I have been frequently asked about this change of career, and my answer is: "I always wanted to discuss art with lawyers, and discuss law with artists."

But seriously, there was no one single reason. Rather, the decision was made based on the "totality of the circumstances." There was a "preponderance of evidence" that mainstream contemporary art had departed the traditional roles in aesthetic engagement and spiritual inquiry, and had become a multi-layered for-profit business. Perhaps this disillusion led me to question the prospect of spending the rest of my life studying and commenting on the contemporary "Emperor's New Clothes."

On the other hand, it was precisely the love of art that made me quit a career in art. You may be surprised to learn that art historians and art critics seldom "enjoy" art, because art is an object for them to study and work with. Appreciating art as a human being is a luxury they can't afford. But now I can go to galleries and museums, look at an artwork, and enjoy every minute of it.

Webber: Why did you choose the University of Minnesota Law School for your legal education?

Wang: Like most law school applicants, I applied for a number of law schools and received several offers. As I was deciding which offer to accept, I paid visits to a number of campuses. My visit to Minneapolis played a key role in my decision-making process, but, that was in early summer . . .

To learn the whole story, please indulge me for a few minutes and read the opening paragraphs in my book "New Tales of the Twin Cities: The History, Law, and Culture of Minnesota," the first Chinese language book about Minnesota, published last year by Thomson Reuters.

"It was summer, 2003, when I paid a campus visit to the University of Minnesota Law School. The sky was high, and the lakes were glassy. Minnesotans were out hiking, biking, kayaking, and walking dogs. If summer were a song, the song sang itself. The Chinese translation of "Minnesota" (明尼苏达) made perfect sense to me in the summer. The first Chinese character means bright and clear, the third character means wake or recover, and the last character means eminent, distinguished, or thorough. The translation appears to be faithful, expressive, and elegant, I said to myself.

"With "bright" and "clear" in mind, I agreed. Three months later, I came back to Minneapolis as a 1L—and as the only Chinese student in the U of M Law School Class of 2006.

"What I hadn't realized was that in Minnesota, summer was a loan that must be repaid in winter. When I again strolled around Lake Harriet during final-exam week in December, the lake had changed its face dramatically: it was now quiet and bleak. The only songs I could hear were the elegy in my heart, a curse directed at the person who had translated Minnesota as 明尼苏达, and an Edward Munch-style "scream" inside.

"I spent my first winter break in Beijing, which is notorious for its Mongolian wind. Compared to Minnesota's wind chill, however, Northern China's winter blow is a nuisance at best. I remember being at the U.S. Embassy in Beijing, applying for a student visa to re-enter the U.S., in order to continue my legal education. After examining the I-20 form that the University of Minnesota International Office had issued, the visa officer looked up at me rather sympathetically and said: "Minnesota, eh? It's . . . cold." Before I could even respond, he had stamped my application—"Approved," as if he were worried that I might change my mind.

"The most difficult part of Minnesota's winter is neither the cold, nor the snow, nor even the wind chill — it's the gray sky. In this regard, the first character 明 (bright and clear) of the Chinese translation is scandalously misleading. Cold is refreshing, wind clears the mind, and blizzards harden the will; but gloomy skies add nothing but depression and sorrow to never-ending Contracts lectures in the windowless classrooms of Mondale Hall and to sleepless nights in the law library. You begin to think hard, soul-searching deep thoughts. During a Minnesota winter, it seems, it is much easier to relate to Henrik Ibsen, Søren Kierkegaard, and Igmar Bergman, than to Benjamin Cardozo, Oliver Wendell Holmes, or Sandra Day O'Connor."

Webber: I am glad you survived, passed the bar exam, and became a member of the Minnesota Bar. Could you tell us of your experience with the bar exam?

Wang: I took the Minnesota Bar Exam in July 2006, passed it, and was sworn in as an "Attorney and Counselor of Law" on October 27, 2006, by the justices of the Minnesota Supreme Court.

Like many of my classmates, I took bar preparation courses. If you are very self-disciplined, the preparation course is not necessary. But if you are like me, then you probably also need a classroom full of sweating applicants, to remind you that this is serious business. One thing many of us realized after the exam — "spoiler alert" to law students — the law school courses, the bar exam preparation course, and the bar exam are three totally different things! The bar exam is just like any standardized exam: hard, but fair. If you give 40 days of serious attention to preparation, you will pass it.

Looking back, the 40 days of preparing for the bar exam, and the 40 days of preparing for the LSAT before law school, were two of my happiest times. I was focused, motivated, determined, had a clear goal and, every day I was making progress toward achieving my goal. Your fate is totally in your own hands. This is precious.

Webber: How did you land in Thomson Reuters? Could you tell us your experience with the job search?

Wang: As you can tell, I am one of the "non-traditional" law students. I was older than most of my classmates; I was one of the few non-native English-speakers in my class, and my publication list — a few dozen journal articles and essays — was too long for law firms. Neither did I envision myself practicing corporate finance in a downtown firm.

I received a scholarship from the University of Minnesota and, all through law school, I worked as assistant training program manager for the Office of International Programs and the China Center. During the second year of law school, I worked on a global strategy and due diligence project for Thomson Reuters (then Thomson Legal and Regulatory). After I had completed the project, I was offered a job, which I accepted.

Thomson Reuters is the world's leading source of intelligent information for businesses and professionals. I lead special research projects and facilitate company joint initiatives with the academic and business communities. I also develop and manage Continuing Legal Education programs and diversity training programs and serve as a resident expert on legal, regulatory, language, and international project management for Thomson Reuters.

I consider myself the most fortunate in term of career development. As the common saying goes: "you work for company, but you also work for people." My supervisor and colleagues at Thomson Reuters are great professionals and wonderful human beings.

Webber: I understand you also practice immigration law. Regarding your current practice, please explain challenges versus benefits of being an immigrant.

Wang: In my company, I have been advising human resources involving various aspects of work visas and legal permanent residency under EB1 (b) and EB1 (c). Also, I practice immigration law part time, mostly pro-bono, for prominent artists and scholars under EB1 (a). I also serve as the official liaison to United States Citizenship and Immigration Services (USCIS) for the American Bar Association (ABA).

The benefits of being an immigrant practicing immigration law are quite obvious: first of all, immigration law is just part of my life. From F1 student visa to Optional Practical Training (OPT), from H1B work visa to permanent residency, I have gone through the whole process for myself and for my family: I-20 form, financial support affidavits, visa interviews, labor certificate, expert support letters, 140 petition, adjustment of status, work permit, travel documents, advance parole, etc. You have to deal with them all the time.

Secondly, language is of the utmost importance in cultural communication and legal representation of immigration cases. Martin Heidegger says that "language is the house of being, in its home man dwells." If I were not bilingual, I would not be able to manage cross-border projects and represent Chinese clients.

Third, my academic background in arts and literature is indispensible in representing artists and scholars petitioning for legal permanent residency to the United States as "alien with extraordinary ability." Being a member of both the academic and art communities allows me to competently and zealously advocate for them and present compelling cases on their behalf. I travel between different parallel universes: art, business, law, without being disoriented—thanks to my 10 years academic training in the arts.

Admittedly, challenges abound. The language and cultural barriers we immigrants overcome are frequently underappreciated, for example, and people sometimes judge the competence and intelligence of others by family name and accent. As a Chinese immigrant in particular, I am sorry to say that, even though the Chinese Exclusion Act was repealed in 1943, we still feel the shadow it casts in American society.

Webber: How has your practice evolved? And how do you see it continuing to evolve?

Wang: My work at Thomson Reuters has evolved from legal information product development and international project management, to legal, regulatory, and compliance research and strategic partnerships. My immigration practice has evolved from non-immigration visas to employment-based immigration. I have received many requests for representation from leading artists, scholars, and business executives from China, and a big challenge for me is finding time to handle these requests.

Webber: We know you also teach law at several law schools and universities, could you tell us more about your teaching?

Wang: In 2006 when I graduated from law school, I was invited to join the faculty of School of American Law at China University of Political Science and Law (CUPL). CUPL is the largest law university in the world, and School of American Law is the first American style law school in China. CUPL is also a strategic partner of Thomson Reuters. I travel to China once a year to teach block courses on Comparative Constitutional Law, Immigration Law, and Legal Research in American Law based on West's Analysis of American Law – the Key Number System, now the intellectual property of Thomson Reuters. I have also lectured at many law schools in China: Beijing Foreign Studies University Law School, Peking University Law School, and Tsinghua University Law School, to name a few.

From 2009, I began to teach comparative law and legal research courses at the University of Minnesota Law School and William Mitchell College of Law in the U.S.; the University of Lucerne and the University of Bern in Switzerland; the University of Milan in Italy, and the University of Vienna in Austria. My overseas teaching involves intense block courses of one or two weeks, four to five hours per day.

Immigration law is a very important part of my teaching: refugee, asylum, citizenship, due process, and equal protection. I appreciate the opportunities to interact with bright young students and high caliber faculty members around the world.

But going forward, I probably will reduce my teaching commitments and use my time to better serve ethnic minority communities in Minnesota by practicing immigration law. Recently I was appointed to Governor Dayton's Diversity and Inclusion Council's Civil Engagement Committee, and I look forward to working with my fellow Minnesotans to ensure that all Minnesotans have equitable opportunities to participate fully in the policy development within our democracy.

Webber: Finally, I would like to ask you to share three fun facts about the place you were born — Beijing.

Wang: One, according to Chinese census, there are about 22 million residents in Beijing, and another 5 million non-residents living and working in Beijing.

Two: the Beijing Subway, which began operating in 1969, now has 18 lines, 319 stations, and 527 kilometers (327 miles) of track, is the second longest subway system

Chang Wang, left, giving a lecture in China

in the world, and is first in annual ridership with 3.41 billion rides delivered in 2014.

And three, this is actually not "fun": the air quality in Beijing is beyond one's worst nightmare. According to the U.S. Embassy in Beijing, it is "crazy bad."

When I was growing up in the 1970s and the 1980s, the sky was blue and the river was clear. It took just a few decades to completely destroy the environment. Beijing is suffocated by hazardous smog of PM2.5, the small particles smaller than 2.5 micrometers (100 times thinner than a human hair) and a leading cause of lung cancer. The World Health Organization's guideline for PM2.5 level is less than 25, Beijing is 200 on average, and frequently off the chart—over 500. You see blue sky less than 30 days per year, and never see stars at night.

Webber: Per Google Maps, how many miles is it from Beijing to your office in Minnesota?

Wang: 7,533 miles or 12,124 kilometers.

Dancing With the Dragon*

Chang Wang and Joe Pearman

The Democrats

Pearman: Since their current field is smaller, our first analytical commentary will concern the Democrats. Before we begin to break down the individual candidates, do you feel it would be helpful to contextualize the race from the perspective of U.S.-China relations? At least one of the Democratic candidates has a long and sometimes fraught history with the Communist Party, and an understanding of how the race looks from the other side of the Pacific could clarify and contextualize all candidates' views.

Wang: I agree, and I feel it would also be beneficial to examine the two primary mental schemas Westerners, and public figures in particular, use when thinking about China. These two schemas color most, if not all China-related discussions in the West, unduly influence public opinion through media outlets, and distort the policy-making process. I like to call these schemas "panda-hugging" and "dragon-hunting."

*These are Chang Wang and Joe Pearman's conversation on how the Communist Party of China was likely to react to the Republican and Democratic candidates for President of the United States in the 2016 race. They originally appeared in the November/December 2015 and January 2016 issues of *China Insight*. They have been slightly modified for this writing.

Pearman: In other words, arguing for closer trade and engagement with China, versus leeriness of its growing influence.

Wang: Precisely. In my opinion, both of these viewpoints are flawed, in that they spring from oversimplifications and misperceptions. I'll start with the panda-huggers. There's one gentleman I feel typifies them: ex-Australian Prime Minister Kevin Rudd. I vividly remember watching him give a TED Talk on the virtues of closer engagement with China. This TED Talk exemplifies panda-huggers' dilemma.

Now, Mr. Rudd claims to both speak and write Chinese. To prove this, he produced several characters on his iPad. They *were* real characters, but the calligraphy was incredibly sloppy, like something a kindergartener might produce. No Chinese person, and no one who truly understands the Chinese, would ever publicly display characters like that. To do so would be to publicly demonstrate incompetence, rather than good faith or engagement, as Rudd seemed to believe. But that clarifies the problem with the "panda-huggers." They believe in trade; they believe in engagement, but they attempt both using knowledge that is either insufficient or just plain wrong. This makes them look dangerously naïve.

Pearman: They seem reminiscent of the writers of guides on "Doing Business in China" who claim that the most important thing to do is present your business card with both hands.

Wang: Exactly, it's the same mindset. And I also feel the dragon hunters have the wrong idea about China. Intelligence writers talk about the growing buildup in the South China Sea and China's assertiveness on the world stage as signs of war. They're closely related to the people who claim that China is buying up the United States' debt so that it can one day take over the country.

Pearman: Our debt being held by China is a major concern, according to a recent Pew poll. 89 percent of the country feels it's a serious issue, and it's considered the *most* serious, ahead of job losses, cyberattacks, and human rights, among other problems.

But this doesn't make a lot of sense. According to the Washington Post, less than half of *all* U.S. debt is held internationally. The Chinese hold less than 10 percent (though they may have used the Belgians as proxies to acquire more). And there's no danger that Xi Jinping is going to arrive in Washington one day and demand payment in full or land deeds to California by the end of the month; government debt doesn't work that way.

Wang: I blame the media for the fact that the public perception of China's American debt holdings is so skewed. The Chinese government's Red Elite isn't interested in taking over America; they love America! They buy property in New York and California; they send their children to American universities. Holding debt is simply another form of investment, and it binds the two countries closer together. But "The Chinese Are Buying U.S. Debt!" gets more attention than "The Chinese Are Investing in America."

Pearman: In other words, the Chinese have every reason to hope America stays prosperous. They may try to steer us certain ways and gain more influence, but they definitely want to see us happy and prosperous.

Wang: Exactly. You don't want to destroy your largest trading partner. And this is why I also am skeptical about the dragon hunters' claims of another World War in the South China Sea. Military parades, anti-American rhetoric, and the Senkaku Islands are stunts pulled for *domestic consumption*. It's for the benefit of the people, to bind them closer to the government.

Pearman: I remember during the flare-up over the Islands last year; I was reading about street demonstrations against the Japanese. If the government was willing to allow spontaneous popular demonstrations, it must have appreciated the content. And it's also worth noting that the last time the People's Liberation Army went to "war" (other than peacekeeping deployments and anti-terrorist operations), it was against the students in Tiananmen.

So, to sum up what you've said, Westerners tend to discuss, and understand China in one of two ways, both of which miss the mark. They either naively try to engage, or they prepare for a war that, barring some catastrophic blunder, won't ever happen. So what would be the *right* approach?

Wang: For that, I think you need to understand what the Chinese leadership wants and values: and that's consistency in business. The Communist Party of China (CPC) has traditionally, ironically, leaned Republican, because Nixon "opened" China. Until he died, Nixon was the CPC's favorite "Old Friend of the Chinese People;" now that title goes to his Secretary of State, Henry Kissinger. (Kevin Rudd probably aspires to the title after Kissinger passes.)

Classic Republican rhetoric makes sense to the CPC. Republicans talked mutual advantages and trade, exactly what the post-Mao leadership saw as the path to the future. Democrats, traditionally, spoke of human rights, or even brushed one of the Three Forbidden T's: Tiananmen, Tibet and Taiwan. In 2007, when Former President Carter visited Beijing, he wanted to support human rights law research in Chinese law schools. He could not find an audience in government or academia, even though he was the one who established full diplomatic relations with China.

Pearman: What's interesting is that both parties, since the 90s, have made free trade a major part of their platforms. George H.W. Bush might have originated NAFTA, but it was Bill Clinton who guided it to fruition, and Barack Obama who pushed for the Trans-Pacific Partnership.

Wang: The Chinese leadership has appreciated this sea change greatly. Put simply, whoever wins, they are unlikely to lose. Of course, there are one or two notable exceptions in this race . . .

Pearman: This seems like a great opportunity to segue into a discussion of the Democrats. Let's start with the two front-runners: Hillary Clinton and Bernie Sanders. Both have some interesting connections to China. Bernie, of course, feels like a blast out of the New Deal past, strongly endorsing unions (and their accompanying skepticism about free trade). When Hillary Clinton was Secretary of State, she endorsed the TPP, but she's come out against it in recent months. Moreover, as Secretary and as a candidate, she tangled with China several times.

While Ms. Clinton was Secretary of State, a human rights activist named Chen Guangcheng sought refuge in the U.S. embassy in Beijing from persecution by the Chinese authorities. To the CPC's irritation, Clinton eventually negotiated Chen's move, with his family, to the United States. This episode is prominently featured in Clinton's memoir, "Hard Choices." Not surprisingly, that book is banned in China. Recently, Clinton labeled Xi Jinping "shameless" for hosting a woman's rights summit after feminist activists were imprisoned in China.

So, professor, how serious is this? And will the CPC be concerned about the possibility of Ms. Clinton becoming president?

Wang: I predict that whatever the CPC may say in public, in private, you'd find them surprisingly understanding about Ms. Clinton (if you could ever persuade them to be candid with you, which I doubt!).

Recall what I said about the CPC's fiery rhetoric. They may preach against America, they may rave against Japan, but they have no intention of going to war! And they're likely to view Ms. Clinton's pronouncements in the same way. Chen Guangcheng might have been a bit of a poke in the eye, but he never hurt trade. Nor will any comments on a few imprisoned feminists.

Pearman: In other words, they would describe Ms. Clinton's comments as simply "sound and fury, signifying nothing," part of the messy but ultimately rewarding process of moving another centrist, free-trade candidate into office? And they'd say Clinton was simply playing to her feminist base by bringing up the women?

Wang: Precisely.

Pearman: I doubt they're as sanguine about Bernie Sanders. For starters, his website (unlike Ms. Clinton's) explicitly denounces current U.S. trade policy with China.

Wang: Sanders certainly seems like a threat to the consistency the CPC value. But then again, the president is only one man.

Pearman: That's true. And candidates with an ambitious platform can hit brick walls when they enter office. For instance, when President Obama gained his first term, he had a supermajority and a perceived public mandate. His signature piece of legislation, the Affordable Care Act, was savaged in the process of getting passed, had to survive a Supreme Court challenge, and all but tore his party apart, leading to disastrous losses in the midterms.

Wang: This is true. So I feel that the CPC fears the prospect of a Sanders presidency, but probably more as an annoying and painful hiccup in a stable relationship than as a game-changer. That being said, let me emphasize that I feel that they *do* fear him. He represents a belief in *real* socialism, albeit democratic socialism, and a belief in political openness that is anathema to the Chinese leadership. For instance, the current legality of "dark money" in politics means that it's perfectly possible for the CPC to donate money to influence American elections, as well as for corporations and individuals who benefit from Chinese trade to pour billions into each election cycle. Bernie Sanders strongly supports a Constitutional amendment to overturn Citizens United, and the polls reflect bipartisan animosity toward money in politics. That is only one example of the ways a Sanders presidency could damage the interests of the CPC.

Pearman: Why don't we take another look at the rest of the Democratic field? Before the first Democratic debate, the other candidates were Jim Webb, Lincoln Chafee, Larry Lessig, and Martin O'Malley. After the debate, both Webb and Chafee withdrew their candidacies. Lessig has not yet been featured in a debate.

Wang: But what they said about China during their campaigns and debate were important. Those words reflected the views of their constituents.

Pearman: We'll start with Mr. Webb, former senator from Virginia, Marine platoon leader in Vietnam, and noted author, whose campaign struggled to get off the ground and ultimately fizzled.

Wang: I feel like Mr. Webb definitely wanted to make China a key issue in his campaign, but his methodology was wrong. During the recent debate, he shoehorned a warning against Chinese expansionism into a question about Syria. It seemed to come out of nowhere, and nothing really came of it.

Pearman: I saw the text of that. I feel that Webb was trying to shift the discussion, but it didn't work. If he had become a serious contender in the race, do you think he would have given Beijing pause?

Wang: I do not think they would been comfortable with the prospect of a Webb presidential victory. Human rights criticism from a career politician is one thing; containment rhetoric from a man who fought (indirectly) against China on the ground is another. However, there is no worry anymore; Webb, a potential dragon-hunter, is out.

Pearman: And that brings us to the two former governors, Lincoln Chafee of Rhode Island and Martin O'Malley of Maryland.

Wang: Governor O'Malley seems to have avoided the China issue entirely, other than focusing on encouraging Chinese trade. Governor Chafee's position can be summed up in one tweet: "With China we have agreements and we have differences. Focusing on the former helps resolve the latter." This is more panda-hugging gesture than policy.

Pearman: Do you feel Beijing would react positively to a presidency by either?

Wang: Neither seems intent on rocking the boat. The CPC appreciates this kind of attitude.

Pearman: And finally, there's Larry Lessig, a professor from Harvard Law. His campaign centers around one thing, overturning *Citizens United*. He's at the bottom of the polls by far, but there might be a future for him as a Sanders running mate.

Wang: I doubt the CPC concern itself much with Professor Lessig, but at the same time, we've already established that the end of Citizens United would be detrimental to their interests.

Pearman: So in conclusion, what the Chinese government wants is a continuation of trade, and they are willing to take a little flak over human rights on the campaign trail as long as the money keeps flowing once the new President takes office. When formulating Chinese policy, it's important to reach past the simplistic views of "panda huggers" and "dragon hunters" to recognize the governing pragmatism at the heart of the CPC, and tailor one's responses accordingly. Though Hillary Clinton has had her spats with China, we feel the CPC's view of her is ultimately positive, unlike their probable perception of the second-ranked candidate, Bernie Sanders. In our next issue, we'll take a look at the Republican stable of candidates.

The Republicans

Pearman: In this edition of "Dancing with the Dragon," we present the Republican candidates and where they stand in relation to China, mainly the Chinese government. Owing to the large number of Republican candidates, we're concentrating mostly on the candidates who are involved in Chinese issues

A dragon stamp issued by Chinese Postal Service

and who we feel are likely to stay in the race and have a decent chance to win the nomination. As before, we do not seek to persuade, merely to inform.

Wang: Within the Communist Party of China (CPC), the relationship with the United States is one of the key factors in evaluating the success or failure of CPC leadership. This is rarely known outside China, but it is with utmost importance in understanding U.S.-China relations. Therefore, the CPC is extremely invested in the U.S. economy, politics and the U.S. presidential election.

Historically, the Republicans have a far better relationship with the CPC than the Democrats do. I think we have to begin with an analysis of the man the Chinese leadership would most like to see win the nomination and become President of the United States: Jeb Bush. He's their preferred candidate by far.

Former President George H.W. Bush in Beijing

Pearman: What makes him so attractive to the men in Beijing?

Wang: He's what I would describe as an ideal Western politician, from a Chinese government perspective.

His father was an ambassador to China and a personal friend of Deng Xiaoping, who essentially charted the course of the contemporary economic reform. In fact, President H.W. Bush is one of the "Old Friends of the Chinese People," which is a very select and "honored" group that includes Kissinger and, before he died, Nixon. Jeb Bush is, on his own merit, a mature, pro-business leader. He understands how important it is to respect the dignity and face of your opposite number, and he is more politely sophisticated than blunt.

Pearman: In a way, Jeb Bush seems a good deal like one of the top men in the CPC himself. He's quiet, comes in by way of a political dynasty, and believes in compromise and mutual benefit. Unfortunately, all of that seems to be working to his detriment in the current race.

Wang: I agree, which brings us to the second important point: the sheer level of *energy* in this Republican primary. This is personified, of course, by Donald Trump, but it's also seen in the fire of Ted Cruz, the blunt rhetoric of Chris Christie, and the enthusiasm of Ben Carson's supporters.

Pearman: I can't imagine Beijing is too happy about that. The Party leadership isn't very fond of strong, boisterous popular sentiment, and I can't help but imagine that they view Trump, in particular, as a kind of American Bo Xilai: a dangerous populist demagogue.

Wang: Trump is indeed the candidate the CPC is most afraid of, simply because they have little idea how to *deal* with him. Remember, these men are technocrats with engineering degrees who read their speeches off cue cards. Trying to deal with the aggressive bluster of a Trump, especially when he's stated publicly that he intends to renegotiate America's trade relationship with China, is not something they look forward to. And on another level, all of this political fervor and fighting feels unseemly to them. The Communist Party has a huge number of quarrels, of course, but these are treated as internal affairs, hidden behind a harmonious public front. They view public disputes as endangering the unity of the entire nation.

Pearman: Do you see any of the quarrels or complexity you mentioned having a bearing in how they view the current race?

Wang: I think that the more important question is if any of the candidates really understand how complex China really *is*. There's a tendency to view China as a monolithic entity that can be "stood up" to; in fact, it's really a nation governed by seven men, ruled by a party of 80 million, and containing 1.3 *billion* people. So even if a candidate has experience dealing with a facet of China, that does not mean that that one facet is translatable across all issues Chinese. Nor does a relationship with one person always mean as much as they assume.

Pearman: Going off that, I think there's sometimes too much media coverage on an individual, like Xi Jinping, and what they may want. That leads to the idea of a China that can be dealt with "man to man," when the more important thing to understand, at least in my mind, is the interests of the Red Elite: the wealthy Communist families at the highest ranks of the Party.

Wang: There's definitely a point to that, and it also seems that a great deal of media coverage misses important points in favor of fluff. For instance, Xi Jinping is often presented as a kind of supreme leader to the American public when, despite his strong centralist tendencies, he's still first among equals. And that's part of a larger problem: both the public and the candidates seem not to realize the incredible opacity of China. We don't know much, and what we *do* know is often misinterpreted. I find there's a special problem with propaganda: anti-American rhetoric is blasted over the airwaves every day in China, and Americans assume it's aimed at them. It's not; it's aimed at the civilian population. The Communist Party isn't trying to provoke America; it's pacifying its own citizens, using the time-honored tactic of stirring up anger at a foreign "aggressor" to avoid tough questions at home. I'm sure the CPC would not mind, and even expects, the same tactics from Americans.

Pearman: How do you feel the idea of lost American trade is playing into this election?

Wang: I think it's a big factor, but again, I think the candidates are oversimplifying. The United States has lost a great many jobs to China, true, but those jobs are now leaving, either returning to America or heading out to other nations in the Pacific Rim. Donald Trump might claim that the TPP is a deal designed eventually to include the Chinese, but it's not. It's a way to punish China for trying to circumvent WTO regulations, and it's really a poke in the eye for them. And as far as currency manipulation goes, that has been a disaster for China's own economy: by keeping the value of their currency low, the CPC is guaranteeing high inflation.

Pearman: I've noticed that the candidates tend to feel confrontational toward China, and they fall into one of two categories. People like Trump, Carly Fiorina, and Chris Christie take a secular focus and attack China for its cyber-attacks, economic drain on America, and expansion in the South China Sea. Others, in particular Marco Rubio, have attacked China on the basis of human rights, usually filtered through the lens of Christian faith (the One-Child Policy comes under special fire for its role in encouraging and sometimes forcing abortions). Rubio also tends to be blunt about the authoritarian nature of the CPC, which is understandable, considering his parents (as well as Ted Cruz's) are escapees from Communist Cuba.

Wang: Yes, and this brings up an important point. After Trump, the person the Chinese leadership would least like to see as president on the Republican side is Marco Rubio. They do not want someone with the kind of personal and political stake in human rights that he has in the White House. Rubio also had written an editorial that lays out a detailed plan for American buildup in the Pacific with the purpose of countering Chinese expansionism. The CPC appreciates a harmonious and prosperous relationship with a U.S. that gives them a free hand in the Pacific. So the CPC fears Trump the most, then Rubio, and after him, I think, would be Ben Carson.

Pearman: Would this be another case of not wanting to deal with someone they don't understand?

Wang: Exactly. As a doctor and a devout Seventh-Day Adventist, Carson's worldview is worlds away from theirs; he doesn't really use the same decision-making framework. I feel that they would see him as someone with Mike Huckabee's problem: a man who has trouble remembering when he is supposed to be a politician as opposed to a pastor. There's also Dr. Carson's well-known blunder of stating that China has troops in Syria; the CPC might well ask if he might, as president, act on misinformation like that. In fact, in some ways, Rubio and Carson might be considered *worse* than Trump. While Donald Trump is a populist and a blusterer, he is still a fairly effective businessman, which means he is conversant with the ideas of exchange, compromise, and mutual benefit. His website, for all its grandiosity, still points to *negotiating* with China. He's also expressed skepticism about the necessity of the U.S. military presence in the Pacific. On the other hand, should tensions between the U.S. and China ever heat up, the situation might become very uncomfortable very quickly for Chinese-Americans in the U.S. Trump has already indicated that he feels the decision to intern the Japanese in World War II might have been justified . . .

Pearman: Where do you think Ted Cruz fits into this equation?

Wang: Ted Cruz, I feel, comes across as similar to Trump, with a few key differences. For starters, he has a personal stake in human rights, considering his parents are Cuban émigrés. He's also more noticeably religious. However, he does strongly support trade and the economy, which would probably make dealing with him at least mildly palatable.

Pearman: I don't think our article would be complete without mentioning two candidates who, while low in the polls, have had a notable presence in the debates, John Kasich, former governor of Ohio, a state that struggled owing to outsourcing, but has managed some rebuilding. Carly Fiorina is a former Hewlett-Packard executive who has taken a strong stance against expansionism and cyberattacks. How do you think the CPC leadership would view them?

Wang: I believe that of the two, Governor Kasich would be received more favorably: despite his Rubio-like advocacy of rearming Japan and more troops in the Pacific. he does have a proven record in helping a state do business, which is something the CPC could work with. If nothing else, closer American military engagement with the Japanese would provide excellent propaganda fodder.

Carly Fiorina, on the other hand, would make the Beijing leadership uncomfortable. Historically, very few women have held power in China (the last being the disastrous Dowager Empress Cixi, who effectively derailed modernization in the late 1800s, or possibly the deranged extremist Madame Mao). Hillary Clinton, as we mentioned previously, would be acceptable due to her long list of connections to China; Ms. Fiorina has none. Of course, the CPC expects Hillary Clinton would soften her tunes on the human rights issues once elected, just like her husband did. And finally, Fiorina is blunt and confrontational, which are not qualities the CPC prizes in a female politician.

In the end, the CPC will always prefer Jeb Bush as the Republican nominee (and probably the president).

The Chinese in Trumpland*

Joe Pearman and Chang Wang

"NC Chinese Americans for Trump"

With the unexpected victory of Donald Trump and the start of a new year, Pearman and Wang feel this is the perfect time to examine what may lie ahead for America's 45th president and his relationship with the world's most populous country, its famously opaque leadership, and the many people with ties to both countries. As with their previous articles, they take no position for or against Donald Trump or his policies. Their aim is, as always, to educate and inform.

Pearman: To me, a logical place to start with this article would be to examine one of Donald Trump's most vocal support bases: Chinese-Americans, especially first-generation immigrants. For instance, if you were around Raleigh, North Carolina, shortly before the election, you might have seen a plane towing a banner that said "NC Chinese Americans for Trump."[1] And there were similar shows of

---

*In "Dancing With the Dragon," Chang Wang and Joe Pearman they laid out how the Communist Party of China was likely to view the various candidates for President of the United States. It turned out that Donald Trump has emerged an unlikely victor, these two writers back to take a stab at examining how Chinese government and the Chinese people will relate to this pugnacious and outspoken new administration. These conversation first appeared in February, March, and April 2017 issues of *China Insight*.
[1] The News and Observer; "Chinese-American group funds aerial Trump ad" October 29, 2016

support in major cities around the country, even in the Twin Cities (*China Insight*, January 2017). What do you think is driving that?

Wang: That has been one of the more unexpected features of an unexpected election. But if you unpack it, it makes sense. First of all, some context: according to Associated Press exit polls,[2] roughly one-third of Asian-Americans who voted cast their vote for Donald Trump, which is the same as the percentage of Latinos. In the run-up to the election, I noticed that while most Asian people who might be supporting Trump were doing so quietly, his Chinese-American supporters tended to be vocal. This

gave them an outsized influence and visibility, even if there weren't that many of them. A report from May said there were about 1500 supporters in one "Chinese-Americans for Trump" group.[3] What was important was that they came out for Trump loudly and early on. Another thing to note was that many of the Chinese-Americans working hardest for Trump were first-generation immigrants; some weren't even citizens but permanent residents without voting rights.

Pearman: And that's the exact opposite of what you might expect, isn't it? After all, Donald Trump built his candidacy around a somewhat anti-China philosophy, that

[2]The YBF.com; "ELECTION 2016: This Is The Breakdown Of How Americans Voted By Race, Gender & More + Hillary Clinton Actually WINS The Popular Vote" November 9, 2016

[3]NBC News; "Attracted by Immigration, Education Policies, Some Chinese Americans Stump for Trump" May 25, 2016

China wasn't a partner but rather a two-faced cheater that was stealing American jobs. And you'd think that first-generation immigrants would relate most strongly to their country of origin.

Wang: You are exactly right in reasoning. But what appealed to the Chinese-Americans, particularly these first-generation immigrants, was a combination of Trump's style and his message, and their exposure to it.

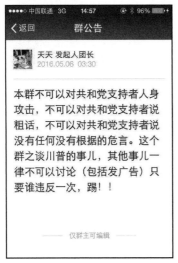

(This WeChat group completely bans any negative comments on and news about Trump and Trump supporters.)

One of the major organizing tools of the "Chinese-Americans for Trump" movement was an app called WeChat. It's a Chinese messaging app that functions as a combination of Facebook and Twitter, and it's extremely popular with Chinese-language speakers in America. It was dominated by pro-Trump discourse. Trump was praised as a tough, no-nonsense, successful businessman; very little that was controversial about him showed up in the discussion. It was also flooded with negative commentary on Hillary Clinton, including fake news like the "pedophile pizza parlor" and the "Clinton Crime Family" stories that allege she had business associates murdered.

Pearman: So in other words, WeChat had its own version of "The Great Meme War," where Trump supporters flooded social media with pro-Trump and anti-Hillary messaging.

362

Wang: And for many of these first-generation immigrants, WeChat is their primary way of consuming news, similar to how a majority of Americans get it from Facebook.[4] So you can understand how influential this messaging was.

Pearman: But what made Donald Trump so appealing?

Wang: Probably there are several different factors. First of all, many of these people are skilled workers or independently wealthy, and came to America for opportunities for themselves and their children. They dislike high tax rates and loathe affirmative action, which they see as unfairly privileging minority groups that portray themselves as victims rather than working. "After all," they say, "I am a minority. I came to this country and I am doing fine. Why don't you man up and get a job?" Few of them take the time to learn about the history of slavery and segregation that led to affirmative action's implementation in the '60s, and most of them were educated in China where liberal education courses, such as sociology and history, are not available. At a civic engagement seminar on both parties' platforms I hosted for local Chinese community, I was asked by a first-generation immigrant: "Why do all black people in this country think of themselves as victims?" And that attitude is typical. What's more, they hate the idea that their children might lose a plum spot in a top university to a less-qualified affirmative action candidate. So there is tremendous appreciation of Donald Trump's "anti-political correctness" rhetoric, a feeling that he will benefit the people who really contribute.

---

[4]Pew Research Center; "The Evolving Role of News on Twitter and Facebook" July 14th, 2015.

Pearman: So instead of claiming identity as an ethnic minority, the Chinese-American Trump supporters see themselves as part of the "Silent Majority": the working, contributing people who are unfairly penalized to support the less conscientious.

Wang: You are absolutely right. These new Chinese immigrants do not identify with the larger Asian-American community, nor do they share many of the values we deem as universal. That leads to the next point: Donald Trump's personality appeals to them. Chinese people appreciate a tough-talking, decisive *male* leader. Remember that China's few recent experiences with national female rulers have been disastrous. There was the Dowager Empress Cixi, who derailed modernization in the late 1800s to keep China weak and under her control. There was Madame Mao, who supported the most destructive aspects of the Cultural Revolution and was so loathed that she was nicknamed "The White-Boned Demon" after a villainous creature in "Journey to the West."

A new biography of Empress Dowager Cixi argues that she was unfairly remembered as a corrupt dictator.

Pearman: Are there any hot-button issues for the Chinese-Americans for Trump?

Wang: Several. Besides affirmative action, they strongly oppose the idea of transgender people being able to use whichever bathroom they identify with. Chinese

364

traditional culture is very conservative, and many Chinese-American Trump supporters see this as a manufactured issue that will allow perverts to target their children. Even though Donald Trump himself has said transgendered people could use whichever bathroom they wanted in his hotels, his campaign and the Republican Party is of course tied to social conservatism, as is his running mate Mike Pence.

Many Chinese-Americans support Trump because of his "law and order" narrative and frequent support for the police. They point to Peter Liang, a New York City policeman who was imprisoned for shooting an unarmed black man in public housing. Liang, they say, was given up by a spineless city administration capitulating to Black Lives Matter sentiment but unwilling to sacrifice a white cop. If the police had proper support, they believe, it would have been recognized that Liang made an unfortunate but legitimate mistake.

Second-generation Chinese-Americans who were educated in the U.S. have objected to this viewpoint, many agreeing with the official verdict that evidence incriminates Liang beyond a reasonable doubt. It is more common for second-generation Chinese-Americans to believe their community ought to be more concerned with civil rights issues. They point to the case of Vincent Chin, who was mistaken as Japanese and beaten to death by an out-of-work auto worker in 1982, which sparked the first modern Asian-American civil rights movement.

There are two competing narratives in the Asian American community today. One states with alarm that racial divides in society are increasing, and says that Asian-Americans should work with African-American, Latino, Native American, and LGBTQ groups as allies in the struggle for justice and preserving the legacy of the Civil Rights movement. The other narrative states that members of all groups should focus more on personal success and less on activism, and should look for recognition as individuals and not as groups. It is unlikely that they will find much common ground in the years to come.

The Eagle and the Dragon

Pearman: Turning from the domestic stage to the international, it would make sense to consider how President Trump's win has been taken by the Communist Party of China (CPC). If you'll recall from our previous article, "Dancing with the Dragon" (China Insight, Nov-Dec 2015 & January 2016), when the Republican primaries were in full swing, we felt that they hoped Jeb Bush would win. He was a moderate, deal- and trade-oriented conservative whose father was once ambassador to China. But we also felt the CPC would look more or less favorably on a Hillary Clinton victory, even though they had clashed over human rights issues during and after her tenure as Secretary of State. Clinton was a pro-trade candidate whose husband had overseen a vast expansion in American free trade. If anything, they would be concerned about her support for the Trans-Pacific Partnership (TPP), which cuts China out of a large and lucrative new trade bloc.

Donald Trump, on the other hand, was a wild card, anathema to a group of men who dress in matching suits and value consistency and pragmatism above all else. What has their response been to the surprise election of this consistently surprising President?

Wang: The CPC has had a bit of a roller-coaster ride in how it perceives Donald Trump. I think it would be fair to say that they were surprised that Donald Trump won the Republican primaries. You might have expected them to support Secretary Clinton, but the problem with that was

Trump's primary victory had turned the entire election into a referendum on trade. Clinton was on the defensive, and had to come out hard against free trade, and by extension, China.

The CPC bided its time until shortly before the election, then official channels came out strongly in support of Trump. I feel there are several reasons for this. First, Trump was well-aligned with their regional interests. Secretary Clinton believes in trade, but she is also a hawk who had supported measures like the TPP as part of the Obama administration's "Pivot to the Pacific." She believes in projecting American power and influence in what China sees as its backyard and natural sphere of influence. With her pro-trade sentiment a no-go in the campaign, the CPC might have worried they were facing Harry Truman in a pastel pantsuit. Donald Trump, in contrast, had taken isolationist positions on the campaign trail; he seemed supremely uninterested in strategic alliance-building, and questioned America's need for bases in Korea and Japan. Also, he had displayed a strong rapport with Russia, Beijing's close ally.

Second, the CPC had come to believe they could deal with Donald Trump. His goals and theirs were far from mutually incompatible; not only did Trump display little interest in controlling the Pacific, but he had publicly praised Beijing's bloody crackdown on student pro-democracy protests in 1989 and more recently embraced dictators like Abdel Fatah al-Sisi in Egypt. Human rights criticism on China seemed unlikely. He had killed the Trans-Pacific Partnership, effectively giving the CPC the go-ahead to create their own trade agreement. Moreover, they had probably come to believe what many reluctant Trump supporters had vocalized: he was a dealmaker who took outrageous public positions to increase his starting advantage in any negotiation. Trump might be talking tough about 45 percent tariffs and currency investigations, the CPC thought, but that could be the same as the anti-American propaganda they regularly blasted over Chinese channels for the benefit of the domestic audience. After all, Trump's son-in-law, real estate scion Jared Kushner, was entering a joint venture with Anbang Insurance Group, the Chinese owners

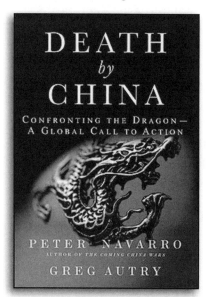

of the Waldorf Astoria[5], which reportedly belongs to the "red princelings," the descendants of China's ruling elite. Could Donald Trump the developer *really* be that bad for business?

More than that, by talking about Donald Trump at all, the CPC had the opportunity to highlight the ugliness and divisiveness of the American election. Election 2016 gave the CPC a way to present democracy as messy and crude, contrasting China's orderly and technocratic rule. To every Chinese citizen who might support a different system of government, the CPC could say "Do you really want to go through *that* every 2-4 years, depending on when the media coverage begins?"

Pearman: So you could say there was an unofficial "honeymoon period" with Donald Trump and the CPC; it depended on their presumption he would turn out to be a regular Republican and shed his populist shell once the election ended. Instead, he strengthened ties to anti-free

---

[5]Minneapolis Star-Tribune; "Ethics Tangles for Trump's Son-In-Law" January 8th, 2017

trade Steven Bannon, tapped domestic steel magnate Wilbur Ross for Secretary of Commerce, and appointed Peter Navarro, an economics professor who wrote "Death by China," as head of the new National Trade Council. And, in a move that confounded the Beltway, he casually made the first official contact between the United States and the Republic of China (Taiwan) since 1979, when he "took" a congratulatory phone call from the President Tsai Ing-wen of Taiwan[6] in early December 2016.

Wang: If I could have been a fly on the wall when that happened . . . It can't be emphasized enough how touchy the CPC is on the subject of Taiwan. There's a saying among diplomats who deal with China: "You don't touch the three Ts." Those are Tibet, the Tiananmen Square protests of 1989, and Taiwan. China, of course, refuses to acknowledge Taiwan's sovereignty, and demands adherence to the "One China" policy, which states that the CPC is the only legitimate government of *all of China, including Taiwan.*

When Donald Trump took the phone call from President Tsai of Taiwan, the CPC censors clamped down. Any search on the Chinese internet for "Taiwan" or "Trump" turned up nothing. After almost a day, official media came out with a short statement from the foreign minister describing the entire thing as a Taiwanese trick, seeking to minimize it as much as possible. This is actually an indicator of the gravity of the affair. It felt like the CPC was *afraid* of the magnitude of the sea change that might have taken place, and afraid of letting their citizens know.

Pearman: Donald Trump treated the phone call as if it wasn't too important. He pointed out that the United

---

[6]CNN.com; "China lodges complaint over Trump-Taiwan call" December 3, 2016

States still maintains a close (informal) relationship with Taiwan, and is pledged to defend it from any attack, and conducts millions in arms sales to the country each year. He presented the phone call, publicly at least, as something it would be silly to get upset over. My own feeling is that Trump actually took it as a calculated move to put pressure on Beijing, a signal that the CPC should expect no concessions in the coming years.

Wang: I understand this point of view, but I must point out just how thoroughly Trump had rattled the delicate balance the U.S., the CPC and Taiwan have managed to preserve for a long time. The CPC, as we have said before, values consistency and normalcy. The Trump-Tsai phone call flew in the face of four decades of U.S. policy, policy that has been deeply beneficial to China and was instrumental in turning it from an international pariah into a global powerhouse. To be fair, this balance has benefitted all parties. Now, the CPC propaganda machines have gone from endorsing Trump to warning him not to "playing with fire," signaling the CPC will approach Trump's administration in the future like wary matadors, not amiable potential partners.

In diplomacy, there are certain rules that everybody follows. Donald Trump has made a career in business and entertainment by tearing up the playbook. Now he seems to be bringing this same approach to politics, probably, as you say, with the intent of letting China know he won't be pushed around as president. The fact that he's not going to meet with Taiwan's president on her trip to the U.S.[7] points to that, as opposed to an effort to re-establish full diplomatic relations. But I'm not sure the CPC understands that. To put this in American terms, they see Trump taking

---

[7]Fox News; "Taiwan's president heads to United States, but won't meet with Trump" January 7, 2017

this phone call as the equivalent of Xi Jinping accepting a cordial New Year's greeting from the Californians who want to secede from the United States. Donald Trump may be doing what has worked for him in the past, but what works in marketing is not guaranteed to work in Beijing.

We will examine how it might all play out in the context of Chinese history and literature.

Lessons Learned

Pearman: In this last part of the three-part series, it seems appropriate to consider some takeaways from candidate Trump's unexpected victory. Many observers have said the 2016 presidential election and the Brexit vote that saw the United Kingdom leaving the European Union are two of a kind. Both elections featured brash, energetic populists focusing on a sense of national loss and economic malaise to defeat a cosmopolitan liberal establishment that was seen as smug and overconfident.

WANG: I agree, and on the point of overconfidence, the first takeaway is this: You only win by winning.

Let me explain. Donald Trump's win over Hillary Clinton could well be compared to Mao Tse-Tung's victory over Generalissimo Chiang Kai-Shek. At the start of the "war," Secretary Clinton had a well-developed and well-funded party apparatus, as well as a solid track record from her time as Secretary of State. Donald Trump's campaign was small and unorganized, and he had appeared to discredit himself as a mainstream politician by supporting the birther conspiracy movement several years before.

But Trump, as we were soon to discover, was Mao's equal in terms of ruthlessness. He hammered Clinton with a constant stream of attacks while mobilizing crucial supporters in rural America, just as Mao sapped Chiang's strength with guerilla warfare while building the Red Army in the countryside. Nothing was sacred for Trump; he insulted Gold Star parents and threatened to sue women who accused him of sexual assault. When China was occupied by the Japanese, Mao let Chiang's government do the bulk of the fighting. Mao sat back, did not fight hard unless forced to, and conserved his forces. He prioritized and calculated; he knew who his real enemy was: the Nationalists.

Clinton made a point of not getting in the mud with Trump, criticizing him on moral standards. Trump, like Mao, recognized there are no rules in war. Can you imagine what a no-holds-barred campaign on both sides would have looked like?

Pearman: I think that by focusing on morals and controversial statements so much, Secretary Clinton made the race about Donald Trump. And when the race was about Donald Trump, he was covered 24-7. And that meant he could always find a way to squeeze a few remarks about trade imbalances and national decline around the edges of his latest gaffe.

Picture Clinton throwing freewheeling press conferences where she lambasted corporate tax shelters and hinted that Ivanka Trump was a Russian honey trap! Imagine if Clinton had promised to appoint Elizabeth Warren as a special prosecutor to investigate and break up corporate monopolies! It would have been outrageous, but you can bet Trump would have a fight for the airwaves on his hands.

Wang: And here is point two. I have been a lawyer for more than a decade, and this election showed me that an election is a jury trial. And in a jury trial, a narrative is what wins.

Let me explain. Consider young, attractive Kate, her older, affluent, and well-insured husband Jack, and Kate's husky, penniless paramour Nate. One day Jack was shot on his drive home from work, and it didn't take long for the police to arrest Kate and Nate. At trial, any defense attorney is going to have a long row to hoe, because "Nate shot Jack over Kate" is a perfect narrative. It's simple and it makes sense, even if it might have nothing to do with the reality. A narrative is a re-construction of the reality.

Pearman: "Make America Great Again" is a narrative. It's patriotic. It's exciting. It fits on the front of a baseball cap. And it lets you read a lot into it, whether you're a laid-off steelworker in Ohio hoping to restore American jobs, or a young mom who wants her kids to go to public school and learn values she agrees with.

"Stronger Together" is not a narrative. It's a statement, and in an increasingly divided America, it seemed unlikely to really catch on.

Wang: Also on the subject of narrative, and going back to the lessons of history, both Trump and Mao could paint their opponents as crooked. The alleged Democratic Party collusion to defeat Bernie Sanders became a stick Trump could (and did) use to hammer Clinton's campaign with over and over, just as Mao could point to the rampant corruption in Chiang's government. The personal characteristics of both Clinton and Chiang became immaterial because they became the embodiment of what people found intolerable about the establishment.

Pearman: And then there were the fake news stories . . .

Wang: Which brings us to the third takeaway: journalism is gone; there are entertainment and propaganda.

In past elections, certain media sources could be relied upon to give the unbiased truth about important issues. CBS (the Columbia Broadcasting System) was especially well known for this; the great rivals Edward R. Murrow and Walter Cronkite helped bring down Joseph McCarthy and

expose the quagmire of the Vietnam War. When Cronkite said "And that's the way it is," people were confident he was right. If you wanted more detail, you could subscribe to your vibrant local paper.

Now newspapers around the country are struggling to stay afloat. Network news carries ephemera; any time a celebrity dies you can count on learning a great deal about the celebrity and nothing much about anything else for a week! There is a plethora of cable news channels, and "news junkies" can choose between conservative Fox, liberal MSNBC, and CNN, which just wants attention. Of course, many people prefer the ease of logging onto the internet. And here you can find a stream of news even better-tailored to your political persuasion: Mother Jones for the labor Democrat, Huffington Post for the cultural liberal, Drudge Report for the Tea Party Republican, Breitbart for the con-servative nationalist. And then there are the great number of people who don't follow the news, and who only get bits and pieces from what their friends talk about or share on Facebook, which is so often fake news, often cranked out by mercenary Macedonian teenagers[8] who write what they know will sell and to hell with the consequences.

---

[8]CBSnews.com; "In Macedonia's fake news hub, this teen shows how it's done" December 2nd, 2016

Pearman: I really enjoy reading the Twin Cities' Star Tribune, even if I often don't have the time to read beyond the national news and a favorite columnist in the local section. Still, I think that when I read the paper, I take away more than I get from online news. Even reading BBC News, which I feel is the best general news source online, requires clicking from chosen article to chosen article, while the newspaper presents a holistic picture.

I can't think of many people my age who read the paper; my local suburban weekly has a massive dedicated senior section. What are we left with when a generation is growing up more exposed to the scrapings of the internet than what is real?

Wang: And in this environment, power belongs to the person with the best propaganda machine. In my opinion, Clinton's campaign was unprepared for the scale of informal discourse in this election, and also for the media's inability to control "fake news" stories. The Trump campaign, on the other hand, enjoyed enthusiastic online support.

Pearman: For instance, the site Reddit has "subreddits" (sections) for the Trump and Clinton campaigns. /r/HillaryClinton has around 33,000 members. /r/TheDonald has over 330,000. And boy, are they pumped.

Wang: In closing, I'd like to suggest a reading list for people who may be struggling to understand this changed political landscape and in search of strategies and tactics to deal with it. This list is in addition to the popular New York Times "Books for the Trump Era."

The first is "The Thirty-Six Stratagems," an essay on various ploys that can be used in battle. 'Loot a burning house;' attack an enemy in disorder. There's the Hillary-Bernie kerfuffle, and Trump taking advantage, in a nutshell. The second title is the Chinese classic "The Art of War," which needs no introduction. 'Hold out baits to the enemy. Feign disorder, and crush him.' Every tweet a piece of bait, evidence of the disorder that guaranteed a Democratic win . . . so ran the prevailing political wisdom. And last, but not least, is another Chinese classic, "Romance of the Three Kingdoms," a historical novel following the breakup of the Han kingdom of China into three separate kingdoms, and the wars among them. It's a saga of plotting, backstabbing, and no-holds-barred warfare. Read it, and internalize its lessons.

Pearman: It's a wild new world out there. We hope that this series may help you, the reader, make sense of a sliver of it. We wish you all a Happy New Year—the Year of the Fire Rooster; we're confident that it will be as eventful as the Year of the Fire Monkey!

What is inclusion?*

Tang Emperor Gaozong (628-83), the third emperor of the great Tang Dynasty (618-907), once visited the home of Zhang Gongyi, who lived together with the improbable number of nine generations of his family. When the emperor asked Zhang for the reasons that such a large family could live well together, Zhang picked up a brush and wrote the character "Ren" a hundred times. "Ren" means "forbearance," a combination of patience, tolerance, compassion, accommodation and self-control.

 Today, it is still quite common for Chinese, and many other Asian families to have three generations under one roof. Protocols are followed, elders are respected, and children are disciplined. People have less expectation of privacy, but a high degree of tolerance for disagreement. Under the circumstance, patience is the cardinal virtue, compromise is a routine.

In 1991, I started my college education in filmmaking in Beijing. The first film we studied in American Film History class was D. W. Griffin's 1916 epic silent film "Intolerance." This complex film consists of four distinct, but parallel, stories that demonstrate mankind's persistent intolerance throughout the ages. "The purpose of the production," according to the producer, "is to trace a universal theme

*Chang Wang received the inaugural *Minnesota Lawyer* – Diversity & Inclusion Award in October, 2017. *Minnesota Lawyer* is a leading legal news publication in Minnesota. This award recognizes those in the legal profession who go above and beyond in their efforts to create a more diverse and inclusionary community. Wang is among "28 individuals and organizations who have laid the foundation of diversity and inclusion in the law that today's practitioners are building upon." This article originally appeared in the October 2017 issue of *China Insight.*

through various periods of the race's history. Ancient, sacred, medieval, and modern times are considered." The film was a personal indictment of moral hypocrisy, persecution, and intolerance. Ironically, "Intolerance" is often regarded as Griffin's cinematic apology for "Birth of a Nation," which was criticized for perpetuating racial stereotypes and glorifying the Klan.

Intolerance always comes with a strong sense of victimhood. From kindergarten to graduate school, Chinese are taught "a hundred years of humiliation," which refers to the period of intervention and imperialism by Western powers and Japan in China between 1839 and 1949. This time is long gone, but as a leading China scholar Professor Orville Schell observed, "China is still living in the syndrome of being the victim, and we don't know when that syndrome will finally be cured."

Recently, we also saw hundreds of Neo-Nazis and Klansman marching in Charlottesville, Va., with torches and chanting "Jews will not replace us!" They feel they are the victims — victims of multiculturalism, victims of tolerance, victims of diversity and inclusion. This strong sense of victimhood, ironically, often felt so personally by people who are privileged and people in power.

Before "Jews will not replace us" and "Build the Wall" was "Chinese Must Go" by Denis Kearney (1847–1907), the California labor leader of the late 19th century who was known for his nativist and racist views about Chinese immigrants — "a demagogue with extraordinary power" who felt victimized by poor and hard-working Chinese immigrants. He deserved some credit for making the "Chinese Question" a national issue and shaping the legislation of the Chinese Exclusion Act in 1882. The Act, signed by President Chester A. Arthur on May 6, 1882, prohibiting all immigration of Chinese laborers, is the first federal law implemented to prevent a specific ethnic group from immigrating to the United States. It was repealed 61 years later.

To the contrary of this type of imagined victimhood in America and in China, Switzerland embraces tolerance, compromise, diversity and inclusion. Switzerland has four official national languages: German, French, Italian and Rhaeto-Romanic, and almost everyone speaks English. In the Parliament, four official languages are spoken, each member can speak his/her own language, and they are not necessarily being translated into other

Front page of *The San Francisco Call* — *Nov. 20, 1901, Chinese Exclusion Convention*

official languages. Members debate and argue in their own languages, and agreement are reached in different languages. Swiss people are fully aware that other people speak, think, and behave differently. You have to acknowledge the facts that all men/women are equal, different languages and cultures are just different, and nobody will replace you. No language, culture and tradition are superior to the others. If you don't understand what other people are saying, it is not their fault, it is your loss.

Swiss Parliament is the modern version of Zhang's nine-generation household. Both are houses of inclusion, where accommodations are made, compromise are sought, and tolerance is routinely practiced.

Inclusion is a state of being valued, respected and supported. It's about focusing on the needs of every individual and ensuring the right conditions are in place for each person to achieve his or her full potential. Inclusion is the culture that connects each individual to the larger community. This culture encourages collaboration, flexibility, equal protection, equal opportunity and fundamental fairness.

Inclusion does not include exclusion: in community and society, exclusiveness should not be accommodated, because exclusiveness will grow like cancer cells, finally eating up all the healthy cells. Swiss and German outlawed Nazi symbolism, denial of the Holocaust is a criminal offense in many European countries. But in the United States, hate speech is protected. In one of the recent First Amendment case, the U.S. Supreme Court wrote, "Speech that demeans on the basis of race, ethnicity, gender, religion, age, disability, or any other similar ground is hateful; but the proudest boast of our free speech jurisprudence is that we protect the freedom to express "the thought that we hate." (Matal v. Tam, 2016). You may be proud, but many are hurt. In the recent decade, the First Amendment has been conveniently utilized to reverse political correctness and to eliminate the progress in equal protection. Thus you saw the proud display of military gear and the swastikas, you hear the chanting of "Blood and Soil" in Charlottesville, where hate claimed victimhood and prepared to attack.

Even His Holiness the Dalai Lama, the human embodiment of inclusion, strongly discourages the worship of an angry and vengeful spirit who favored an exclusive stance. As His Holiness said, "Restricting a form of practice that restricts others' freedom is actually a protection of freedom. So in other words, negation of a negation is an affirmation."

In today's America, we need an affirmation of inclusiveness, an affirmation of equality, and an affirmation of basic human decency.

What is Diversity?*

From left to right: Martin Hyndman, Nicole Hansen, Betsy Lulfs, Carlos Seoane, Chang Wang, Sharon Sayles Belton, Michele Engdahl, at 2015 Diversity in Business Award ceremony, July 23rd, 2015.

People can tell from my heavy accent that I was originally from an exotic part of the world. I was born and raised in Beijing where I spent the first 28 years of my life, from K-12 to college, work, and graduate school at Peking University. I was confident I had an identity and that identity had little to do with diversity.

That identity evaporated when I became a graduate student at the University of Illinois and later a law student

*In July, 2015, *Minneapolis/St. Paul Business Journal* awarded Chang Wang a "Diversity in Business Award". This article originally appeared on Thomson Reuters Blog and in the September 2015 issue of *China Insight*.

381

at the University of Minnesota Law School, where I became the member of a minority group and was forced to write, reason, and argue in another language.

"In which language do you dream?" a Swiss law student at the University of Bern asked me. She speaks four languages. So does every student in the class I teach at that University, some even more.

"Don't kill insects. They might be your relatives in the past lives," a Tibetan monk told me. Buddhists believe in reincarnation. Therefore, you should demonstrate a reverence for all sentient beings.

Not until the second year of law school did I begin to dream in English . . . and swear in English; not until I began to listen to Mozart did I realize that some people hear musical notes, rather than words; not until I saw Kandinsky did I discover that fine artists "think" in colour and shapes. Not until I had my own first dog did I truly share the joy, sadness, and pain an animal experienced emotionally; and not until I settled in Minnesota did I realized that we all live in parallel universes, separated by language, history, time, and space. Yet we are all so similar.

Diversity to me is seeing commonalities among different races, genders, and classes, and seeing differences and divergence in the same race, gender, or class.

Diversity does not only mean race or gender diversity; diversity is an open-minded way of understanding, i.e., empathy. Empathy is the capacity to understand what another person is experiencing from within the other person's frame of reference, the capacity to place oneself in another's shoes.

Can we imagine how Little Rock Nine felt when they were yelled at and spat upon by a mob, as they were escorted to school by federal troops?

Can we feel the humiliation the U.S. citizens of Japanese ancestry felt when they were forced to relocate and endure incarceration during the World War II, with their loyalty to the United States questioned?

Can we feel the horror and desperation of the Dakotas when they faced the well-trained and well-armed troops during the 1862 U.S.-Dakota War; and similarly, the horror and desperation of Tibetans facing the "invincible" People's Liberation Army of the Chinese Communist Party in 1959? The horror and desperation that both the Dakotas and the Tibetans felt, when they feared that the extermination of their lives and their civilization were inevitable?

And can we feel the pain and suffering of the refugees who have fled Syria, Iraq, and Afghanistan, to escape the violence and try to find a way to survive, hour by hour, day by day, without medication, food, even water?

Can you sense the confusion, disorientation and bewilderment of a pet dog when he was abandoned on the street? And can you sense the tremendous gratitude and trust he puts into you when you rescue him from the death shelter?

And can you feel and share the joy and exhilaration James Obergefell had when he heard Justice Kennedy deliver the opinion of *Obergefell v. Hodges*?

If we can feel those pains and sufferings, those joys and happiness, we have obtained the capacity to empathize with another sentient being, and we realize, as President J.F. Kennedy said "We all inhabit this small world. We all breathe the same air. We all cherish our children's future. And we are all mortal."

Then we no longer see people as white, black, Asian, Jewish, Latino; male, female, LGBT; we no longer identify people in a caste system or by their family names.

Instead, we see people in thousands of different categories:

    people with intellectual curiosity regarding useless information;

    people who can understand Fibonacci numbers and see them everywhere;

    people who have photographic memories;

    people who can reason and argue in four different languages;

    people who spend every summer vacation up North;

    people who spend their summers backpacking in Italy;

    people who believe every good business decision comes from some kind of formula;

    people who regard corporate bureaucracy as a threat to innovation;

    people who appreciate self-deprecating jokes;

    people who believe the murder of editors of *Charlie Hebdo* was justified;

    people who believe in universal values: life, liberty, and pursuit of happiness;

    and people who believe their own culture is exceptional and superior to others . . .

The categories are endless, and continually changing and evolving. By labelling people by race, gender, and class, it may be a little better way to describe and understand other human beings.

The law of attraction states that "like attracts like." This means that people with a low frequency attract each other, while people with a high frequency also attract each other. I am thrilled to find people with the same frequency in Minnesota, at Thomson Reuters.

I remember 20 years ago when I graduated from college, my professor said something which none of us understood at the time: "What exactly is happiness? Happiness is working with the people you like and respect and who also like and respect you."

Now I understand what he meant, and I agree.

Diversity in Business*

Minneapolis/St. Paul Business Journal (Journal): *what's your favorite part of your job?*

Chang Wang: The constant learning of new developments in law, technology, and ideas.

Journal: *what is your favorite memento?*

Chang Wang: A Khata (Tibetan Silk Scarf) blessed by His Holiness the Dalai Lama; also, a small cross, made of olive wood, that I brought back from Assisi, Italy, the birthplace of San Francesco d'Assisi (St. Francis of Assisi).

Journal: *an event or person that changed your career?*

Chang Wang: Rick King, Chief Operating Officer— Technology, Thomson Reuters, my teacher and mentor. Without Rick's trust and mentoring, none of my career accomplishments would have been possible. Rick is a senior business executive with profound intelligence, superb management skills, and tremendous integrity. In short, he is a wise man with a big heart who teaches me modesty, honesty, compassion, confidence, determination, patience, tolerance, and professionalism.

Journal: *what's something about you that would surprise people?*

Chang Wang: my undergraduate major was filmmaking: screenwriting. I have been keeping active connections with the film community and recently, played a major character in an independent film.

---

*In July, 2015, *Minneapolis/St. Paul Business Journal* awarded Chang Wang a "Diversity in Business Award". This interview originally appeared in the *Minneapolis/St. Paul Business Journal* on July 24th, 2015. © Minneapolis/ St. Paul Business Journal

Journal*: who is a hero who inspires you?*

Chang Wang: My late grandfather Zhou Bo, a World War II veteran, war correspondent, and senior editor of the largest newspaper in central China. He taught me integrity, humility, civility, perseverance, tenacity, empathy, forgiveness, and optimism.

Journal*: What is one thing you would change in the world?*

Chang Wang: I would like to see a worldwide network of no-euthanasia dog shelters that house and comfort all homeless and unwanted dogs.

Journal*: if you had to give only one business tip, what would it be?*

Chang Wang: do the right thing; don't just do things right.

Journal*: I absolutely do not want to live without . . .*

Chang Wang: My family and my dog, friends, freedom from fear, freedom of expression, the *Heart Sutra* and the *Diamond Sutra*, Chinese poetry, Beethoven, Mozart, Tchaikovsky, the BBC, PBS, sunshine, lakes, espresso and gelato.

Diversity in Business Award*

Elaine Dunn

Chang Wang, attorney and chief research and academic officer of Thomson Reuters and regular contributor to China Insight, is one of the honorees to receive 2015 Diversity in Business Award from Minneapolis/St. Paul Business Journal. The award recognizes some of the Twin Cities' leading business leaders, owners and executives from ethnic minority community and the GLBT community. The winners are those who play strong leadership roles inside and outside their jobs and serve in industry associations or community organizations. China Insight interviews Wang as he reflects on important persons and events in his life and career.

China Insight: Congratulations on receiving another award—this time from the business community—in addition to the two awards you recently received: China 100 Distinguished Chinese Alumni Award from the University of Minnesota and the Asian Pacific Distinguished Contribution Award from the State Council on Asian Pacific Minnesotans. Please tell us how you settled in Minnesota and came to work for Thomson Reuters.

Chang Wang: I grew up in a scientific and technological family and community in Beijing. Both my parents are

---

*This interview by Elaine Dunn, Chief Editor of *China Insight*, originally appeared in the July 2015 issue of *China Insight*. © China Insight senior scientists at Academia Sinica, the national academy of science in China. I was born and raised in the Zhong-guan-cun neighborhood, the "Silicon Valley" of China, where thousands of high-tech companies, research institutions, and dozens of China's top universities and technology colleges are located. In fact, my parents' residence is on the same block as the Thomson Reuters China's IP & Science Office in Beijing! I went to Beijing Film Academy for my undergraduate studies and received a Bachelor in Fine Arts degree in filmmaking. I then went to Peking University for graduate studies and received an M.A. in comparative literature and cultural studies. For nearly two years, between college and graduate school, I worked as an editor and correspondent for Science Times, a major Chinese newspaper. In 2000, I came to the United States and studied art history at the University of Illinois. After receiving my second master's degree in 2003, I came to the University of Minnesota Law School for my legal education. I received my juris doctor degree in 2006, passed the bar, and have worked for Thomson Reuters ever since. Thomson Reuters is the world's leading source of intelligent information for businesses and professionals. I lead special research projects and facilitate company joint initiatives with the academic and business communities. I also develop and manage Continuing Legal Education programs and diversity training programs and serve as a resident expert on legal, regulatory, language, and international project management for Thomson Reuters.

China Insight: You have published four books, and each one of them has a dedication. "The End of the Avant-Garde: Comparative Cultural Studies" was dedicated to your late grandfather Zhou Bo. "Inside China's Legal System" was dedicated to your "teacher and mentor" Rick King. "Legal Research in American Law" was dedicated to the

University of Minnesota and Thomson Reuters, where you "found and read the law," and "New Tales of the Twin Cities: The History, Law, and Culture of Minnesota" was dedicated to "all the earlier settlers of the Land of 10,000 Lakes, and to all the strong, good-looking, and above-average Minnesotans who live there today." Why did you dedicate the first book to your grandfather?

Chang Wang: My late grandpa Zhou Bo was a World War II veteran, war correspondent and senior reporter for a newspaper. He taught me integrity, humility, civility, determination, perseverance, tenacity, forgiveness and optimism. He played a very special and important role in my life.

Grandpa was born in 1923 in Shanxi Province, northwest China. He was a son of a moderate landlord and studied traditional Chinese literature and art in his hometown. However, his studies were interrupted by the anti-Japanese war. In early 1940s, he joined the Chinese Communist Party and the legendary 8th Route Army of The National Revolution Army. He led a team of soldiers fighting the Japanese army in northwest China and also was in charge of reporting from the frontline. During the wars, he seldom stayed in one village for more than a week. After the Civil War ended in 1949, Grandpa was honorably discharged from the army. When peace finally came, he had a chance to pursue his real passions—literature, art and journalism. He worked for Henan Daily, the biggest newspaper in central China and was appointed senior reporter in the 1950s. He was a strong supporter of then President Liu Shaoqi's social democratic policy. President Liu, the nominal national leader who ranked No. 5 in the Chinese Communist Party, was murdered by Chairman Mao's Red Guards in Henan in 1969 during the Cultural Revolution. President Liu was labeled a "traitor" from his death until

1980. I remember later my grandfather showed me the pictures of him interviewing President Liu in the '60s and told me the heartbreaking story that President Liu desperately clung to a copy of the Constitution of China as he was beaten to death by the Red Guards. Grandpa served the country with dignity, honor, and a pure faith in social democratic equality. He despised corruption and party politics. In 1989, when the Tiananmen tragedy occurred, he was disgusted and disillusioned.

Over the years, I sent him all my publications. He enjoyed reading them even though he was not familiar with the topics of Separation of Powers or Freedom of Expression. He sent me his calligraphies and paintings. In his last years, he could hardly paint, draw, or even read anymore. After I had settled in Minnesota, every time I went back to China, I could only spend one or two days with him and Grandma, mostly in the hospital. I never had a chance to tell him what I do, what kind of life I have in Minnesota, and how much I love him. I missed the opportunity forever. But I know he is always here with me. I know he would be pleased to know that I am writing a treatise on comparative constitutional law.

China Insight: You credited your "teacher and mentor" Rick King, Chief Operating Officer — Technology, Thomson Reuters, for all your career accomplishments. Is Rick the most important individual who changed and shaped your career?

Chang Wang: Yes. Without Rick's trust and mentoring, none of my career accomplishments would have been possible. I am most fortunate to work on Rick's team at Thomson Reuters. Under his leadership, Thomson Reuters has built strong partnerships with science and technology communities, universities, and government agencies; and we enjoy many benefits from these collaborative relation-ships. I am honored to participate in joint initiatives with the law school, business school, and the international offices at the University of Minnesota, Minneapolis Institute of Arts, Minnesota State government, the Supreme Court of Minnesota, Minneapolis-St. Paul International Airport and Minnesota Public Radio.

Rick is a senior business executive with profound intelli-gence, superb management skills, and tremendous integ-rity. In short, he is a wise man with a big heart who teaches me modesty, honesty, empathy, compassion, confidence, patience, tolerance and professionalism.

In addition, I consider Rick a true example of "diversity in business." Diversity does not only mean race or gender diversity, diversity is first and foremost an open-minded way of understanding, i.e., empathy. Empathy is the capac-ity to understand what another person is experiencing from within the other person's frame of reference, the capacity to place oneself in another's shoes. Rick excels in positive psychology: his unique capacity of empathy is inspiring and motivating.

China Insight: What do you think the major difference in your life and career between east and west: China and the U.S.?

Chang Wang: I consider myself most fortunate to be able to appreciate the beauty and charm of Chinese arts and culture, while functioning freely in the American system of equal protection and fundamental fairness. In fact, there are only two things that can bring me close to tears: Chinese literature and American law. To illustrate the major difference between the two parallel universes, I would like to share with you a paragraph from the preface to "My Life in China and America," the autobiography of Yung Wing, the first Chinese student to graduate from an American university. It said, *"Would it not be strange, if an Occidental education, continually exemplified by an Occidental civilization, had not wrought upon an Oriental such a metamorphosis in his inward nature as to make him feel and act as though he were a being coming from a different world, when he confronted one so diametrically different? This was precisely my case, and yet neither patriotism nor the love of my fellow countrymen had been weakened. On the contrary, they had increased in strength from sympathy."*

Asian Pacific Leadership Award*

Elaine Dunn

Chang Wang, a regular contributor to *China Insight* and chief research and academic officer of Thomson Reuters, said his first reaction to learning he is one of this year's recipients of the Council on Asian-Pacific Minnesotans' Asian Pacific Leadership Award was, "I smiled." That response is not hard to believe, coming from a most down-to-earth individual.

The Asian Pacific Leadership Awards honor, recognize and celebrate the work of individuals and organizations who have demonstrated continuous commitment to and leadership in the Asian Pacific Minnesotan community. Wang will be honored for his outstanding contributions to education, legal service, and diversity in business at the

---

*Chang Wang received the Asian Pacific Outstanding Contribution Award from the Minnesota State Council on Asian-Pacific Minnesotans, for "his outstanding contributions to education, legal service, and diversity in business." The award was presented to him on May 8, 2015. The Council on Asian-Pacific Minnesotans (CAPM) was created by the Minnesota State Legislature in 1985 pursuant to Minnesota Statute 3.9226, subdivision 1, to fulfill three primary objectives: to advise the governor and members of the legislature on issues pertaining to Asian Pacific Minnesotans; to advocate on behalf of those issues; and to serve as the bridge for and between Asian Pacific Minnesotans and non-Asian Pacific Minnesotans. In 1993, to honor the achievements and contributions of Asian/Pacific Americans, the US Congress, by Public Law 102-450, designated the month of May each year as "Asian/Pacific American Heritage Month." This article first appeared in the May issue of *China Insight*. © China Insight

Council's Asian Leadership and Heritage Dinner on May 8 at The Prom Center in Oakdale.

His nomination letter reads, in part, "as an educator, he has inspired thousands of students to be global citizens; as an author, he demonstrated an astonishing breadth of scholarship: from Chinese law, comparative law, and legal research, to cultural studies, art history, and Minnesota history; as an attorney, he is keen to civil rights and the plight of minorities, and is committed to pro bono service; as a business manager, he is an advocate of innovation and a perfect example of thought leadership and corporate responsibility . . . "

When China Insight asked what the motivating force behind his very "full plate" was, he replied with nary a bit of hesitation, "The prospect of collective happiness."

Wang, a native of Beijing and a graduate of the University of Minnesota Law School, practices in the Twin Cities area. Besides holding associate and adjunct professorships at seven top law schools in the U.S., China and Europe, he has published four books on law and cultural studies, including the first Chinese language book about the State of Minnesota, "New Tales of the Twin Cities: The History, Law, and Culture of Minnesota."

He credits his "teacher and mentor" Rick King, Chief Operating Officer for Technology at Thomson Reuters, for his accomplishments. "Without Rick's trust and support," Wang said, "none of my career accomplishments would have been possible. He is a business executive with profound intelligence, superb management skills, and tremendous integrity. In short, he is a wise man with a big heart . . . I dedicate this award to Rick King and his wife Gina King, two of my favorite 'transplant' Minnesotans. They help me appreciate Minnesota, and life in general, in the most positive ways."

Chang Wang dedicated Asian Pacific Outstanding Contribution Award to his "teacher and mentor" Rick King (left), Executive Vice President and Chief Information Officer, Thomson Reuters.

A lifelong learner and an avid reader with a personal library of 6,000 books in Chinese, English and Italian that run the gamut from poetry to art history to astrophysics to social psychology to information technology and other topics, he mentioned the following books had made "significant impact" on his life because:

"The Gulag Archipelago" by Aleksandr Solzhenitsyn, taught me history is nightmare;

"Animal Farm" by George Orwell, taught me that the nightmare is real;

"The Importance of Living" by Dr. Lin Yutang, taught me the beauty of traditional China;

"My Life in China and America" by Yung Wing, taught me about parallel universes;

"A Brief History of Time" by Stephen Hawking, taught me time does not really exist (that does not mean we are immortal, though);

"Se una notte d'inverno un viaggiatore (If on a winter's night a traveler)" by Italo Calvino, taught me the unlimited potential of imagination;

"Destructive Emotions" by His Holiness the Dalai Lama and Daniel Goleman, taught me being happy is the common goal of faith and science; and finally

"Justice" by Michael Sandel (one of my favorite Minnesotans), taught me there are right things to do.

Wang plans to forge ahead with his law practice, teaching, research and writing, but hopes to contribute more to the Asian Pacific community by getting more involved in community affairs.

The Asian Pacific community of the Twin Cities is fortunate to have such a dedicated and knowledgeable member among us. *China Insight* is grateful for Wang's contribution and extends our sincere congratulation on his award.

Chang Wang receiving "China 100 Distinguished Chinese Alumni Award" from Dr. Eric Kaler (left), president of the University of Minnesota, in 2014.

Chinese Community Held
Civic Engagement Seminar*

Elaine Dunn

According to the Pew Research Center, there are approximately four million Chinese (including Taiwanese) in the U.S. as of 2011. A report from the Council of Asian Pacific Minnesotans (based on U.S. Census Bureau 2010 statistics) indicate that the Chinese population of Minnesota grew from 16,060 in 2000 to 24,643 in 2010, with 13.5 percent and 7.6 percent of the Asian populations in Hennepin and Ramsey counties being Chinese.

On Oct. 15, Peking University Alumni Association — Minnesota (PKUAA-MN) and Tsinghua University Alumni Association–Minnesota (TAA-MN) held a joint seminar on civic engagement and the 2016 election at the Ramsey

*This report first appeared in November/December 2016 issue of *China Insight*.
© China Insight

County Library. Board members from two alumni-associations attended the seminar, along with an audience from the local Chinese community. Chang Wang, a PKU alumnus and a regular contributor to China Insight, delivered the keynote speech in Mandarin.

Peking University (北京大学) and Tsinghua University (清华大学) are two of the most prestigious universities in China. More than 200 alumni from both universities work and live in the Twin Cities. In addition, there are more than 3,000 Chinese students and scholars currently studying at the University of Minnesota, making the University of Minnesota the largest Chinese-student community in the United States. A significant portion of the

双城华人讲坛系列 第十四讲

了解民主制度，参与公共事务

详细介绍美国的三权分立体制，
民主党和共和党的基本理念，
选举知识，及最高法院大法官的作用。

今年的选举无论对民主党还是共和党都至关重要。
未来的总统将有可能任命三、四位最高法院大法官。
这将对您和下一代人的生活产生深刻影响。

时间： 2:00 – 4:00 PM, Sat. Oct. 15, 2016
地点： Roseville Ramsey County Library
2180 North Hamline Ave
Roseville, MN 55113
http://www.rclreads.org/about/locations/rcl-roseville
Open to public. Parking is free.
主办： 明州北大、清华校友会联合举办
联系： 郭宏 gliao6009@gmail.com
612-986-0728

演讲人:王昶先生

王昶： 毕业于明尼苏达大学法学院，获法律博士学位。纽约州、哥伦比亚特区、明尼苏达州和联邦法院执业律师。现任汤森路透集团首席研究和编审学术员。美国明尼苏达大学法学院、明尼苏达大学本科荣誉项目和大都会州立大学商学院兼职教授。王昶著有四部著作《先锋的终结：比较文化研究》，《中国法律体系》，《美国法律文献与信息检索》，《新双城记：明尼苏达的历史、法律和文化》。

Chinese student body at the U of M are graduates of Peking University and Tsinghua University.

Wang is chief researcher at Thomson Reuters, an attorney, and a member of Civic Engagement Steering Committee of the State of Minnesota, which is responsible for developing best practices to ensure cabinet-level administrative agencies make an effort to communicate with historically disenfranchised communities. Under the leadership of Commissioner Kevin Lindsey, Deputy Commissioner Rowzat Shipchandler and Civic Engagement Director Nick Kor of Minnesota Department of Human Rights, the Civic Engagement Committee crafted Minnesota's Civic

Engagement Plan 2016, as a government effort to facilitate meaningful dialog with all members of the public
in its work and in the development of policy. The Civic
Engagement Committee is part of Governor Mark Dayton's
Diversity of Inclusion Council.

Starting with an overview of the United States
Constitution, Wang detailed the guiding principles of the
U.S. government: the rule of law, separation of powers,
checks and balances, an independent judiciary and representative democracy. Also presented in a non-partisan
way were the different views of the Democratic and the
Republican platforms' key issues: economics, abortion, gun
control, gay marriage, military spending, energy, the death
penalty and immigration.

The audience, approximately 30 percent of whom were
students, showed intellectual curiosity about the topics of law
and separation of powers rather than ideological differences
of the two parties. There were also questions representing
concerns of the first -generation Chinese-American community: transgender bathrooms; violence against Chinese
small-business owners; and affirmative action (which may
hurt Chinese students with strong academic backgrounds).

Wang stressed that the audience should look at all these
issues from both sides and watch analyses from both left-
and right-leaning media such as MSNBC and Fox News.
In addition, Wang mentioned the importance of learning
about U.S. history, and the civil rights movement in particular, to understand where "political correctness" came from.

When China Insight asked Wang what stood out for him
about the event, he said, "About gun control, I was shocked
to learn one audience member had not heard of the
National Rifle Association. I told him to do some research
on the organization. That same person also expressed an

interest in observing/monitoring the voting, I told him to
call the Minnesota Secretary of State's office to volunteer."

Wang wrapped up his presentation by logging on to
the Minnesota Secretary of State's multilingual website on
election and voting, which includes a Chinese version, and
showed the audience how to register to vote and research
the candidates.

He encouraged the Chinese community to participate in
the political process by learning to understand the history
and complexities of the political issues, engaging in public
service, voicing their concerns through appropriate channels, and developing meaningful dialogs with other communities. "If you do not participate, you do not exist in the
political world." Wang concluded, "If you do not vote, you
do not matter."

Man of Many Talents*

Elaine Dunn

The name Chang Wang should be familiar to *China Insight* readers. Wang was the recipient of the Council of Asian-Pacific Minnesotans' Asian Pacific Leadership Award, the University of Minnesota "China 100" Distinguished Chinese Alumni Award, and the Minneapolis/St. Paul Business Journal's Diversity in Business Award in 2015.

He also has been a regular and consistent contributor to

this publication since 2013. His articles "Dancing with the Dragon" (November 2015-January 2016), "Doing Business with China and the Chinese People" (January-June 2015), "Last Lecture" (January and October 2014), "Living Within Parallel Universes" (February and March 2016), and "Luckiest Generations"

---

*This article originally appeared in the September 2016 issue of *China Insight*.
© China Insight

(April-September 2016), to name a few, offer depth and insight into the Chinese psyche and social norms.

Not only is he a good writer, practicing attorney, law professor, business manager, and published author, Wang has also recently taken on another role: an actor! He played the part of a Chinese ambassador in a locally produced movie, "Domestics," with understated panache. Those of you who have had to deal with The People's Republic of China's officials will appreciate how well Wang handled his part.

Asked why and how he got involved in the movie, Wang said: "The filmmakers and I were connected by a mutual friend Jim Hilbert, a professor at Mitchell Hamline School of Law. The filmmakers watched my interview on Youtube and offered me the role. I guess I was the guy they were looking for: a middle aged mean Chinese man with a heavy accent. As you know, I majored in filmmaking in college, and many of my friends are in the film and television industry, so acting in a film is not uncharted territory for me. In fact, I found acting is much easier than lawyering!"

The movie was shot in 12 days and produced by human rights lawyers and award-winning filmmakers John Shulman and Jeanne-Marie Almonor. Shulman and Almonor's goal was to "give voice" to groups targeted by big business and misguided government. The plot, in my untrained film critic opinion, tried to address too many social issues (school segregation, racism, corrupt government, anti-union sentiments, terrorism, biased media and, to a lesser degree, generational issues). The many flashbacks further hindered following the storyline.

BUT . . . as the filmmakers indicated at the June 26 Minneapolis screening, the movie is their way of speaking out for the various groups who cannot do so for themselves.

As of June, private screenings had taken place in Atlanta, Chicago, Detroit and Minneapolis. *China Insight* will include movie schedules when available. When in the cinemas, watch and draw your own conclusion.

Civics 101: The Judicial Branch, with Minnesota State Supreme Court Chief Justice Lori Gildea and Professor Wang*

Scott Augustin

Chief Justice Lorie Gildea (left) and Chang Wang.

By day, Chief Research & Academic Officer Chang Wang is a brilliant and hard-working Thomson Reuters employee. But by night, he's an attorney, law school and college

---

*This article originally appeared on Legal Current (www.legalcurrent.com) on March 9, 2017. © Thomson Reuters

professor, author and budding actor (as a serious Chinese guy in dark suits).

Recently, Professor Chang Wang brought his students from two different local universities to a private meeting with Minnesota State Supreme Court Chief Justice Lorie Gildea for memorable lecture on the judicial branch, the balance of power, and the unique role of a Supreme Court Chief Justice.

Appointed as Associate Justice on January 11, 2006, Gildea was appointed Chief Justice on July 1, 2010, by Governor Pawlenty, and then stood for election and won in 2012. One week a month, she told the class, the Minnesota Supreme Court again hears cases in the State Capitol Building's newly restored and spectacular courtroom, where she met with the class. Cases are also heard in the Minnesota Judicial Center.

Chief Justice Gildea discussed the separation of powers, her unique duties as chief justice (from overseeing committee) to testifying before Minnesota legislators about funding for the judicial branch). She also discussed the paths cases take to find their way to her courtroom, then generously answered questions from the students.

At the end of the meeting, Chang presented the Chief Justice with a copy of the newly published *Constitutional Law: Lectures, Cases, and Resources* (Thomson Reuters and China University of Political Science and Law Press). Chang Wang's two-volume, 1200-page textbook picks up where his first bilingual legal research book on American law, Legal Research in American Law, leaves off. The set includes annotated case briefs of 39 U.S. Supreme Court cases, 24 lectures from Wang on Constitutional Law and more. Importantly for this meeting, the text book includes the first-ever Chinese translation of the Constitution of the

State of Minnesota, as well as Chinese translations of Magna Carta, the United States Constitution, and the Constitution of the Commonwealth of Massachusetts (the oldest constitution in the United States).

According to Wang, it was an especially appropriate learning environment for the subject matter and a masters-level course for these undergrads in the constitutional powers granted the judiciary and how they manifest in everyday life. "It was wonderful of Chief Justice Gildea to so generously share her experiences as a lawyer and Chief Justice with these students," he said. "These students are bright and I hope that some of them were inspired enough by her words to take a serious look at the practice of law. We'll always need more good lawyers."

(And good authors, and good professors, and good actors.)

Afterword

Coming "Home" Crazy

It was summer, 2003, when I paid a campus visit to the
University of Minnesota Law School. The sky was high, and
the lakes were glassy. Minnesotans were out hiking, biking,

---

*This article originally appeared in *New Tales of the Twin Cities: The History,
Law, and Culture of Minnesota*, the first Chinese language book about the
State of Minnesota. The book is authored by Chang Wang and published by
Thomson Reuters in 2014.

Coming Home Crazy: An Alphabet of China Essays is a book by Minnesotan
author Bill Holm (1943 – 2009). Writing about traditions that endure in Chinese
rural areas as well as the absurdities of bureaucracy experienced by an
American teacher and traveler in the 1980s, this collection of short essays
captures the variety of daily life in contemporary China. The title of the book
was inspired by Du Fu (杜甫, 712 – 770 AD), one of the most prominent
Chinese poets of Tang Dynasty (618 – 707 AD).

kayaking, and walking dogs. If summer were a song, the song sang itself. The Chinese translation of "Minnesota" (明尼苏达) made perfect sense to me in the summer. The first Chinese character means bright and clear, the third character means wake or recover, and the last character means eminent, distinguished, or thorough. The translation appears to be faithful, expressive, and elegant, I said to myself.

Professor David Bryden, criminal law professor at the Law School, graciously showed me around campus, Downtown Minneapolis, and Uptown. He and his wife Rebecca convinced me that the University of Minnesota Law School would be the best choice for my legal education.

With "bright and "clear" in mind, I agreed. Three months later, I came back to Minneapolis as a 1L—and as the only Chinese student in the U of M Law School Class of 2006.

What I hadn't realized was that in Minnesota, summer was a loan that must be repaid in winter. When I again strolled around Lake Harriet during final-exam week in December, the lake had changed its face dramatically: it was now quiet and bleak. The only songs I could hear were the elegy in my heart, a curse directed at the person who had translated Minnesota as 明尼苏达, and an Edward Munch-style "scream" inside.

I spent my first winter break in Beijing, which is notorious for its Mongolian wind. Compared to Minnesota's wind chill, however, Northern China's winter blow is a nuisance at best. I remember being at the US Embassy in Beijing, applying for a student visa to re-enter the U.S., in order to continue my legal education. After examining the I-20 form that the University of Minnesota International Office had issued, the visa officer looked up at me rather sympathetically and said: "Minnesota, eh? It's . . . cold." Before I could even respond, he had stamped my application — "Approved", as if he were worried that I might change my mind.

The most difficult part of Minnesota's winter is neither the cold, nor the snow, nor even the wind chill – it's the gray sky. In this regard, the first character 明 (bright and clear) of the Chinese translation is scandalously misleading. Cold is refreshing, wind clears the mind, and blizzards harden the will; but gloomy skies add nothing but depression and sorrow to never-ending Contracts lectures in the windowless classrooms of Mondale Hall — and to sleepless nights in the law library. You begin to think hard, soul-searching deep thoughts. During a Minnesota winter, it seems, it is much easier to relate to Henrik Ibsen, Søren Kierkegaard, and Igmar Bergman, than to Benjamin Cardozo, Oliver Wendell Holmes, or Sandra Day O'Connor.

Years later, when I heard Lewis Black's sarcastic comments that, "In Minnesota's winter, you want to be a moose, because then you will have fur; you want to be a bear, so you can hibernate." I responded with a forced smile.

Nevertheless, spring and summer re-visit after six months, the melody plays again, and your heart melts. You forget all the "cries and whispers" and all your winter doubts. The simple truth is that if we had no winter, spring and summer would not feel so pleasant!

I have spent the last 11 years in Minnesota. That's the longest time I've spent in one place during my adulthood — even more time than I've spent in my hometown of Beijing. I've always wondered whether my choice of Minnesota was one of pure serendipity, was influenced by subconscious forces, or was simply a matter of destiny. Do I resonate with the songs and rhythm of Sioux and the Ojibwe at Powwow? Do I share the same longing for natural beauty and spiritual seclusion that motivated earlier Scandinavian and German settlers? Do I embrace Minnesota's cultural diversity and pluralism as enthusiastically as do progressive Minnesotans? And do I really understand the hidden message of "Minnesota Nice"?

It has been said that Minnesota is a good place to live if you can get out of here when you need to. The phenomenon of "snowbirds" (retired individuals who head south each winter for six months) might weaken the argument that winter is an indispensable part of Minnesota experience. But as a linear descendent of Chinese literati, I salute Jin Shentan (金圣叹), a 17ᵗʰ Century Chinese writer, who wisely concluded that it is the ultimate enjoyment to read a banned political book during an evening blizzard. Mentally and physically, I don't need to be in the city of Beijing to feel close to home, thanks to ultra high-speed broadband and the free flow of information in the Land of the Free.

People on the East Coast or the West Coast may not distinguish Minnesota from the rest of the Midwest, but Minnesota does deserve special attention. This is the place that produced some of the finest authors in the country: Sinclair Lewis, F. Scott Fitzgerald, Garrison Keillor, Jon Hassler, Bill Holm, Jonathan Franzen, and Vince Flynn; the Twin Cities is the home of several top notch orchestras, museums, theatres, and thousands of artists and performers, not to mention the sports teams; this is the land where thousands of Somalian, Hmong, and Tibetan sought and received protection and comfort; and this is the land that borders one of the largest fresh-water lakes in the world.

Of course, Minnesota is also the state where the 1862 Mankato Massacre happened; the state from which a number of controversial political figures have emerged, and the State whose government shut down for 20 days in 2011.

But at the end of the day, if you add up all of Minnesota's positives, they undeniably outnumber the negatives.

Finally, I'd like to share with you my Twin Cities Top Ten List, my top-ten Minnesota pleasures:

Listening to oral arguments in the Minnesota Supreme Court's old state-capitol courtroom;

Browsing the Asian Art Collection at the Minneapolis Institute of Art;

Listening to Minnesota Public Radio;

Browsing used-book stores in Uptown;

Walking around Lake Harriet and Lake of the Isles;

Taking a cruise on the Mississippi River;

Enjoying a weekend concert by the Minnesota Orchestra;

Watching a play at the Guthrie Theatre;

Checking out special exhibitions at the Minnesota Science Museum;

Shopping at the Mall of America.

In August, 2003, I came to Minneapolis with two suitcases and a used car. Today, I call the Twin Cities home. On October 16, 2014, I received a China 100 Distinguished Chinese Alumni Award from the President of the University of Minnesota. It would be quite unnatural if I were not moved by the recognition of Minnesotans.

As I re-entered the U.S. at Minneapolis-St. Paul

International Airport after my last trip to China, the
Immigration officer looked at my documents and asked:
"How long have you been out of the country?"

I replied "Two weeks."

He inquired "What did you do?"

I responded "Giving lectures overseas."

He stamped my passport and handed it back to me:
"Welcome back home."